Catch-up and Competitiveness in China

This book examines the role of corporate structure, including the role of corporate headquarters, in the success of large firms. It considers these issues in relation to large global corporations, thereby providing a 'benchmark', which is then used as a contrast in a discussion of corporate structure and the role of corporate headquarters within large Chinese firms, many of which have evolved from former government ministries. It includes a detailed case study of firms in the crucially important oil and petro-chemical sector. Overall the book shows what a huge competitive battle China's emerging 'national champions' face with their global competitors, and puts forward policy implications for both large Chinese firms and the Chinese government concerning how business systems should be reformed further still in order to construct globally competitive large industrial corporations.

Jin Zhang is Leverhulme Research Fellow in the Judge Institute of Management and Fellow of Wolfson College at the University of Cambridge. Her main research interests are international business and China. She is currently undertaking research on China's large corporations and their position within the global business system.

RoutledgeCurzon Studies on the Chinese Economy

Series editors: Peter Nolan, *University of Cambridge*
Dong Fureng, *Beijing University*

The aim of this series is to publish original, high-quality, research-level work by both new and established scholars in the West and the East, on all aspects of the Chinese economy, including studies of business and economic history.

Catch-up and Competitiveness in China

The case of large firms in the oil industry

Jin Zhang

RoutledgeCurzon
Taylor & Francis Group

LONDON AND NEW YORK

First published 2004
by RoutledgeCurzon
11 New Fetter Lane, London EC4P 4EE

Simultaneously published in the USA and Canada
by RoutledgeCurzon
29 West 35th Street, New York, NY 10001

RoutledgeCurzon is an imprint of the Taylor & Francis Group

© 2004 Jin Zhang

Typeset in Times by LaserScript Ltd, Mitcham, Surrey
Printed and bound in Great Britain by
MPG Books Ltd, Bodmin

British Library Cataloguing in Publication Data
A catalogue record for this book is available from the British Library

Library of Congress Cataloging in Publication Data
A catalog record for this book has been requested

ISBN 0–415–33321–0

For my mother and father Qian Manyu and Zhang Ketai

Contents

Figures

Tables

Foreword

Good research illuminates for us phenomena about which we have little prior understanding. Truly great research forces us to reexamine that which we thought we already knew, and in so doing, helps us better understand ourselves and our broader world. Jin Zhang's *Catch-up and Competitiveness in China* represents exactly that kind of truly great research.

No one would dispute that China through the course of the twentieth century has hurtled through breathtaking transformation. For many of the most learned scholars, these changes, taken together, are understood as an extended process of integration, integration on China's part into a global system of norms, institutional standards, ideas, and economic transactions. The global system in this view is taken as constant – a fixed, albeit abstracted, benchmark by which latecomers can be measured, and a fixed goal toward which they are, or at least should be, aiming. Empirical investigation then turns toward the moving target of China, but investigation considering primarily the extent to which this nation has approached the abstracted global standard of "best practice."

In her richly empirical work, Jin Zhang challenges this entire approach and the fundamental assumptions behind it. Central to the work is the observation that just as China entered its most determined phases of market transition and institutional change changes that undoubtedly involved integration into the global economy the global economy itself was undergoing revolutionary change. Moreover, the simultaneous transitions, that of China and that of the broader global system, happened to be moving if not in wholly opposite, then in at least difficult to reconcile directions. That is an extremely original observation, one that forces us to reconsider the nature of radical change in global commerce, and the implications for developing and developed nations alike.

We are living in an era of profound shifts in the way in which production of goods and services is organized. That which once took place within the confines of a single firm or a single coordinated national system now takes place across numerous firms spread across borders and linked through densely complex networks of production. Production systems have been deverticalized, supply chains have been extended, outsourcing and subcontracting have spread rapidly, and a host of new entrants often from developing countries have been brought into the production process. At the same time, for all this fragmentation, and for all the dispersal of activities to new players, supply chains have become densely linked. Boundaries between firms have blurred, the coordination between them has deepened, and the value to be realized through integration has soared. New types of leading firms have emerged, firms that may be far narrower in focus than the champions of yore, but firms that have achieved massive scale and concentration within that focus. Such firms have built extraordinary capabilities often through massive investment in R&D, information technology, managerial talent, and global branding to extend their reach over vast supply chains, chains they may no longer own, but ones that they decidedly control. What has emerged, as Jin Zhang beautifully illustrates in her study of the petroleum sector, is a new type of global production system and a new type of leading firm a firm that is massive not just in scale, but more important, in its capacity from a powerful center to shape activities extending across the firm and far beyond.

What does this mean for developing nations, nations like China that have dramatically reshaped their domestic business systems to meet an international benchmark, but one that has rapidly receded into obsolescence? For the past twenty-five years, China has pursued extraordinary and extraordinarily positive, in many respects market transition, transition that has involved sweeping decentralization, deregulation, and liberalization. In pre-reform China, the industrial sector was populated by organizations that were firms in name only. More accurately, they were production arms of the state, organizations that had little if any power to allocate resources, set strategy, control personal, or handle financing. Today, though some of the old names persist, the old organizations are basically gone. The most traditional mechanisms of socialist planning and state intervention have been dramatically reduced, if not wholly eliminated. Prices have been liberalized, the firm separated from the state, and the doors of competition thrown open. Production organizations that once stood at the commanding heights of the economy the state-owned behemoths of the past have been simultaneously confronted with new competitors, granted unprecedented autonomy from the state, and charged with the task of managing loosely connected networks of subsidiaries and constituent firms. In their effort to build markets, the architects of Chinese reform have pushed decentralization, downward dispersal of authority, and the granting of autonomy to economic producers. As a result, in China today we can meaningfully talk aboutˆfirms,¤ firms with real autonomy and power to shape their competitive stance in the market. Yet, precisely because marketization has proceeded through decentralization and dispersal of authority, the firms that now exist often pieces of the larger production organizations of the past – tend to be small in scale, haphazardly diversified, and poorly focused. China, therefore, finds itself today integrating into a global economy dominated by vastly powerful, capable, massive, and concentrated enterprises, at the very same time its own firms precisely because of market reform have been dispersed, diffused, and downsized.

The point is neither that China's reforms nor the global economy's transition should be judged negatively. Rather, the point, one made so clearly by this volume, is that the challenge of industrial catch up has become not just more complex and daunting than in the past, but frankly, fundamentally different. The price of entry into the catch up game, transition to a market system institutionally, has benefits that make it worth purchasing, but so too does it leave domestic firms in a decidedly deep hole with respect to leading international players. Simply to play the game, the developing nation must push changes at the business level that run counter to those taking place in the world's leading firms. To marketize, China has decentralized, dispersed authority, and spread autonomy down to the lowest level business units. To dominate competition internationally, leading global firms have – in the particular respects that Jin Zhang highlights – recentralized, reconcentrated authority, and refocused autonomy upward toward the corporate center. Given these trends, one cannot help sensing the magnitude of the challenge faced by those hoping to play the game of catch up. It is truly breathtaking.

This is a volume that, through extraordinarily careful empirical analysis, permits us to understand not just the Chinese business system, but the entire global business system in a new light. It represents a wonderful contribution to the literature, and a wonderful contribution to our understanding of the times in which we are living, times of extraordinary organizational transformation.

Edward S. Steinfeld
Cambridge, Massachusetts
December 2003

Acknowledgements

This book would not have been possible without the support from many people and institutions. I am most grateful to Professor Peter Nolan for his intellectual inspiration and unstinting support throughout the course of this study. The many discussions with Professor Nolan help to clarify the ideas and sharpen the argument of this study. I am indebted to Dr Wang Xiaoqiang for sharing with me his ideas on China's reform and providing me research materials.

The research involved extensive fieldwork with BP, Shell, CNPC, and Sinopec between 1999 and 2002. Research trips were made to the headquarters of BP and Shell in London as well as their business streams. The study of the CNPC and Sinopec consisted of research trips to the headquarters of CNPC and Sinopec and CNOOC in Beijing, Daqing, Zhenhai, and Shanghai Petrochemical Corporation. I am enormously grateful for the managers with BP and Royal Dutch/Shell who helped to arrange my field study with openness and professionalism. My field study with the Chinese companies took place at the most turbulent and sensitive period of restructuring. I am extremely grateful for the managers and officials with the Chinese companies for showing their enthusiasm towards my study, for discussing with me their deep knowledge of the Chinese oil industry, and for sharing with me their deep thoughts and concern over restructuring the oil industry. For reasons of confidentiality, I cannot list their names here. I wish also to thank Dr Liu Yan for her help with some of the field visits in China.

I wish to thank the following institutions for funding my PhD research: Clare Hall, Cambridge, Cambridge Overseas Trust, British Council, Suzy Paine Fund, the Cambridge Trust for Political Economy, Imperial Chemical Industries (ICI), and the China Big Business Programme (CBBP) in the Judge Institute of Management at Cambridge University. I am extremely fortunate to have advice and help from Mr Michael Hilton from the Foreign and Commonwealth Office and Mr Michael T. Simmons, OBE, former Manager of Asia Pacific Liaison with ICI, at the crucial stage of fundraising for the research.

This study is based on my PhD dissertation at the University of Cambridge. The research necessary (in both China and the United Kingdom) to comprehensively revise my dissertation for publication in this form was made possible by the generous financial support of the Leverhulme Trust, which

I gratefully acknowledge. I am grateful to Peter Sowden, editor at RoutledgeCurzon, for his valuable advice.

I wish to thank the wonderful group of Professor Nolan's PhD students at the University of Cambridge. Their research covers various industries including aerospace, automobile, banking, brewing, coal, insurance, IT hardware, media, oil, retailing, telecommunications, white goods as well as business ethics and corporate governance. The weekly seminars in Jesus College and the Judge Institute of Management were immensely valuable. The comments from my colleagues on my research have been extremely stimulating.

Nevertheless, I carry full responsibility for the content of this study.

Abbreviations

Arco	Atlantic Richfield Company
AVIC	China Aviation Industry Corporation
BCEO	Business Chief Executive Officer (BP)
BU	Business unit
CBRC	China Banking Regulatory Commission
CEO	Chief Executive Officer
CMD	Committee of Managing Directors (Shell)
CNPC	China National Petroleum and Gas Corporation
CNSPC	China National Star Petroleum Corporation
CNOOC	China National Offshore Oil Corporation
CPMES	China Petroleum Material and Equipment Supplies Company
E&P	Exploration and Production
EDLTIP	Executive Directors' Long Term Incentive Plan (BP)
EPS	Earnings per share
ERP	Enterprise Resource Planning
ExCo	Executive Committee (BP)
Excom	Business Executive Committee (Shell)
FIE	Foreign invested enterprises
FMIS	Financial management information system (PetroChina)
FOB	Free on board
FSU	Former Soviet Union
GCEO	Group Chief Executive Officer (BP)
GHC	The Group Holding Companies (Shell)
GIAAP	Group Appraisal and Approval Procedures (BP)
GOM	Global oil major
GTL	Gas to Liquids
HR	Human resources
HSE	Health, Safety and Environment
HSECP	Health, Safety and Environment Commitment Policy (Shell)
IFAN	Investigation and Fraud Awareness Network
IPO	Initial public offering
IT	Information technology
JV	Joint venture

KPI	Key performance indexes
LNG	Liquefied natural gas
LPG	Liquefied petroleum gas
M&A	Mergers and acquisitions
MCI	Ministry of Chemical Industry
MGMR	Ministry of Geology and Mineral Resources
MOFTEC	Ministry of Foreign Trade and Economic Co-operation (China)
MPI	Ministry and Petroleum Industry (China)
NOC	National oil company
OECD	Organisation of Economic Co-operation and Development
PAB	Petroleum Administration Bureaux
PC	Performance contract
PE	Polyethylene
PIA	Purified Isophthalic Acid
PP	Polypropylene
PSC	Production sharing contract
PTA	Purified Terephthalic Acid
PWF	Public welfare fund
R&D	Research and Development
REMCO	The Group Remuneration and Succession Review Committee (Shell)
RICP	Risk and Internal Control Policy (Shell)
RMB	Renminbi
ROACE	Return on average capital employed
SARS	Stock appreciation rights
SASAC	State-owned Assets Supervision and Administration Commission
SBPCI	State Bureau of Petroleum and Chemical Industry
SDPC	State Development and Planning Commission
SDRC	State Development and Reform Commission
SETC	State Economic and Trade Commission
SGBP	Shell General Business Principles
Sinochem	China National Petroleum and Petrochemical Import and Export Corporation
Sinopec	China National Petrochemical Corporation (before 2000) China Petroleum and Chemical Corporation (since 2000)
SOE	State-owned enterprise
SPC	State Planning Commission
SPCC	Shanghai Petrochemical Corporation
SSR	Statutory surplus reserves
TPEDH	Tarim Petroleum Exploration and Development Headquarters
TSR	Total shareholder return
Unipec	China International United Petroleum and Chemical Corporation
WTO	World Trade Organization

1 Introduction

When China set on the course to reform its economy in the late 1970s, the country marvelled at the technological achievement of the advanced economies and was convinced that technology lay at the heart of the catch-up process. Science and technology is the primary driving force of productivity (Deng Xiaoping). Scientists and engineers were sent to the advanced economies to learn advanced technology. Their eagerness and great effort in learning earned them the 'sobriquet of "technological vacuum cleaner"' (Brodie, 1990: 271). Indeed, the technological level and potential plays a vital role in the competitiveness of an industrial sector and the competitiveness of a nation in the international economy (Dosi *et al.*, 1988; Tyson, 1992). However, in a global economy, technology is one of the elements in an articulated system including the science base of the production and management process, the R&D strength, the human resources available for technological innovation, the adequate utilisation and level of diffusion of new technologies (Castells, 1996: 103). At the firm level, a competitive strategy based on low cost should incorporate the factors of technological as well as managerial excellence (Katz, 1987).

In contrast to the reform policies of swift privatisation adopted by other command economies, China's approach to restructuring its large-scale state sector has been incremental (Naughton, 1995; Nolan, 1995). Large Chinese firms have been experimenting with 'institutional innovation' and achieved significant progress in raising levels of industrial output, technology, and management know-how, and understanding market competition (Nolan and Wang, 1999). During the course of two decades, large state-owned enterprises (SOEs) evolved from former government ministries, have undertaken an evolutionary transformation in their organisational structure. A consistently stated goal has been to construct internationally competitive large firms (Nolan and Zhang, 2002). In the late 1990s, alongside the emphasis on 'technological innovation' (*jishu chuangxin*), China increasingly stressed the notion of 'organisational innovation' (*zuzhi chuangxin*) in reforming the large firms in strategic sectors such as oil, aerospace, telecommunications. Each step in the attempt to create large competitive firms has involved intense policy debate in China.

In the late 1990s, China's State Council initiated the strategy of 'restructuring and flotation (*chongzu shangshi*)' to reform the large SOEs which evolved from former government ministries. Since then, PetroChina, Sinopec, CNOOC, China Unicom, China Telecom, and Chalco were all listed successfully in the international stock exchanges in New York and Hong Kong. The restructuring process before the flotation involves massive asset reorganisation, personnel relocation and workforce downsizing. The structure of a modern industrial corporation has been established with the help of international consultants and investment bankers[1]. The model is to create a shareholding company with the parent company in control of the majority of shares, usually more than 50 per cent. The new shareholding company has the core businesses for listing whereas the parent company retains the non-core assets as well as social security-related entities. Typically, the world's leading firms in each of the industries become 'strategic investors' in the listed Chinese companies, whereas Hong Kong's large companies become 'overseas investors' in the listed Chinese firms.

Whereas China has been pursuing an *evolutionary* path to reform its large SOEs during the last two decades, the world's leading firms have undergone a *revolutionary* change in the same period. This epoch of global business evolution witnesses a fundamental transformation of the nature of the leading world firms (Nolan, 2001). China has joined the World Trade Organisation (WTO) at the beginning of the twenty-first century. As the country begins to integrate closely into the world business system, how competitive are China's aspiring large firms in terms of both business and organisational capabilities?

This study attempts to answer this question by studying the function of corporate headquarters within the global large firms and the Chinese large SOEs. The function of corporate headquarters is crucial in understanding the operation of modern business enterprises (Chandler, 1990b) and has become a fundamental question in strategic management (Rumelt *et al.*, 1990). However, there are few structured descriptive studies in this area to establish the direction and extent of changes at the corporate headquarters level (Ferlie and Pettigrew, 1996).

On the other hand, the reform of the Chinese SOEs has attracted abundant studies on the SOEs' reform, behaviour and performance (Child, 1994; Hassard *et al.*, 1999; Hay *et al.*, 1994; Jackson, 1992; Jefferson and Singh, 1999; Laaksonen, 1988; Naughton, 1995; Sachs and Woo, 1994). In addition, various aspects of SOE management have been researched such as the decision-making process, human resource practices, international joint ventures and trade unions (Campbell, 1989; Child and Lu, 1996; Brown and Porter, 1996; Ding *et al.*, 2002; Hong and Warner, 1998; Warner, 1995). There has also been research on the politics of management (Forrester and Porter, 1999) and institutional regulation (Lo, 1997). There is only a tiny amount of in-depth case studies of large Chinese SOEs[2] in their attempt to reform and become competitive (Byrd, 1992; Nolan, 1998; Steinfeld, 1998). Nolan (2001) makes an original and unique contribution to the analysis of institutional change in China's large companies. However, there has been negligible research on the headquarters' function during the long restructuring process of China's large companies which evolved from former governmental ministries in an attempt to construct internationally competitive large firms.

This study examines the organisational structure and the role of corporate headquarters within global large companies in the epoch of the global business revolution. It studies the organisational restructuring of China's large companies which evolved from former governmental ministries and in the attempt to construct internationally competitive large companies. The study systematically compares and contrasts the business and organisational structure of the leading global firms and the large Chinese companies. The investigation covers aspects of setting business policy, strategic planning, resource allocation, brand management, performance monitoring, financial control, procurement, reward policy, research and development (R&D), and information technology management.

The research is conducted in respect to large firms in the oil industry. The oil industry is the second most capital-intensive industry after the automobile industry (Ruigrok and Van Tulder, 1995). It is characterised by high barriers to entry and exit. Moreover, the oil industry has always been regarded as an industry of 'strategic importance' for a country. The consolidation in the late 1990s has transformed the industry on a global scale with Exxon Mobil, Royal Dutch/Shell and BP as the top three global players. This research analyses the case of BP and Royal Dutch/Shell, two UK-based companies, studying their business structure in the late 1990s.

The oil industry is regarded as one of China's 'pillar industries' (*zhizhu chanye*). The restructuring of the oil industry is significant for the reform of China's large SOEs and for the country's effort to construct large competitive modern companies. Following the nation-wide restructuring of the industry in 1998, the company-wide restructuring for flotation in 1999–2000 created two giant integrated companies, PetroChina (PetroChina Company Limited) and Sinopec (China Petroleum and Chemical Corporation). The two companies have been successfully listed on the international market and have entered the league of top ten publicly-traded oil companies in the world. In China, the oil sector is held up as a beacon for other sectors to study in restructuring to face the challenge of globalisation and consolidation. Moreover, the institutional experiment in China's oil industry is being closely watched by all concerned to understand the future course of China's industrial strategy regarding large firms and their relationship with the leading global firms. China's oil industry is of great importance for the global political economy, with major implications both for the main supplying regions, for the high-income countries, and for the firms based in those countries.

The study consists of nine chapters. Chapter 2 examines some of the theoretical and empirical issues with regard to the functions of the corporate headquarters. Since the 1980s, there has been a body of literature announcing the demise of the Chandlerian vertical corporation and advocating the rise of horizontal network enterprise (Castells, 1996). Many management writers advocate the transformation of vertical bureaucratic structures into network-based organisations – 'debureaucratising' the corporate structure, 'delayering' the middle management, and downsizing the workforce (Kanter, 1989; Kay, 1993). 'Flat and flexible' structure is the preferred structure to enable businesses to cope with the uncertainty of the global economy. This process is characterised by decentralisation of authority, power, responsibilities and resources from the corporate headquarters to the lower levels in the company hierarchy. The function of corporate headquarters is a void in this structure.

The network model of which the key process is decentralisation of authority, power, responsibility and resources has its weaknesses. First, the network model generalises the trend of decentralised organisation and does not distinguish between the characteristics of different industries and firms of different sizes and ignores the pattern of historical development of firms such as those in the oil industry. BP and Shell were indeed decentralised companies before the network model came into fashion. Second, the model does not recognise the centralisation and decentralisation at different levels in a company. While the divisional or subsidiary managers gained more autonomy from decentralisation, they are under close and remorseless scrutiny from the centre. Third, the model does not differentiate between the types of decisions devolved from the corporate headquarters to the divisional or subsidiary level. There are strategic decisions critical to the survival of the company as a whole in the global competition and operating decisions relevant to particular circumstances. Whereas managers of business units are empowered by operating decisions, the headquarters maintains its decision-making power in critical strategic areas such as mergers and acquisitions, investment and divestment, entry to or exit from a particular market or product line. The case of BP and Shell demonstrates that the headquarters has stripped the autonomy enjoyed by the powerful 'feudal baronies' of the company and centralised control in critical areas, ranging from capital investment to performance monitoring.

In the Chandlerian model of multidivisional structure, the creation of the corporate general office is an organisational innovation from the centralised multi-business structure. It is an attempt at decentralisation. In the last decade of the twentieth century, the Chandlerian model was transforming itself into different business models. Studies (Volberda, 1998) suggest that there is a much larger variety of flexible organisational forms from which corporate management can choose in order to achieve a balance between flexibility and controllability in the constantly changing environment.

The 1990s is an epoch during which global big businesses have undergone profound transformation. This revolutionary process featured massive industrial concentration (Nolan *et al.*, 2002) and competitive advantage at the firm level focusing on core businesses, downsizing and outsourcing, global brand-building, R&D and IT expenditure, and financial resources (Ruigrok and Van Tulder, 1995; Nolan, 2001). '(T)he global business revolution has produced an unprecedented concentration of power in large corporations headquartered in the high-income countries' (Nolan, 2001: 28). One important aspect of this process is that the global large corporations have fundamentally transformed their organisational structure. What is the function of corporate headquarters in the epoch of the global big business revolution? Is the headquarters in large corporations *the command centre* leading a unified company to compete in the market? Or rather, has it become *the service centre* for its subordinate units? The question of the function of corporate headquarters in this revolutionary process remains as fundamental as ever.

Chapter 3 provides empirical evidence on the function of corporate headquarters in the case of BP and Shell. Both companies have adopted the 'business unit' structure, delegating decision-making power from the head-quarters to business units. However, the establishment of the business unit structure does not mean that the autonomy of the business unit, usually confined to business operating matters, is without surveillance. The headquarters has the ultimate power in setting policy and goals, making strategic business decisions, and monitoring the performance of business units. The activities of the business units are subject to the broad policy guidelines and budgetary control devised by the headquarters. More importantly, the business units are constantly monitored by the headquarters. The corporate headquarters is the locus of power within the global giant firm.

Chinese large firms have come a long way from government ministries to listed companies. In the case of oil and petrochemical industry, this evolution covered a period of half of the twentieth century (1949–2000). From the 1950s to the 1970s, China's oil industry developed in the fashion of military 'massive campaigns' (*da hui zhan*) (Chapter 4). Under the leadership of the State Council, the Ministry of Petroleum Industry was responsible for planning campaigns for exploration and development and organising human and material resources nation-wide to support the campaigns. It undertook and co-ordinated the production, transportation and marketing of oil and oil products based on the overall national plan formulated by the State Planning Commission. It negotiated investment funds from the government and allocated them to its subordinate petroleum administrative bureaux (PAB) all over the country. The various PAB were production units responsible for carrying out production and investment plans.

From the 1980s to 1997, China's oil and petrochemical industry experienced significant institutional change, which was examined in Chapter 5. In 1983, the assets of the Ministry of Petroleum Industry, the Ministry of Chemical Industry and the Ministry of Textile Industry were merged and corporatised into the China Petrochemical Corporation (Sinopec). In 1988, the assets of the Ministry of Petroleum Industry were corporatised into the China National Petroleum Corporation (CNPC). In the meantime, CNPC experimented with the 'oil company' (*you gong si*) model. CNPC and Sinopec carried government administrative responsibilities such as formulating technological standards for the industry, and devising environmental regulations for the industry. CNPC and Sinopec were entrusted by the State Council to manage the state's assets and were made responsible for generating revenue to hand over to the government treasury. However, the two corporations did not devise production plans and did not have rights over product pricing, marketing as well as capital investment above 500 million yuan for CNPC and 200 million yuan for Sinopec. These business decision-making rights were tightly controlled by the central government. In this sense, CNPC and Sinopec were 'administrative entities', rather than 'economic entities'.

During the same period, the enterprise reform gave great emphasis to enhancing enterprise autonomy at the level of production units. The subordinate enterprises of CNPC and Sinopec were able to retain a greatly increased share of profits. They had the autonomy to make investments not only in core businesses but also in diversified businesses. They were able to finance expansion through bank loans and bonds and were responsible for debt repayment. They were listed in the domestic and international capital markets, which reduced the ownership rights of CNPC and Sinopec over them. They negotiated and set up joint ventures with multinational companies. In the case of Sinopec, strong subordinate enterprises initiated mergers and acquisitions in order to increase their market share of particular products. The functions of the CNPC and Sinopec headquarters in financial control, performance monitoring, procurement, and R&D were weak. This put CNPC and Sinopec into an awkward situation. In executing government functions, the headquarters of CNPC and Sinopec were simply an extension of various government administrative responsibilities. In exercising business functions, the headquarters of CNPC and Sinopec did not have the rights in product pricing, capital investment above a certain amount, and product marketing. Meanwhile, they did not have effective control over their subordinate enterprises even in the most important aspect of financial affairs and performance monitoring. They exercised their control over subordinate enterprises mainly through the appointment of senior manager in subordinate enterprises.

The growing autonomy at the enterprise level caused tension between the headquarters and their subordinate enterprises (Chapter 7). Under CNPC, Daqing, the largest oil field in China with annual production volume of 50 million tonnes, became increasingly ambitious for development as an independent entity across the value chain from upstream to downstream. Under Sinopec, Zhenhai, the second largest refinery in China with annual primary distillation capacity of 8.5 million tonnes in 1997, also aspired to become the largest refiner in East Asia and to expand its existing petrochemical businesses through mergers and acquisitions. The question 'where is the headquarters?' arises.

The reorganisation of China's oil and petrochemical industry in 1998 indicated that the headquarters of CNPC and Sinopec had won the struggle to become 'the headquarters' with the support of the Chinese government (Chapter 5). Through the 1998 reorganisation, CNPC and Sinopec each became an integrated oil and petrochemical company. The subsequent restructuring for floatation in 1999 and 2000 established the 'one-tier' legal person system (*yiji faren zhi*) and dashed the subordinate enterprises' aspiration for independence. CNPC and Sinopec Group each created a 'child company' – PetroChina and Sinopec – that amalgamates the core businesses and floated in the international market (Chapter 6). PetroChina and Sinopec obtained from the government the rights in product pricing, production, and investment in core businesses. They are centralising their control over their branch companies in capital investment, financial control, and marketing. They are investing in establishing an integrated information technology system in the company to facilitate the centralisation process. They began to monitor the performance of managers through performance contracts. The task of centralisation is formidable, considering the enormous autonomy the subordinate enterprises used to enjoy. At the level of the individual enterprise, this restructuring process resulted in the change of position from an increasingly autonomous enterprise back to a production unit (Chapter 7).

Chapter 8 compares and contrasts the business and organisational capabilities of the large global firms with that of their Chinese counterparts in relation to the headquarters' function. The global large corporations such as BP, Royal Dutch/ Shell and Exxon Mobil became strategic investors of the floated PetroChina, Sinopec and CNOOC. Moreover, each of the global giants has a great number of joint ventures with their Chinese competitors. Whereas Exxon Mobil, Royal Dutch/Shell and BP have lodged themselves in oligopolistic positions in the world oil and petrochemical industry, CNPC and Sinopec face a critical challenge for survival and growth. In the process of competitive struggle, the large Chinese corporations are at disadvantage with the world's leading firms.

The study concludes (Chapter 9) that in the epoch of global business revolution, the function of corporate headquarters of global leading firms, as exemplified in the oil industry, is of critical importance for the growth of the firm. The fundamental function lies with leadership and control as well as planning and monitoring. The model of a fluid business organisation with minimum control from the centre is detrimental to China's effort to construct modern corporations in the oil industry. The internal business structure of large Chinese companies is conflictual, which poses a threat to their competitiveness. The large Chinese companies still have enormous difficulties to integrate their businesses and enhance their organisational capabilities. However, the interaction of large Chinese firms with the global leading firms is an extremely complex and prolonged process. The eventual institutional structure of the large Chinese firms is far from certain.

The study contributes to the debate on organisational structure and the nature of corporate headquarters as well as to research on large Chinese SOEs. The study finds that the locus of power within a global giant firm is the corporate headquarters. This is of special importance to the large Chinese companies striving to enhance their competitiveness. The study presents policy implications for the Chinese large firms as well as for their government in reforming their business systems with the objective to construct globally competitive large corporations. China has begun to integrate closely into the global economic system as a result of its entry to WTO. The study presents policy implications for the global leading firms in their co-operative as well as competitive relationship with their Chinese counterparts.

2 The function of corporate headquarters

China's reform of its large state-owned enterprises (SOEs) has followed an evolutionary path. After the early 1980s, China's SOEs adopted the 'director responsibility system' and the 'contract management responsibility system'. They also experimented with lease, merger, bankruptcy, joint stock holdings, joint ventures with foreign partners, as well as domestic and international listings. In the 1990s, the strategy for further reforming the state-owned sector was to 'grasp the big and let go the small' (*zhua da fang xiao*), which was initiated in the ninth five-year plan (1996–2000) and remained the strategy for continuous reform in the state-owned enterprises in the tenth five-year plan (2001–5). With these institutional innovations, China has been experimentally changing the SOEs through a combination of central policy, local initiative, and interaction with international investment (Nolan and Wang, 1999). Throughout the course of reform, a consistent stated goal of China's industrial policy has been to construct globally powerful companies that can compete on the global level playing field (Nolan and Zhang, 2002). From the late 1990s, for those SOEs which evolved from former government ministries, the strategy has been to restructure and float in the international market (*chongzu shangshi*). The restructuring aims to establish the modern enterprise system (*xiandai qiye zhidu*). The productive assets of the large enterprises were reorganised into a joint stock company with a multidivisional structure and a system of boards and supervisory boards. The process involves large-scale asset reorganisation and massive workforce 'splitting off' (*fen liu*). As the large Chinese firms began operating under the new organisational structure, they faced critical issues in building up both business and organisational capabilities. The role of corporate headquarters is central in the process of establishing the modern enterprise system. This chapter examines some of the theoretical and empirical issues with regard to the function of corporate headquarters within large corporations.

The firm as an administrative organisation

In *The Theory of the Growth of the Firm* (originally published in 1958 and republished in 1995), Edith Penrose acknowledges the centrality of large firm (multi-plant firm) in a growing economy and the importance of 'big business' competition. Large firms can enjoy 'managerial economies' – 'marketing, financial, and research economies' (Penrose, 1995: 92). Compared with small firms, large firms have 'apparent superiority in research, … easier access to capital, and [an] ability to attract and hold the confidence of consumers' (Penrose, 1995: 260). Moreover, there exists competition among large firms. Their dominant market position is not stable as the market grows increasingly bigger and consumers' taste changes to favour more innovative brands. The decline in large firms' performance weakens the barrier to entry for potential competitors. On the other hand, the constant threat from the competitors and the effort to secure their market position encourages large firms to invest heavily in innovation and research.

> A strong case can be made for the big firm and for 'big business' competition, especially with the rate of development of new technology and new and improved products, and it may be that economists have been slow to recognise some of its advantages. Part of the reason for this, I think, can be traced to the influence on economic analysis of the so-called 'theory of the firm', which has tended to confine the theoretical approach to the firm within the frame of reference provided by the traditional categories of monopoly and competition and by the problems of price and output determination. In consequence, this part of economic theory has attained a high state of refinement, but, … , it does not provide suitable tools for the analysis of the growth and, in particular, of the innovating activities of firms treated as administrative organizations free to produce any kind of product they find profitable.
>
> (Penrose, 1995: 261)

Penrose treats the firm as an administrative organisation and a collection of productive resources rather than the textbook 'firm' defined as a cost curve and demand curve operating under the logic of optimal pricing and inputs. '(T)he productive function in a modern economy is carried out by autonomous administrative organisations with mind and capacities of their own. … The firm has the power to mould the environment, and to add new possibilities to its own information' (Marris, 1967: 112–13).

The internal organisation is of central importance to the growth of the firm. The firm's administrative arrangement serves as a conduit linking managerial resources to material and financial resources. Managers have administrative control over productive assets and are able to operate in any field of business activity, produce any products they find profitable and virtually in any place in the world they choose. The growth of the firm can be achieved through expansion in its original business activities, vertical integration, diversification, and mergers and acquisition. Moreover, as long as the firm's managerial functions, known as 'managerial services', keep pace with the firm's growth, there is usually no limit to the size of the firm.

According to Penrose, the 'management' of a firm includes individuals providing 'entrepreneurial services' as well as those supplying 'managerial services' (Penrose, 1995: 31–2). Moreover, the managerial competence of a firm to a large extent depends on the quality of the entrepreneurial services available to it.

CORPORATE HEADQUARTERS

The headquarters, 'central management' in Penrose's terminology, of the Penrosian industrial firm consists of 'the board of directors or committees thereof, the president, and the general managers of the firm' (Penrose, 1995: 16). It is the accepted highest authority within the administrative framework of the firm as well as the decision-making body of the firm. It is responsible for establishing or altering the administrative structure of the firm, laying down general policies, and making decisions related to financial and investment matters and the filling of top managerial posts. The headquarters is engaged in providing both entrepreneurial services and managerial services.

Entrepreneurial services   The availability of the particular type of entrepreneurial service is of strategic importance in determining a firm's growth (Penrose, 1995: 35). These services refer to the contributions to a firm's operation of the introduction and acceptance of new ideas in relation to products, location and technology, to acquiring new managerial personnel, to changing the administrative organisation of the firm, to raising capital, and to devising plans for expansion, including the method of expansion.

Managerial services   The managerial services refer to the execution of entrepreneurial ideas and proposals, and to the supervision of operations. The expansion of the firm is achieved by experienced managerial personnel performing two-fold managerial services – planning and co-ordinating. Co-ordination is needed in the process of capital budgeting as well as in handling the relationship between the major activities involved in expansion and the activities of the rest of the firm. Moreover, co-ordination is essential to revise the firm's administrative structure for the expansion, and to devise policies of responsibility and authority relating to the execution of the expansion and operation of the expanded activity: 'Hence, in addition to the administrative task of planning the expansion itself, there is the task of maintaining the necessary integration with the rest of the firm and, at the same time, working out flexible administrative arrangements so that the execution of the expanded programme will not be handicapped by bureaucratic bottle-necks' (Penrose, 1995: 208).

The headquarters' ability to plan and co-ordinate the firm's expansion is fundamental to a firm's long-term growth. Whereas the long-term policy is devised by the headquarters, authority and responsibility are increasingly delegated down the hierarchy. However, absolute delegation of responsibility is impossible. The ultimate responsibility must accumulate in full measure at the top of the hierarchy, which is a necessary condition for continued growth beyond a relatively small size of firm (Penrose, 1995: 50–1).

The multidivisional corporation

Empirical research shows that the large industrial enterprise became 'the engine of modern economic growth in the century spanning the 1880s to the 1980s, an era of industrial capitalism when technological advance provided the most powerful dynamics for the sustained growth of nations and the global economy' (Chandler, 1997). At the centre of this engine are the organisational capabilities of a large industrial enterprise (Chandler, 1990a; Lazonick, 1991). These organisational capabilities, together with the innovative multidivisional structure, are central to the growth of large industrial corporations.

The multidivisional structure is an organisational innovation that enabled large American industrial firms to adapt to opportunities created by the new developments in markets and technology. Hence in managing the fast-expanding multi-business enterprises, the modern business enterprise, characterised by the multidivisional structure, reached its maturity in 1920s. In the decades thereafter, it diffused to most of the American enterprises where the 'visible hand' of management in administrative co-ordination proved more profitable than market co-ordination (Chandler, 1977).

Chandler (1962, 1977) systematically analysed evolution and perfection of the multidivisional structure (Figure 2.1). This analysis was rationalised by Williamson (1975, 1985). There are four levels of administrative positions. At the top is the general office where the top executives set goals, plan strategy and

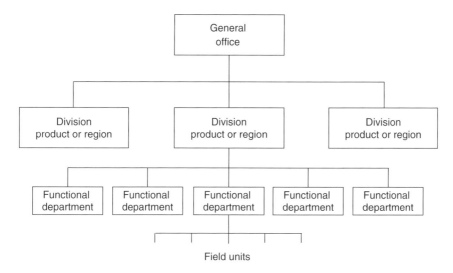

Figure 2.1 The multidivisional structure.

Source: adapted from Chandler, 1962.

devise the policy framework for the lower managers. Each division is responsible for a major product line or carries out activities in a geographical region. The divisional managers co-ordinate and administrate the functional departments in areas such as manufacturing, marketing, purchasing, research, and finance. Each of the functional departments, in turn, supervises the field units. These units can be a branch, an office, a plant or a laboratory and they are at the lowest level of the multidivisional structure.

THE CORPORATE HEADQUARTERS

Chandler considers that the creation of the multidivisional structure with a corporate headquarters (general office in Chandler's terminology) at the top is a creative organisational innovation (Chandler, 1962: Chapter 6). The multi-divisional enterprise was led by a powerful general office whose executives concentrated on entrepreneurial activities.[1] The divisions under the general office had autonomy in carrying out operating responsibilities.[2] This structure relieved the top executives from their administrative load. They were responsible for strategic decisions that were of critical importance to the survival and growth of the enterprise. The strategic decisions include allocation of existing resources and acquisition of new resources for development and expansion. The financial office and advisory staff in the general office studied new business areas for development and provided information on the performance of operating units and the whole company. All these greatly assisted the top executive who now gained the time and independent information to make strategic decisions for the company. Meanwhile, the responsibilities for co-ordination and appraisal were greatly eased. The general office staff provided routine checks and supplements on product flow, cost determination, and product design that were now carried out by the operating divisions. Appraisal of divisional performance became more accurate since the general office had detailed reports on all aspects of a division's financial performance.

The divisional managers had autonomy in running their businesses. They were responsible for the prices of specific products, for the design and quality of existing products and for the development of new ones, for supply and marketing, for technological improvements, and for the transfer of the product from the supplier to the consumer. However, these responsibilities were to be made within the framework set by the broad policy guides and a financial budget devised by the general office, and within the carefully defined interrelationships between the operating units and the general office.

In Williamson's analysis (1975), the general office in the 'M form' firm is principally concerned with strategic decisions, involving planning, appraisal, and control, including the allocation of resources among the operating divisions. Relieved from the load of making operating decisions, the general office is responsible for strategic decisions. In addition, the general office performs the function of internal auditing and control to overcome the 'information impactedness'[3] conditions and to exercise control over the operating units

(Williamson, 1985). In addition, the 'elite staff' of the general office perform both advisory and auditing functions, which enable greater control over the behaviour of operating divisions.

Moreover, Williamson considers that the M form firm should operate as a miniature capital market. He argues that one important reason for inefficiency in capital market control is its information impactedness (Williamson, 1975: 142) with regard to the internal conditions of firms. Its power to audit firms and its access to firms' incentive and resource allocation mechanisms is very limited: 'The most severe limitation of the capital market is that it is an external control instrument' (Williamson, 1975: 143). Williamson argues that in the M form firm, the headquarters is more efficient than an external capital market in incentive programmes, internal auditing and resource (cash flow) allocation. The existence of the general office is beneficial for establishing employment policy and making sure that divisional managers ensure that the behaviour of the operating units is consistent with the goals set at a higher level. Furthermore, the general office is more effective in reviewing the accounting records and files of its subordinates and in dealing with situations involving disclosure of sensitive information. In addition, the general management can assign cash flows to investment with higher rate of return on capital by evaluating investment proposals from the divisions.

HEADQUARTERS' FUNCTION

The two basic functions of corporate headquarters of industrial multi-business enterprises are entrepreneurial and administrative (Chandler 1990b; Williamson, 1990). They are intimately related to each other. Analysing the growth of firms in the 1970s and 1980s in relation to the experience of IBM, GE and Du Pont, Chandler (1990b) pointed out that the headquarters' ability to carry out these two basic functions is one of the three factors[4] that contribute to the size and boundaries of enterprises.

Entrepreneurial function The entrepreneurial function is 'to determine strategies for maintaining and utilising in the long term the firm's organisational skills, facilities, and capital and to allocate resources – capital and product-specific technical and managerial skills – to pursue these strategies' (Chandler, 1990b: 327). This function helps to create value.

Administrative function The administrative function is 'to monitor the performance of the operating divisions; to check on the use of the resources allocated; and, when necessary, to redefine the product lines of the divisions so as to continue to use the firm's organizational capabilities effectively' (Chandler, 1990b: 327–8). This function helps to prevent loss.

Addressing the functions of headquarters in a multidivisional structure from the economizing (efficiency analysis) perspective, Williamson (1990: 375) maintains:

A well-functioning headquarters unit is one that simultaneously is alert to market opportunities and hazards, creates an internal operating ethos and rules of the game to which division managers relate and are responsive, and recognises both its own limitations and those endemic to large firms in general. Such a management is engaged in both entrepreneurial and administrative roles.

The ability to employ effectively the organisational capabilities – the collective physical facilities and human skills within the corporation – is essential to the corporation in achieving economies of scale and scope in order to maintain the firm's growth and to compete in national and international markets. The ability of the top management to fulfil their entrepreneurial and administrative roles is most critical to the long-term health and growth of the corporation. 'One of the most critical tasks of top management has always been to maintain these (organizational) capabilities and to integrate these facilities and skills into a unified organization – so that the whole becomes more than the sum of its parts' (Chandler, 1990a: 594).

The multidivisional structure enables the headquarters to make long-term strategic plans for the whole corporation. Meanwhile, operating decisions are delegated to managers at a lower level. In addition to co-ordinating business activities among divisions, top management has to ensure that the delegated decision-making power should serve the overall goals of the corporation. Therefore, the administrative function of the headquarters in monitoring and controlling the performance of the divisions is highly important. There needs to be a balance between centralised control and delegation of power in order to serve the interests of the multidivisional structure. The key to the success of the multidivisional structure in the United States was 'the delegation of authority over operational decision making without loss of control by top management over the implementation of enterprise strategy' (Lazonick, 1991: 33). Moreover, the 'organisational integration' of the structure achieved through the training and motivation of managers is essential for the corporation to achieve superior performance. Setting up the multidivisional structure cannot in itself guarantee effective management and good performance. In-depth studies on General Motors reveal that the multidivisional structure is an administrative form in which decentralisation is balanced by central control (Drucker, 1946; Sloan, 1965): '(G)ood management relies on the reconciliation of centralisation and decentralization. Decentralization should be balanced with co-ordinated control' (Sloan, 1965: 429). This balance is achieved by the administrative and incentive mechanisms. Being a 'boss', the headquarters unifies the 'aggressive, highly individual, and very independent divisional top executives into one team' (Drucker, 1946: 52), thereby achieving the synergy of a unified company.

HEADQUARTERS IN THE TRANS-NATIONAL CORPORATION

Recent research on the function of the headquarters in trans-national corporations reveals that the headquarters' power of control remains as important as before despite the fact that the mechanism of control becomes more sensitive and co-ordination oriented (Bartlett, 1986). The headquarters management must co-ordinate strategic objectives and operating policies to ensure the unity of the whole company. They must co-ordinate the flow of supplies, components, and funds throughout the company. They must monitor global developments, collect, accumulate and transfer useful knowledge and experience throughout the company.

In a trans-national business organisation, while the centre sets the strategic direction, multiple groups within the company make a great contribution to the development of strategic management. While the headquarters still provides central supporting services to the world-wide operations, the headquarters and operating units have become increasingly interdependent. While the centre still monitors the performance of its subordinates, its control role becomes less mechanistic and hierarchical. In trans-national corporations, the headquarters' role in developing the overall strategic direction, supporting, and monitoring remain just as important as it is in multinational companies and global companies. However, the key role of the headquarters 'tends to evolve into a more sensitive coordinating task in which it builds and maintains the complex linkages required in the trans-national corporation' (Bartlett, 1986: 397).

Corporate styles and industrial characteristics

Goold and Campbell's book *Strategies and Styles* (1989) makes a unique and important contribution to research on the function of the corporate headquarters with different corporate management styles. The book examines the relationship between the headquarters and the business units of sixteen leading British multinationals and demonstrates that the headquarters can choose a management style that adds value to the businesses in its portfolio. Analysing the headquarters' influence on the process of planning and control over the business units, Goold and Campbell identify eight management styles. They examine in detail the headquarters' role in the three most common styles – strategic planning, strategic control and financial control. The characteristics of the three styles are summarised in Table 2.1.

The strategic planning company pursues maximum competitive advantage for the businesses in their portfolio. It co-ordinates global strategies and makes a great effort to search for the optimum strategy. The company strongly emphasises and tenaciously pursues long-term goals. The headquarters plays a vital role in developing and reviewing business units' strategies. It sets up extensive and demanding planning processes, contributes to strategic thinking, and co-ordinates development across business units. However, control tends to be flexible and less tightly enforced in the strategic planning company than in the strategic control and financial control company. It stresses decentralisation, and values strategic direction. Nevertheless, performance targets are set flexibly and reviewed within the context of a long-term strategic process.

Table 2.1 Corporate styles and characteristics.

Styles	Characteristics
Strategic planning	• Complex but coordinated corporate structure • Extensive planning process • Strong central leadership • Flexible controls • More focus on long-term goals and strategy
Strategic control	• Decentralised profit centres and divisional co-ordination • Extensive and strategic planning process • Business autonomy • Tight controls • Balance long- and short-term objectives
Financial control	• Separate profit centres • Budgetary planning process • Business autonomy • Focus on short-term objectives • Tight controls

Source: Goold and Campbell (1989).

The strategic control company seeks both competitive and financial strength. It focuses on the quality of strategic thinking, allows businesses to develop long-term strategies, and motivates the business units' managers to develop plans. Instead of giving directions as in the case of a strategic planning company, the headquarters reviews the business plan as a check on the quality of strategic thinking. However, the control process is tightly exercised to ensure that both financial and strategic objectives are realised.

The financial control company focuses more on financial performance than on competitive position. The growth of the company is mainly through acquisitions, and long-term strategic planning for growth is limited. The main criterion for success is profits. The headquarters closely reviews the annual budget and sets profit targets. Tight financial controls are exercised while the planning influence of the headquarters is low.

The typology of management styles and the role of the headquarters are further developed into the role of 'parenting' in devising corporate strategy (Goold *et al.*, 1994). The argument is that in the multi-businesses companies, the 'corporate parent' – the corporate hierarchy outside of the businesses – has an essential role in making corporate strategy decisions.

It is the parent that decides what new businesses to support, what acquisitions to make, and whether to form joint ventures and alliances. It is the parent that determines the structure of the corporation, defines budgeting and capital expenditure process, and sets the tone for corporate values and attitudes. It is the parent that comes under intense scrutiny during hostile takeover bids, or when large shareholders are dissatisfied with their returns. The parent is at the heart of corporate strategy decisions.

(Goold *et al.*, 1994: 6)

Chandler further differentiates the role of headquarters of large industrial corporations in different industries. He developed the thesis that the function of the corporate headquarters varies with the characteristics of the industries in which enterprises operate. He employed the terminology of Goold and Campbell for the three styles of companies – financial control, strategic control and strategic planning – to discuss and illustrate his point.

> In industries in which new product development is a critical component of inter-firm competition, where R&D expenditures are high, state-of-the-art facilities costly, and marketing requires specialised skills, the corporate office needs to concentrate on the entrepreneurial (value-creating) function. Here it needs to play a strong role in the strategic planning process if it is to utilise fully the company's existing competitive strengths in technologically advanced businesses and to determine paths for new product and process development. Nevertheless, as the IBM story suggests, strategic planning for all lines in a high-technology global industry by a single dominant firm may become too complex for a single office to handle. Strategic planning may then be delegated to the operating subsidiaries, with the corporate headquarters providing no more than broad strategic direction. In more mature industries where the nature of the final product remains stable, where R&D expenditures continue to be essential but primarily for improving product and cost-cutting processes, and where facilities are costly and marketing complex but the facilities and skills required have been well established; in such industries the corporate office can more easily delegate strategic planning to the operating divisions and maintain strategic control by setting targets and establishing long-term goals for the corporation as a whole. Finally, as the experience of the conglomerates reinforces, in the service industries and mature manufacturing industries where the products remain much the same, where the technology of production is not complex, where facilities are less costly and where competition lies more in distribution or R&D, financial controls alone have usually been enough to prevent losses and maintain profits in multibusiness enterprises.
>
> (Chandler, 1990b: 357–8)

The network corporation

In the 1980s and the early 1990s, comment on the management of post-Fordist organisation[5] mainly focussed on the decentralisation of authority, power, responsibility and resources. There are accounts of the emergence of smaller and more flexible organisational forms (Bahrami, 1992) operating with more network-based forms of management (Powell, 1990; Thorelli, 1990). Multinational corporations are seen as moving towards a network form of organisation (Ghoshal and Bartlett, 1990).

Castells' *The Rise of the Network Society* argues that network-based organisation has become *the* dominant organisational form in the 'information economy'. This organisational form is termed the 'network enterprise'. It is

> that specific form of enterprise whose system of means is constituted by the intersection of segments of autonomous systems of goals. ... The performance of a given network will then depend on two fundamental attributes of the network: its *connectedness*, that is its structural ability to facilitate noise-free communication between its components; its *consistency*, that is the extent to which there is sharing of interests between the network's goals and the goals of its component.
>
> (Castells, 1996: 171)

Drawing on empirical evidence from the East Asia (Japan, Korea, and China) business corporations, he argues that the predominant form of business organisation in East Asia is the 'network enterprise'.

> The building block of such systems is not the firm or the individual entrepreneur, but networks or business groups of different kinds, in a pattern that, with all its variations, tends to fit with the organizational form that I have characterised as the network enterprises.
>
> (Castells, 1996: 173)

Castells argues that the success of Asian Pacific business model based on networks external to the corporation challenges the validity of Williamson's (1985) interpretation of the large multidivisional corporation as an efficient organisational form and Chandler's (1961, 1977) model of multidivisional corporation.

> Thus, Williamson's influential interpretation of the emergence of the large corporation as the best way to reduce uncertainty and minimize transaction costs by internalizing transactions within the corporation, simply does not hold when confronted with the empirical evidence of the spectacular process of capitalist development in the Asian Pacific, based on networks external to the corporation.
>
> Similarly, the process of economic globalization based on network formation seems also to contradict the classical analysis by Chandler that attributes the rise of the large multi-unit corporation to the growing size of the market, and to the availability of communications technology that enables the large firm to take hold on such a broad market, thus reaping economies of scale and scope, and internalizing them within the firm.
>
> While market size was supposed to induce the formation of the vertical, multi-unit corporation, the globalization of competition dissolves the large corporation in a web of multidirectional networks, that become the actual

operating unit. The increase of transaction costs, because of added technological complexity, does not result in the internalization of transactions within the corporation but in the externalization of transactions and sharing costs throughout the network, obviously increasing uncertainty, but also making possible the spreading and sharing of uncertainty.

(Castells, 1996: 190 and 193)

Castells predicts that the large corporations can only survive by transforming their organisational form from 'vertical, rational bureaucracies' into 'an articulated network of multifunctional decision-making centers' (Castells, 1996: 166). The implication is that the survival of large corporations relies on their disintegration into a network of centres, each with decision-making autonomy.

In the 1990s, big businesses underwent massive restructuring of their organisational structure and adopting new business model, focussing on core businesses, downsizing the workforce, and outsourcing non-core business activities (Ruigrok and Van Tulder, 1995). The term 'network' is widely used in discussions on the changing business structure and the emerging new organisational forms in business. Generally, the network perspective is applied to research both on network-based management within the corporation and network relationships outside the corporation (Child and Heavens, 1999). Research on the internal networks of the corporation focuses on the relationship between the business units operating in different countries and the global corporate headquarters. The multinational corporation is treated as an inter-organisational network. It is suggested that the relative power of the headquarters and the national units is determined by the degree of linkages and interactions within and across the national organisational sets involved in industrial activities (Ghoshal and Bartlett, 1990). The external networks of the corporation or the strategic networks examine firms embedded in a network of relationships, both horizontal and vertical, with other organisations – suppliers, customers, competitors, or other entities – across industries and countries. These strategic networks include strategic alliances, joint ventures, long-term buyer–supplier partnerships and other similar ties (Gulati *et al.*, 2000).

The restructuring of global big businesses considerably enhances the notion of inter-firm network relationships. The knowledge learning and sharing emphasises the network relationships of business units of a corporation. However, in the model of a network enterprise, who 'governs' the components to guarantee the 'connectedness' and 'consistency'? Where is the locus of centrality and power?

East Asian corporations

Evidence of the East Asia management system forms a critical part of Castells' argument which challenges the Chandlerian model of the multidivisional corporation. In fact, as we shall see, this evidence shows that the corporate headquarters has the power of control over, and co-ordination throughout, the whole corporation.

Aoki's research on the Japanese management system reveals that it is characterised by 'the duality principle' (Aoki, 1988: 53) – a decentralised/centralised information structure is complemented by a centralised/decentralised personnel administration system. Toyohiro Kono's research (1984, 1999) on the function of corporate headquarters in Japanese large corporations found that participation and consensus was widespread, but only at the sub-system level. The headquarters, which is usually large and strong, has the central authority. Kono pointed out: 'It is a misconception that the Japanese organization has a decentralized authority structure, and the bottom-to-top approach is popularly used' (Kono, 1984: 298). The headquarters has the final authority in making strategic decisions, operational decisions and administrative decisions. Until the 1990s, in successful Japanese companies, important functions were centralised in the head office (Kono, 1999). These functions include devising corporate strategy, developing strong competence through the expert staff in functional departments such as marketing, technology and quality assurance and personnel development, and providing centralised services to produce strong competencies.

Kono argues that a strong head office has far more advantages than disadvantages. Indeed, it is essential to the success of Japanese corporations. Based on a survey of major Japanese manufacturing corporations, Kono (1999) summarised that the corporate headquarters has three functions: formulating corporate strategy, building core competencies, and providing expert services. His findings are as follows:

- The strong headquarters can initiate and determine better strategies for the whole company. The headquarters can take innovative action to capitalise on business opportunities by mobilising corporate resources. The concentration of resources into growth products would have been impossible under a decentralised product division structure. Moreover, the headquarters can also bring together project teams to plan and implement risky new ventures by accommodating them in the incubator department of the head office. A large headquarters office can also take aggressive action in expanding operations on a global scale by establishing production centres around the world. In addition, whenever future opportunities or threat arises, which are not the responsibility of the product divisions or which cover the fields of more than two divisions, the headquarters can take action to utilise the opportunities or to fend off the threat. Information on product improvement and productivity enhancement is collected and utilised at the lower levels but it has to be diffused to other departments with the help of the headquarters. Delegation of authority is not always the best approach. The problem is what sort of information should be collected where, and how to generate successful new ideas.
- The strong headquarters accumulates knowledge on personnel management, production systems, quality control and marketing systems. Strong staff

support is available for every functional area, in order to create and develop the companies' core competencies. A strong headquarters also enables a company to flatten its organisational structure.

- A large headquarters can provide a pool of competent talent, which can be mobilised to support foreign investment and new projects. To innovate, companies need to have personnel and resources available.

KOREA

The Korean *chaebol* is a hierarchical structure (Chen, 1996; Steers *et al.*, 1991). All the firms in the *chaebol* are controlled by a central holding company owned by a family that is deeply involved in management. The most powerful body in the group is the chairman's office. It is in charge of the group's administration and planning, and monitors performance (Kang, 1989: 75). Financial and personnel administration are the two most effective control measures involving loose supervision and direct participation of the *chaebol*'s top management (Janelli, 1993: 124) Top managers participate directly in constructing public financial statements and making various reports to government agencies. They also conduct shareholder meetings in a manner disguised to minimise external interference over the company's finances. In the area of personnel management, top managers control the appointment to the board of directors and supervise a set of personnel policies from recruitment, training, promotion, to dismissal. With the expansion of businesses, professional managers are hired and decision-making power is delegated. However, the *chaebol* family and centralised management remain (Janelli, 1993; Chen, 1996).

CHINESE FAMILY BUSINESSES[6]

Much research on the Chinese business organisation has focussed on Chinese family businesses (Redding, 1993; Whitley, 1994, 2000). The top management positions in the family business are filled by key family members whose personal goals are identical to the corporate goals. Therefore, the business organisation becomes a social organisation oriented towards relationships (Chen, 1996: 87)'. The organisational structure of Chinese family business is simple and informal. Very few large businesses developed large functional departments such as R&D, public relations, labour relations and market research. The management style is authoritarian, centralised and 'paternalistic' (Whitley, 1994: 77). Business practice is not typically based on formal rules. The top executive has the ultimate power in making strategic decisions, which often rely on their intuition and/or experience. Operating responsibility can be delegated to lower level managers, but the delegation remains at a low level. Control over decisions relating to employee rewards and discipline remains in the hands of the top management. On the other hand, Chinese businesses cultivate external relationships to nurture their businesses. This forms a flexible network of businesses connected by personal trust. This gives the Chinese businesses the flexibility to respond quickly to changes in market demand (Chen, 1996: 84–94).

However, as Redding points out, the vast majority of Chinese family businesses are small and they usually specialise in one field of expertise. The exception of the large corporation came into being only under two conditions – an extremely knowledgeable chief executive officer with acute business senses and a 'soft' environment usually under political patronage allowing the development of a monopolistic position. 'The alternative route to growth which is the building of a complex multiproduct or multimarket organization, fully integrated under a complex bureaucratic control system, and professionally managed, does not appear to be normal route' (Redding, 1993: 179).

CHINESE SOE[7]

The reform of the Chinese state-owned enterprises started in early 1980s through adoption of the director responsibility system (DRS) and the contract management responsibility system (CMRS). The DRS was introduced from 1984 to 1986 with the aim of separating the enterprise management from party control. Under the DRS, the enterprise director had the commanding power and responsibility for the internal and external operations of the enterprise (Child, 1994). The CMRS was introduced from 1987 with the objective of separating the enterprise management from ownership of state assets represented by the government and went through two periods: 1987–90 and 1990–5. Under the CMRS, the government and the state-owned enterprise established a profit-sharing scheme, a total wage bill control scheme for employees and a contractual technological investment project (Chen, 1995). A survey of six state-owned enterprises of different sizes in Beijing (Lu and Child, 1996) shows that up to early 1990s, the large industrial enterprise had a governance structure similar to that of a joint-stock company. The board or group headquarters had the managerial authority over the manufacturing units. However, an in-depth case study in the oil and petrochemical industry revealed that the group headquarters transformed from previous government ministries had weak authority and control over the subordinate enterprises (Nolan, 2001).

The global business revolution

The last decade or so of the twentieth century was characterised by a fundamental change in global business at both the industry and firm level. This revolutionary process was facilitated by the explosive development in technology, particularly information technology and was influenced strongly by the shareholder movement from the 1980s onwards, the rising power of global financial institutions due to the formation of new forms of financial organisational and financial devices, and by the ideology of globalisation. The huge mergers and acquisition explosion in the 1990s was characterised by consolidation of the 'strong with the strong'. Pushed by the shareholder movement, companies came under stringent scrutiny by the financial market to 'deliver' shareholder value. Companies that failed to do so were either taken over or dissolved through the market. The ideology of globalisation advocated by the firms and governments of the advanced capitalist countries became immensely powerful in the 1990s. Giant firms that have accumulated competitive capabilities in technology, brand and financial resources in the past decades sought to gain first move advantage to lodge themselves in a dominant position in the process of globalisation. While cost-cutting was still the preoccupation, companies pursued the creation of new 'shareholder value' by investing in newly opened markets and in new technologies. This required colossal financial and organisational capabilities.

The 1990s saw a rush of global giants to merge or form alliances with their competitors, which took place in every industrial sector. The breakthrough in communication technology and faster transportation facilitated this wave of consolidation. This process fundamentally transformed the global industrial structure in every sector. The fundamental change in the world oil industry from the 'seven sisters' to the 'three brothers' – Exxon Mobil, Royal Dutch/Shell and BP – dramatically illustrated this process.

Giant firms underwent internal management reorganisation to get 'fit' for the fast changing environment. Practices of de-layering, downsizing, outsourcing, privatisation were adopted widely. The corporate headquarters were downsized to cut overheads and many of their activities were outsourced. As discussed above, many predicted that the 'disintegrated' hierarchical Fordist corporation would be replaced by the network-based corporation. These predictions usually imply that corporations will base their business activities on networking with different business entities. However, as the large firm has 'disintegrated', the extent of comprehensive planning and conscious co-ordination across the whole value chain has increased and it is the core system integrator that is central for this comprehensively planned and co-ordinated activity (Nolan, 2001: 41–5). The core system integrator typically has strong financial capabilities to fund large new projects and to invest in information technology and high-level R&D. It is capable of developing a global brand and attracting the best human resources. It interacts intimately with the major segments of the whole value chain, both upstream and downstream. With the globalising process of business activities in the last decade or so, core system integrators plan and co-ordinate the development of the firm on a global scale. What is the function of corporate headquarters in this structure?

Summary

The Chandlerian modern industrial enterprise with its multidivisional structure involves delegation of decision-making power from the headquarters to the divisions. This by no means implies that the autonomy of the division, usually confined to business operating matters, is without control. The headquarters in the multidivisional structure has the ultimate power in setting policy and goals, making strategic decisions, and monitoring division performance. The activities of the divisions are subject to the broad policy guides and budget control devised by the headquarters. They are constantly monitored by the headquarters.

In the large modern industrial enterprise, despite differences in managerial styles, power ultimately lies with the headquarters. The headquarters has the power to determine the goals of the corporation as a whole as well as the goals of the divisions. It has the power to determine investment decisions and strategies for growth such as mergers and acquisitions. It has the power to devise policy as a framework to guide the divisions' activities. It has the power to define the limits of the authority of the divisional managers as well as to appoint, appraise, reward, promote and remove divisional managers. It has the power to constantly monitor the progress and performance of the divisions. The power of corporate headquarters lies in its ability to plan and control.

The ultimate location of power in the corporate headquarters is a characteristic shared by East Asian corporations. The headquarters in the Japanese large enterprises and the Korean *chaebol* has the authority to make strategic decisions, to deal with the relationship with government and shareholders, and to set up personnel administration policies. For the mostly small Chinese family businesses in a less formal hierarchy, ultimate power lies in the hands of the owner as the top executive. At the end of the 1990s, the case of the Chinese large state-owned enterprises transformed from previous governmental ministries stood out as an exception. The structure was usually that of a holding company. The headquarters had limited control over business and internal administrative activities in the subordinate enterprises.

The notion of the network enterprise is helpful to capture the changing method of organising business activities, which is characterised by co-operation and interdependence between partners. However, this approach paid little attention to the dynamism of distribution power, or to the nature of relationships between components of the network. An important exception to this, is research on northern Italy which shows that the salient business networks have started to change: '(A) segmented oligopoly is evolving in which large Italian and foreign firms have started to exploit the flexibility of the region, but now in a vertical manner' (Ruigrok and Van Tulder, 1995: 31).

In the epoch of global business revolution, the very boundary of firms has become blurred (Nolan, 2001) due to the increasing outsourcing and partnering activities upstream and downstream across the value chain. The core system integrator is central in planning and co-ordinating activities on a global scale. Further research on the functions of the headquarters within the core system integrator is necessary to understand more deeply the headquarters' function in conducting business activities world-wide, the interaction with large businesses from developing countries, and the impact of these activities on the global political economy in this century. I will explore this issue in the following chapter in relation to two giant oil and petrochemical companies, BP and Royal/Dutch Shell.

3 Corporate structure and headquarters' function

BP and Shell

Until the late 1990s, most of the world's leading oil and petrochemical companies operated under a matrix structure involving complex layers of hierarchy and bureaucracy. Regional head offices enjoyed considerable independence including autonomy in capital expenditure. Shell had 'a proliferation of regional baronies', which 'encouraged too many committees and turf battles' (*Financial Times*, 16 February 1996). The complex reporting structure and the powerful regional head offices made it difficult to link the performance of individuals and operating units to that of the whole group. The typical attitude was that '(w)hen things went wrong it was usually someone else's fault' (ibid.).

During the 1990s, the global oil and petrochemical giants undertook fundamental restructuring of their management systems. They stripped out regional lines of command and established structures with fewer management layers and clear lines of accountability. Businesses are now organised into business units, each of which is an autonomous profit centre and responsible to internal and/or external customers. They operate in compliance with the company's policies and are held accountable for their fulfilment of performance targets. This chapter examines the business unit structure adopted by BP from the mid-1990s in relation to the function of corporate headquarters. It also examines the unique management structure of Royal Dutch/Shell and its lines of command and accountability after its restructuring in the late 1990s. The chapter concludes by presenting the common features related to the function of the corporate headquarters shared by BP and Shell.

BP

Organisational structure

BP's business unit (BU) structure has three layers. At the top is the board of directors and group chief executive officer (GCEO). The four business streams – Exploration and Production, Gas and Power, Refining and Marketing, Chemicals – and their chief executives are led by the board and GCEO. Under the four business streams, there are 150 business units engaged in a variety of business activities from upstream to downstream (Figure 3.1).

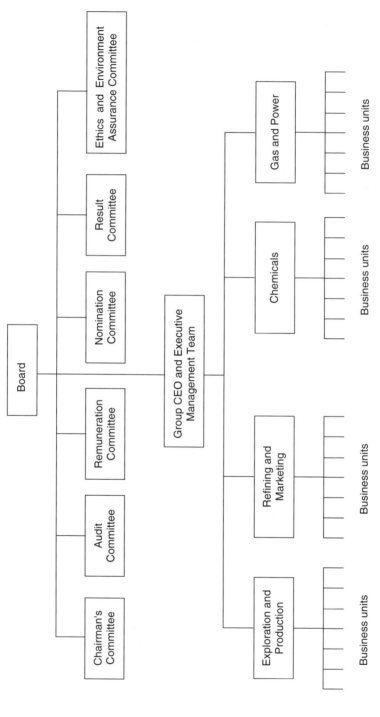

Figure 3.1 Organisational structure of BP, 2000.

Source: BP.

THE BOARD AND THE GCEO

In 1997, BP's board of directors adopted a set of governance policies that cover its own activities, its relationship with the shareholders and the GCEO. BP's board of directors consists of eighteen members, six of which are leaders of executive management including the GCEO, (currently Lord Browne), the Deputy Group Chief Executive, the Chief Financial Officer, and three Business Chief Executive Officers (BCEOs) responsible for upstream, downstream and chemicals. The other twelve members are all non-executive directors, accounting for two-thirds of the total number of directors. The Chairman and the Deputy Chairman are Non-Executive Directors. The Company Secretary reports to the Non-Executive Chairman and is not a part of the executive management. The board has a board process policy that defines its activities and responsibilities as well as the rules for conducting its activities. The board processes policy, formulates the cycle of board activities and the setting of its agenda, the qualification of board membership, the rules of conduct for board members at meetings, the provision of information to the board, the process for directors to obtain independent advice and the assessment of the board's performance. It defines the role of board officers, the establishment and composition of board committees and their responsibilities, the appointment and role of the Company Secretary, and the remuneration of Non-Executive Directors. The chairman of the board is responsible for implementing the board's policies and for training directors.

The board and the shareholders The governance policy with regard to the relationship between the board and the shareholders specifies that the board represents and promotes the interests of shareholders. The board is accountable to shareholders for the performance and activities of the whole company. The board communicates with shareholders through the publication of BP's annual report and accounts, the quarterly performance announcement at the London Stock Exchange and the New York Stock Exchange, and the annual general meetings (AGM) of shareholders. The AGM provides shareholders with the opportunity to hold a dialogue with the board about their concerns. However, BP has 1.1 million shareholders across the world and direct interaction with the board is limited. In addition, BP makes regular presentations on BP's performance and future prospects to the representatives from the financial community in the United Kingdom and the United States. These presentations are simultaneously broadcast over the internet and with an open conference call for shareholders.

The board and the GCEO As the representative of the shareholders, the board delegates the authority of business management to the GCEO. The board sets general policies and monitors the performance of the GCEO. The board set out the long-term goal for the company that it expects the GCEO to deliver. It also sets out the restrictions on the manner in which the GCEO may achieve the objectives in the executive limitations policy, which include issues related to

HSE (health, safety, and the environment), internal control of the company, financial distress, risk preference, business ethics, treatment of employees and political considerations. The GCEO explains to the board his annual and medium-term plans to achieve the company's long-term goal. The annual plan includes a comprehensive assessment of the risks involved in delivering the targets. Each month, the GCEO reports to the board on the progress of carrying out the plan, the actual results achieved and a forecast of the results for the year. The board reviews the reports and judges the GCEO's performance. In these systematic reviews, the GCEO must discuss with the board all 'strategic projects or development' as well as 'material matters' that are currently or prospectively affecting the company's performance, which specifically include 'any materially under-performing business activities and actions that breach the executive limitation policy' (BP website).

BUSINESS STREAMS AND BUSINESS UNITS

Each of BP's four business streams – Exploration and Production, gas and power, refining and Marketing, Chemicals – is led by a chief executive officer (BCEO) who is himself (herself[1]) board executive member and is accountable to the GCEO. Each business stream leads a group of business units.

In 2000, the chemical stream was divided into nineteen business units, each led by a BU leader. Leaders are tagged to an Executive Vice President who sits on the Chemicals Executive Committee (ExCo). Each vice president is responsible for a business line: polymers, performance products, intermediates, and feedstocks. Under each business line, each BU leader runs a particular category of products or a certain product in different part of the world. For example, under the business line polymers, there are six business units: engineering polymers and carbon fibres, polyethylene Asia, polyethylene Europe, polypropylene, erdölchemie, styrenics (Figure 3.2).

The business unit model has enabled the structure of BP to become 'flat'. There is only one management layer between the board and the GCEO and the business units, compared with eight layers ten years ago. Under this structure, the GCEO, the BCEOs and BU leaders are able to manage their business affairs autonomously and react rapidly to new situations. However, they are subject to constant scrutiny from their superiors based on performance measurement and intervention in delivering performance targets. The GCEO is accountable to the board of directors. The BCEOs are held accountable for the GCEO and the BU leaders are accountable to the BCEOs. The strict performance review process ensures accountability. The management process ensures that the performance targets of each business units conform to the objective and strategy of the whole company. Moreover, the organisational arrangement such as Peer Assistance creates a unified company identity to ensure that the whole company or the peer groups can act as one when needs arise. The accountability process has been described by insiders as involving a culture of 'remorseless monitoring' of lower levels by higher levels.

Business lines

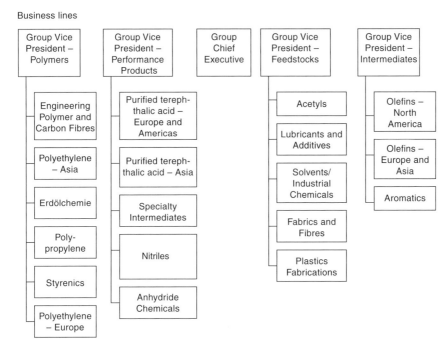

Business units

Figure 3.2 Business lines and business units: BP Chemicals, 1999.

Source: BP Chemicals.

The function of corporate headquarters

Formulating business policies

A crucial function of the headquarters is to formulate policies. The business policies address what the company stands for and set a framework for the company to conduct businesses.[2] In a sense, the business policy is the 'constitution' upon which BP organises its activities.

The stated overall goal of BP is to contribute to 'human progress'. The mission is to produce products and services that create a better quality of life, while itself producing and consuming the products in ways that 'respect both human rights and the natural environment':

> [BP] enable[s] customers, governments, communities and our own people to participate in a new constructive dialogue. We aim for a radical openness – a new approach from a new company: transparent, questioning, flexible, restless and inclusive. We will be the magnet for people who want to change the world with new ideas, delivering a performance standard that challenges the world's best companies.

The business policies focus on five areas – ethical conduct; employees; relationships; health, safety and environmental performance; and control and finance. Each of the five areas includes both a policy commitment and policy expectations. The business policy also specifies that BP should apply these policies in joint projects where BP is the operator. Where BP is not, BP will seek to influence its business partners so that the joint operation adopts similar policies. Line managers of BP are accountable for policy implementation and for providing assurance on compliance within their area of responsibility.

The policy expectations set out in more detail what the policy commitments mean in practice. They describe the boundaries for what is and what is not acceptable practice in BP and clarify what people can expect in dealing with BP.

ETHICAL CONDUCT

Policy expectations on ethical conduct include: respect for the law in the countries and communities in which BP operates; never to offer, solicit or accept a bribe in any form; to hold no secret or unrecorded funds of money or assets; to avoid situations where loyalty to the company may come into conflict with personal interests or loyalties; not to employ forced labour or child labour. Fees paid for services must be for legitimate business purposes.

As to facilitation payments, they can only be made in specified situations. Employees are expected to refer to the guidance within the BP Group Guidelines on Business Conduct. In consultation with regional presidents, BU leaders must establish local guidelines and procedures that address issues of local custom and practice. Any such payments must be modest and recorded properly within the accounts. In consultation with Regional and Country Presidents, BU leaders should also put in place local rules to cover the giving and acceptance of gifts and entertainment which reflect this expectation and local custom. Acceptance of gifts or entertainment during the process of a competitive bid or tender exercise is not permitted.

BP does not make political contributions in the United Kingdom. Group companies outside the United Kingdom may make political contributions in the countries in which they operate – but only if the contributions are lawful, of modest size in local terms, are properly recorded in the accounts and are approved in advance by the Executive Vice President, Policies and Technology and endorsed by the General Counsel. In such cases, contributions should only be made to legitimate entities – never directly to an individual.

Before making major investments in a new area, BP evaluates the likely impact of major developments on local communities and indigenous peoples, local infrastructure and the potential for conflict and its implications for security. BU leaders are expected to engage in open dialogue and consultation with local communities and their representatives, non-governmental organisations and government at all levels to ensure that potential issues arising from BP's operations are identified and the risks addressed. Whether BP continues to operate in a country with serious human rights issues will be determined in the light of the company's ability to fulfil the policy commitments in the company's own activities and to act as 'a force for good' over the long term.

The employees should know what is expected in their positions. Team leaders are expected to provide a clear view of the business aims and each employee's part in delivering them and should help everyone to get the information they need to do their job. Team leaders are expected to give everyone in their team open and constructive feedback through face-to-face conversations. Leaders are required to hold a formal conversation with every employee in their team at least once a year to review their performance and identify how it can be improved further.

Employees are encouraged to formulate personal development plans. BP provides coaching and training to employees to build relevant skills. Moreover, mentoring relationships are arranged to facilitate continual learning and growth. Systematic selection and placement processes are used to make the best use of people's skills and abilities. For employees moving overseas, ongoing, open conversations about their future and plans for re-entry into their home country will be provided. When tensions between work and home life arise, employees are expected to discuss them with their manager, who is expected to help individuals obtain constructive support in handling such tensions.

Employees should be given transparent information on the reward process. The relationship between group, business unit, team and individual performance and reward should be explained to employees. BP sets base pay and benefits at competitive levels within each national and business framework and explicitly links annual individual and team awards to business performance. Exceptional rewards are given for exceptional performance. Employees are encouraged to become BP shareholders.

Employees have the opportunity to give feedback to their team leaders on their leadership performance. Leaders should initiate and encourage open and timely two-way dialogue with their teams on all issues relating to business performance. Upward feedback and peer review process are used to provide performance feedback to supervisors and managers. Employees are expected to network both within and between business units and with those outside the company, and to share knowledge, skills and experience across BP. It is intended that the diversity of talent, background and perspective within BP's workforce is deployed to build innovative, high-performance teams.

BP commits itself to handle organizational change that results in job dislocations with care and sensitivity through constructive dialogue and provision of all reasonable options. In-house activities should be outsourced only for better business in the long term. Leadership opportunities and development should be open to all on merit. Employment opportunities below the group leadership must be advertised, specifying when there is a preferred candidate and explaining expatriation and relocation options.

RELATIONSHIPS

Policy expectations on relationships specify BP's conduct in dealing with relationships with individuals; customers; partners, contractors and suppliers; communities; governments; non-governmental organisations; the media; trade bodies and employee representative bodies. The principle is to engage in constructive dialogue with different groups to promote understanding and seek new ways of conducting businesses for mutual advantage.

HEALTH, SAFETY AND ENVIRONMENT PERFORMANCE (HSE)

BP's HSE management system framework include the following thirteen elements: leadership and accountability; risk assessment and management; people, training and behaviour; working with contractors and others; facilities design and construction; operations and maintenance; management of change; information and documentation; customers and products; community and stakeholder awareness; crisis and emergency management; incidents analysis and prevention; assessment, assurance and improvement.

The full set of HSE expectations is mandatory for every activity across BP. Each operation or business unit is expected to implement each expectation based on specific operational risk profile, the local and national regulatory requirement, and voluntary HSE management programmes. Business units or functional units can choose the content, format and terminology of HSE management and audit system within the HSE management system framework.

CONTROL AND FINANCE

Annual performance contracts and medium-term plans must be prepared for all business units and service functions and agreed on with their respective business ExCos or executive vice presidents. The degree of risk involved in achieving the targets set should be appraised realistically. Progress against these targets will be measured and reported accurately and monitored *inter alia* through quarterly performance review meetings. Actual financial performance should be that recorded in the group accounts.

Staff at all levels are expected make decisions within the authority delegated to them and within their competence to do so. They should have the information needed to run their part of the business. All significant decisions on finance, tax and accounting matters will be referred to the appropriate functional team. The appointment of BU controllers or more senior posts requires the approval of the Chief Financial Officer (CFO).

All opportunities of capital investment are evaluated in accordance with the principles of the group investment appraisal and approval procedures (GIAAP). The group's financial and tax structure is placed under central management. Borrowing money must be controlled centrally, using asset-based finance only when it adds value. Responsibility for managing key financial risks (including foreign exchange and insurance) and for executing certain transactions (including borrowing and depositing cash, cash transfers, dealing in all financial and foreign exchange markets) are held centrally. The group manages the interface and relationships with banks and other providers of financial services on an integrated basis. All activities in the group are subject to independent review, the extent of which will be determined by the internal and external auditors.

The key risks to the achievement of any objective should be understood and managed, which includes consideration of risks to information and digital business systems. Adequate controls must be maintained to give reasonable assurance that operations are effective and efficient, that financial results are timely and reliable, that assets and reputation are safeguarded and that laws and regulations are complied with.

Internal control

BP's line managers, function heads and regional presidents are held accountable to their Business Chief Executive for compliance with the business policies in their business units. Regional and country presidents are accountable, through the Group Vice President, Regions and Policies, to the Executive Vice President, Policies and Technology, for supporting and challenging business units on policy implementation throughout their countries or regions. The Executive Vice President, Policies and Technology, provides accountability to the GCEO and the board for policy commitments related to ethical conduct, employees, relationships, security and HSE performance. The CFO is accountable to the GCEO and the board for policy commitment to control and finance.

The process installed to ensure the implementation of BP's business policies covers three broad categories. First, there are performance measures including 'hard measures' such as HSE measures, security measures or staff survey results and 'soft measures' such as the quality of important relationships or the level of staff awareness of the ethical dilemmas they face (see discussions on performance contract below). Second, there is the internal process of reporting and monitoring performance at the level of the business units, functions, regions and the BP group (see discussion on monitoring process below). Third, there is external monitoring and challenge by business ExCos, the Group Vice President, Regions and Policies, regional presidents, country presidents, functional experts and independent reviews. The whole process is intended to be characterised by informed, rigorous and 'hard-edged' discussions, in order to generate mutual personal convictions.

The IFAN (investigation and fraud awareness network) is set up to prevent fraud and investigate serious violations of company policy, breaches of ethical conduct, fraud, and other criminal acts. The IFAN investigators are from internal audit and group Security. Outside consultants are used when needed. BU leaders and function heads are required to report immediately or upon discovery to the Vice President and General Auditor or Vice President Group Security all incidents of fraud or ethical misconduct involving actual or potential losses of $100,000 or more. The Vice President and General Auditor or Vice President Group Security refers to IFAN the reported incidents. Incidents of fraud or ethical misconduct involving actual or potential loss greater than $10,000 but less than $100,000 are to be reported to IFAN directly. In addition to the Vice President Group Security or General Auditor, incidents can also be reported through the internal audit or regional security advisor network for referral to IFAN. Other reporting channels include hotline numbers and e-mails to IFAN. The Vice President and General Auditor and the Vice President Group Security hold regular meetings to review the status of any potential or confirmed breaches of ethical conduct policy and the progress of investigation where appropriate.

Strategic planning

MERGERS AND ACQUISITIONS

Within the two years from 1998 to 2000, BP completed a series of large-scale mergers and acquisitions. The initiative and planning of the process was directly organised from the top of the company. The decisions to pursue M&A were taken confidentially and at a high speed. They were not discussed with shareholders in advance. Nor were they discussed in-depth, if at all, with the leaders of individual business units. For example, the announcement of BP's merger with Amoco in 1998 took many, even senior managers within the company itself by complete surprise: 'We know something was going to happen but we didn't know what or when. And the news came all of a sudden that it was Amoco. This was a well-kept secret deal' (Senior Planning Manager of BP, interview, March 2000). The series of strategic moves created a new BP that secured its position as the third largest global integrated oil and petrochemical company next to Exxon Mobil and Royal Dutch/Shell. The ambition was not only to 'compete with Shell and Exxon for the most attractive projects in the industry' but also want to 'set the pace of competition' (John Browne, BP/Amoco Group CEO, *Financial Times*, 13 August, 1998).

BP/Amoco: August 1998   The merger of BP and Amoco initiated the entire recent consolidation process in the global oil and petrochemical industry. In August 1998, BP announced its trans-Atlantic merger with Amoco in a $55 billion stock and debt deal. The combined company had oil and gas production of 3.1 million barrels of oil equivalent per day (BP/Amoco 1999a: 68). It was placed close behind the world leaders Royal Dutch/Shell and Exxon in terms of market capitalisation, oil and gas reserves and production. The deal greatly strengthened BP's position in downstream marketing in the Mid-West and Eastern United States as well as in the petrochemicals production. The merger was highly significant in that it was one of a series of extremely large-scale transatlantic mergers initiated by European-based companies such as the Daimler/Chrysler merger and the Rolls Royce/Allison acquisition.

BP/Amoco/Arco: March 1999   Following hard on the heels of completing the BP/Amoco merger, in March 1999, BP/Amoco agreed on a $26.8 billion all-stock take-over deal of the Atlantic Richfield Company (Arco). The acquisition of Arco significantly increased BP's oil and gas reserves from 12.9 billion barrels of oil and oil equivalent to 17.5 billion barrels. More importantly, through Arco, the new company had a much wider global reach with oil fields in Algeria, Venezuela, the Caspian and Russia as well as gas fields in the Gulf of Mexico, the UK North Sea, the South China Sea, Malaysia, Thailand and Qatar. The new company has full operational control of the Prudhoe Bay oil and gas field in Alaska with 4.5 billion barrels of oil equivalent oil and gas reserves, equivalent to the total proven reserves of the entire United Kingdom. Through Arco, the new company owns 40 per cent of the Tangguh natural gas site in Indonesia, which has proven gas reserves over 2.5 billion barrels of oil equivalent. The acquisition of Arco also enabled the new company to access the large chain of service stations on the West Coast of the United States, thus effectively establishing a coast-to-coast network across the country. After the acquisition, BP's revenue, oil and gas reserves and production rival those of Shell. It became the world third largest producer after Shell and BASF of acetic acid, polypropylene and PTA (Purified Terephthalic Acid) (*Financial Times*, 12 August, 1998), with leading technology and market share. The deal of BP/Amoco/Arco secured BP's position among the top 'big three' of western oil companies.

BP/Burmah Castrol: March 2000   In March 2000 BP announced that it had agreed to buy Burmah Castrol for $4.7 billion. Castrol is 'one of the great lubricants brands of the world', a name that 'stands for superbly engineered products of the highest quality, and research and development that has consistently kept those products at the forefront of the marketplace' (BP Website). It has become BP/Amoco's leading lubricant brand with its products made available through the group's 28,000 retail sites and to BP/Amoco's massive world-wide customer base.

CREATING A GLOBAL BUSINESS PORTFOLIO

In the 1990s, a vast part of the world market that was not accessible to companies from advanced capitalist countries has been opened up due to the end of the Cold War and the globalisation process. A major function of the headquarters is to enable the firm to benefit from the global development of the industry and from the growth opportunities in the newly opened-up markets. Through mergers and acquisitions, BP has achieved a global presence in upstream oil and gas, downstream refining and marketing and petrochemicals. It is able to construct a global business portfolio that can offer high returns on investment and provide future growth opportunities. In BP, the effort to create a global business portfolio starts from the development trend of the industry and technological develop-ments. The strategy is to rationalise the existing assets and expand into new low-cost assets across the world. Assets that are not distinctive with a strong market position will be divested. Since the late 1980s, BP has divested a sequence of non-core business assets including chicken production and marketing, computer manufacture, coal and mineral production, and a travel agency. As a result of the assets divestment, almost 15,000 employees left the company between 1990 to 1996 (Nolan, 2001: 425). Moreover, alongside the high-speed and massive M&A deals worth about $100 billion from 1998 to 2000, BP plans to rapidly divest assets worth around $10 billion from 1999 to 2001. It aims to construct a portfolio of global business assets with 'the lowest costs, the highest efficiency, and the capacity for growth' (John Browne, BP/Amoco, 1999a).

Crude oil   BP's principle in constructing a crude oil portfolio is to target big and simple oil prospects, to have the lowest lifting costs, to sustain the production in mature areas on a cost effective basis and to divest assets that do not generate high return (BP, 1999a). The strategy is to pursue the large fields and to be a leader in those key areas. From 1994 to 1998, BP participated in nineteen out of the world's eighty giant fields with involvement in discoveries of around 5 billion barrels, achieved with only 3 per cent of the total wells drilled. The most significant discoveries in the late 1990s were the fields in Angola and the Gulf of Mexico. BP's exploration activities in Angola have found a resource base of an estimated 6 billion barrels of oil. The success rate of exploration in Angola is over 80 per cent. The Crazy Horse field which was discovered in deep water in the Gulf of Mexico was estimated to contain at least 1 billion barrels of oil, 75 per cent of which is owned by BP. Another growth location is Chirag-Azeri in the Caspian Sea. For the mature production fields in the United Kingdom and Alaska, technology will be employed to reduce the drilling costs. Drilling costs have fallen from $4.2 million per well by conventional drilling approach in the 1980s, to $2.73 million per well by using horizontal drilling technology of the early 1990s, and further to $1.2 million per well by using coiled tubing technology of the late 1990s. It is intended to dispose of assets that are not distinctive. This includes Canada Oil and BP's share of Altura in the Lower 48. The total amount of divestment of assets would amount to $4 billion in the period from 1999 to 2001.

Natural gas   The primary energy mix in the 1990s showed that the world consumption of oil remained stable at around 40 per cent and incremental demand has been shifting to the natural gas (BP, 1999a). The combination with Amoco increased the share of BP's gas production in its overall portfolio from 18 per cent to 33 per cent. The acquisition of Arco strengthened BP's gas presence in Southeast Asia. In 1999, BP created a new business stream Gas and Power to capture the growth opportunities of natural gas. The strategy for the natural gas portfolio is to maintain the position of leading producer in the North Sea and North America and to achieve growth in new low-cost assets in Trinidad and East Siberia, the Caspian and Alaska in the longer term. In Trinidad, BP found 19 trillion cubic feet of gas in large accumulations at a cost equivalent to 10 cents per barrel of oil. Daily production in 1999 was 1 billion cubic feet of gas together with some oil. The Atlantic LNG Plant in Trinidad was built up over seven years, achieving the world's shortest cycle from planning at the lowest cost per tonne to first delivery for a green-field project. The gas from Trinidad is supplying markets in North America and Europe and will expand into markets in the Caribbean and Latin America.

Refining and marketing   The portfolio of refining assets is to be rationalised based on three criteria: whether the refinery has an advantageous position in supplying BP's marketing business, whether the refinery is well placed to adopt BP's clean fuel strategy, and whether the refinery can add value through integration with other parts of BP's businesses. Assets that do not meet these criteria will be disposed of. BP plans to divest assets worth $2 billion from 1999 to 2001. The Alliance refinery in the United States, with a capacity of 250,000 barrels per day, was sold. Three additional US refineries and BP's interest in its Singapore refinery are on sale. For retail, the strategy is to increase the number of service stations under the direct management of BP or franchise in order to access the full retail margin. BP intends to develop its convenience business combining sales of fuel, merchandise, food and services directly to consumers. This will capture the fast growth in convenience business and compensate for the declining margin from marketing fuels alone. Moreover, BP will focus on investing in markets with above-average growth. In the markets from which BP intends to withdraw its capital investment in retail marketing, BP will divest its service stations to either the jobber or dealer, to be operated under the BP brand. The divestment proceeds are to be invested in the convenience business in BP's core metropolitan markets.

Petrochemicals   Integrated companies can derive significant value through the alignment of their petrochemical manufacturing base with internally generated feed-stocks. BP's chemical stream is expected to add value to the company's hydrocarbon production through producing aromatics and olefins, each of which amount to about 35 per cent of the total chemical production of BP. The strategy is to create large, integrated and cost-effective production sites combining the refining process, feed-stocks and chemical production. This will reduce costs in logistics and increase plant loading through close co-operation between demand and supply. The sites at Grangemouth, Dormagen, Chocolate Bayou and Lavéra are being expanded or upgraded. BP is also integrating its assets along the Gulf Coast in the United States and its assets in Shanghai and Zhuhai in China. Moreover, implementation of best practice in the manufacturing process will achieve cost reduction. For example, BP's aromatics production unit in Texas City will introduce leading-edge process technology and control systems to create a fully automated and integrated facility that links supply from the refinery to demand from the PTA and PIA (Purified Isophthalic Acid) production. A similar scheme will be applied to most of BP's sites to improve manufacturing efficiency. The product portfolio focussed on three core areas: aromatics and derivatives, including PTA, olefins and derivatives, including PE and PP, and related businesses in which BP has a leading position in technology and/or in market share. BP's PTA has 37 per cent of the global market share in 1998 (BP Amoco, 1999b). Around 70 per cent of acetic acid and 90 per cent of acrylonitrile produced world-wide are under licence from BP (BP, 1999a).

Renewable energy   BP recognises that hydrocarbons will dominate world energy consumption for several decades to come, but the energy mix will continue to change. More renewable energy sources will emerge. In 1999, BP Solar merged with Solarex to form BP Solarex, through which BP intends to develop its solar business, increasing the revenue from $200 million in 1999 to $1 billion by 2007. BP Solarex owns the world leading thin film photovoltaic technologies. Its Apollo thin film module achieved 8.3 per cent efficiency with a corresponding power output of 72.1 watts, the highest wattage for any monolithically integrated thin film module in the world (BP Press Release, 25 November 1999). BP Solarex produces over 30 megawatts of solar products each year, accounting for 50 per cent of the world off-grid markets. It has manufacturing sites in the United States, Spain, India and Australia and sells in around 160 countries in the world. In 2000, BP converted 200 service stations world-wide to solar power (BP, 2001). Moreover, BP has been engaged in fuel cell technology and has been working with the world's leading auto manufacturers on technological projects. It aims to be a fuel marketer for hydrogen and its derivatives. BP will fuel Daimler-Chrysler's hydrogen-powered buses.

Managing the BP brand

After the mergers and acquisitions from 1998 to 2000, BP owns a portfolio of powerful brands: BP, Amoco, ARCO, and Burmah Castrol. In May 2000, Sir John Browne, as he was then, announced that the group company was to launch a single, global brand – bp. The objective is to create a powerful global brand in an increasingly globalising market and to achieve economies of scale in order to remain profitable. A single, global brand makes expenditure on sales promotion more efficient and effective. BP spent $7 million on research for the new brand, on designing the new logo and service stations, and on legal copyrights for the brand. A total amount of $200 million investment was planned for the launch of the single brand in two years, equivalent to the expenditure needed to support the separate brands. Moreover, a single, global brand is expected to help unify BP's employees world-wide around a common vision of the future. Each of the previous brands was to be integrated into a single BP brand. The Amoco sites in the United States were to be re-branded as 'bp' but continue to supply Amoco-branded petrol. Since the targeted customer segment of ARCO is different from that of BP or Amoco, the ARCO brand was to be retained on the USA's West Coast. Castrol will also be retained as BP's leading lubricant brand. However, all activities, products and services will be endorsed under the umbrella of the new bp identity.

The existing images of BP and Amoco have been around in the market for about twelve and twenty years, respectively. BP has learnt from the fast moving consumer goods (FMCG) industry in which there is an average re-imaging cycle of less than ten years. It is launching a new retail strategy to re-image its service stations. The full-scale prototype of BP's new site offers a thin film solar canopy, retains the best of BP and Amoco products, incorporates a new convenience retail design and supports the brand attributes of being green. The new site is also expected to be fully digitised for e-commerce transactions.

Evaluating performance

PERFORMANCE CONTRACT

The performance contract (PC) is the 'vehicle' that links the business unit structure with higher levels. It signed between the GCEO and the board, between the GCEO and the four BCEOs from the four business streams, between the BCEOs and the business ExCo members, and between the ExCo members and the BU leaders. The performance contract is not only signed between the leaders in the structure, but also covers almost all the employees in BP from CEOs to secretaries. Each person is held accountable for his/her work and is expected to provide assurance to others for their performance. It also guarantees the reward the employees get once they deliver what has been specified in the contract.

The performance contract is written by the BU leader but should be approved by the ExCo member under whose responsibility it lies. Often it involves lots of discussions and negotiations between the BU leader and the ExCo member over the issues covered in the PC. But the authority is the ExCo member since he/she must make sure that overall he/she is able to deliver the targets set in their contracts with the BCEO. The same process takes place between the BCEO and GCEO; ultimately John Browne must stand before the investors to make sure BP delivers. Year after year, the targets set in the performance contract can only become higher and higher, better and better. This is, as one senior manager observed is 'the way that BP extracts value' (Interview, March 2000). The BU structure and PC practice was first adopted by John Browne when he was the Chief Executive of the exploration and production stream and was introduced in the whole company in 1995 when he became the GCEO of BP.

The performance contract is written and signed on an annual basis on a single sheet of paper. It generally consists of two types of targets: long-term aims and specific performance targets for delivery. Long-term aims indicate the aspirations, usually in five years' time, and the strategic imperatives necessary to achieve the aspiration. Performance targets cover a wide range of criteria from hard financial, operational and HSE targets to wider responsibilities such as personnel development and relationships with government, academia and industry in which the BU has operations. Each performance target and delivery target has a weighting percentage that amounts to 100 per cent with dates of delivery. The risks of hard targets are measured by probabilities of delivery.

For example, Table 3.1 illustrates the performance contract for an upstream business unit for 1997. The first part of the contract specifies the long-term aim to build a portfolio of competitive options to deliver BP net production sustainable from 2005 and to participate in the growth of regional gas market. The second part, 'business assurance', addresses issues related to HSE, business conduct, networks including peer group process, human resources and targets for protecting and enhancing BP's reputation. In the third part, specific targets are set for operational and financial performance for exploration and production. Financial measures for production include lifting costs, cash flow, net income and capital expenditure. Financial measures for exploration include base capital expenditure, the exploration write-off target, and discovery costs. The final part presents the options for business appraisal and development. Table 3.2 illustrates the performance contract for a business development business unit in the chemical stream for the year 2000. In that year, the joint venture project was at the stage of preparing for a feasibility study report. Hence operational targets were not applicable in the performance contract. Financial performance measures cover net profit, EBITDA, capital expenditure, net cash flow, and ROACE. HSE and human resource targets were also specified. There was much emphasis on building up relationships with decision-makers in the country in which the joint venture will operate, and on developing the BP group's agenda in that country.

MONITORING PERFORMANCE

In BP Chemicals, the vice presidents each hold quarterly business review meetings with the business units under their responsibility. At these sessions, progress against the targets set out in the performance contract for the current year is discussed. This covers financial performance and other key areas such as health, safety and the environment, people and cross-business issues. The meeting is recorded.

Leadership meeting   In addition to quarterly reviews, a chemical leadership meeting is expected to be held twice a year. It is attended by senior management of the chemical sector, including ExCo members, BU leaders, senior works general managers and function heads. These meetings are action-oriented to tackle the key short- and long-term issues and opportunities facing the business. They also help to shape the roles and responsibilities of the senior management team. In addition, business units conduct strategy reviews and present them to the ExCo. The strategies of the business units require agreement from the ExCo.

Peer groups   The peer groups form a linking network of related business units within a particular business stream, particularly those facing similar technological, operational or relationship issues. In structure, they resemble a federation. They can act together to raise funds for supporting a project or to share knowledge for constructing a project. For example, the business unit of the Jinshan project (a joint venture between BP and Shanghai Petrochemical Corporation) can team up with other projects producing the same products in the region of Southeast

Table 3.1 Performance contract for an upstream business unit.

Emerging area asset

Aims Commit to build a portfolio of competitive options to deliver BP net production target sustainable from 2005 and to participate in the growth of gas in the regional market.

Business assurance

HSE	• Zero LTLs and Spills in BP activities • Demonstrate exchange of best practice with partner X
BCE	• Business conduct letter signed without qualification
Networks	• Contribute to the better working of partner Y • Be proactive in the exploration Forum and peer group process • Provide a clear asset technology plan by end of 1Q • Integrate the aims into deep water operational network
HR	• Policy compliance demonstrated with measure publishes quarterly
Reputation	• Enhance reputation as a key element of future business build and verify through independent review

Production

Production	• Influence partner X to achieve targets measured by probability
Financial	• Lifting cost target • Cash flow target • Net income target • Capital expenditure (capex) target

Exploration

Financial	• Base capex target • Exploration write-off target • Discovery cost target
Drilling	• BP operated deep water wells delivering target • Influence Partner Y to deliver an equivalent BP dry hole cost
Activities	• Spud wells to test two deepwater prospects • Test at least one other prospect under favourable terms
Reserves	• Discoveries; other targets

Appraisal and Development

Options	• Ensure partner Y achieve allocation • Bring Project N to sanction as a commercially attractive project accessing the regional market • Unlock the value of asset A through e.g. trade/sell • Review asset B and ensure partner Y optimise value

Business development

Options	• Offer two commercially attractive growth options with targets in 2000–2005 • Monitor licence round timing and develop position to nominate

Manager signature and date

Source: BP.

Table 3.2 Performance contract for a business development business unit.

2000 Performance Contract (Business Development Business Unit)

Long-term aims

Aspiration	• By end 2005, to create with partners a world-scale, competitive, 50:50 joint venture petrochemical company.
Strategic Imperatives (Weighting %)	• Agree a final scope and viable business case • Develop standards, processes and objectives for JV consistent with BP policies • Complete and submit the feasibility study (FS) to government department • Form JV, with integrated management team

2000 Deliverables

Financial performance (Weighting %)	• Profit target • EBITDA target • Capital expenditure target • Net cash flow target • Self help target • ROACE target
Operational targets	Not applicable
HSE targets (Weighting %)	• Targets for both employees and contractors
Peer group metrics	Not applicable
2000 milestone deliverables (Weighting %)	• Define and agree the complex location, scope and scale and timetable for FS completion • Complete project appraisal and select • Complete setting business priorities, VIP and appraise and select stage peer reviews
Objectives	• Build a constructive relationship between BP and partners at all levels – Actively manage programme of relationship-building with other key decision makers including, other investors in the same location, and participants in other similar projects
Stretch targets (Weighting %)	• Agree expanded initial scope • Complete FS report
Wider responsibilities (Weighting %)	• Contribute to development of group agenda in the country and enhancement of cross-BU activity • Managing visiting delegations to ensure maximum benefit to BP and the project • Maintain and develop BP links with government, academia and industry within the country
People and organisational development (Weighting %)	• Implement the 5 BP People Management commitments for all BU staff

Signature of BU Leader and business stream CEO and date

Source: BP.

Asia as a peer group. They can join together their resources in personnel, knowledge and expertise to raise funds or they can draw their experts together to share know-how in conducting business in the region. Peer group matrix is an entry for evaluation in the performance contract.

Peer review   Peer review is conducted among peer groups. It involves business units challenging each other in performance. Business units must justify their promises to their closest colleagues set out in the performance contract. They must prove that they deserve the resources in competition with other business units. The assessment is based on performance data: 'It is also a powerful tool to share knowledge and experience' (Senior Manager, interview, March 2000).

Peer assistance   In the case where the project team has little experience in a certain area, they may ask for assistance from their peers who have experience and expertise to share with them. Psychologically, it is very important because 'you are not alone' (Senior Manager, interview, March 2000). It contributes to the bonding among people working in different business units and establishes a unified corporate identity that says 'we are BP people'.

Setting reward policy

REWARDS FOR EXECUTIVE DIRECTORS

The remuneration for executive directors includes fixed components, a long-term performance-based component and a short-term performance based component.

Fixed component   The fixed component includes salary, pension, benefits and other share schemes and resettlement allowance. Salaries are reviewed periodically in line with the global markets. A remuneration consultancy conducts regular surveys and analyses the remuneration levels in a group of international companies with comparable size, complexity and global spread of operations. Executive directors are eligible to participate in pension schemes, all-employee share schemes and savings plans, and regular employee benefit plans including health and life insurance, which are applicable in their home countries.

Long-term performance-based component   In April 2000, BP adopted the executive Directors' Long Term Incentive Plan. The plan consists of a share element, a share option element and a cash element. The share element compares and measures BP's performance against oil majors over a period of three years. The peer companies for the year 2000 were Chevron, ENI, ExxonMobil, Repsol YPF, Royal Dutch/Shell, Texaco and TotalFina (BP, 2000b). In the period from 1999 to 2001, the performance measures included shareholder return against the market, earnings per share (EPS) and the return on average capital employed (ROACE). The Remuneration Committee review and approve the specific performance measures and the chosen peer companies for comparison on an annual basis. Performance units are made at the beginning of each period and converted to an award of shares at the end of the period based on performance against the oil majors. The maximum award can be made only when performance has been ahead of the peer group on all measures. No award is made if performance is below the median. After the award is made, the shares are held in trust for three years before they are released to the individual directors. The share option element reflects BP's performance against a wide selection of global majors. The Remuneration Committee take into account the ranking of BP's total shareholder return (TSR) against the TSR of the FTSE Global 100 group of companies over the three-year period. In special cases, the Remuneration Committee may grant cash-based incentives rather than share-based incentives.

Short-term performance-based component   The short-term performance-based components includes the annual bonus. The Remuneration Committee set and review annually the specific measures for the bonus award and the level of bonus. Performance targets for the bonus award cover financial targets and leadership objectives. The financial targets include savings in cash costs and the performance improvement relative to competitors and market expectations. The leadership objectives include HSE, people, organisation and investment issues.

REWARD FOR EMPLOYEES

Each of BP's business streams establish industry benchmarks to measure the business stream's performance. For example, BP Chemical selects twenty-five competitor petrochemical companies around the world and monitors their performance. A chart is worked out indicating a range from the best to the worst and the average performance, which is then used as a comparator with which to evaluate BP Chemical's performance. Ten years ago, BP Chemical under-performed the industry average. Over the years, its performance improved and now it out-performs the industry average and is locked in the top five range. On the relevant BP presentation slide, the chart resembles a whale. The employees' bonus is determined in relation to this 'whale' in the second quarter of every year. There are individual, business unit, and group bonuses. If the group as a whole does not deliver, neither the individual nor the business unit bonus are made available, no matter how outstanding the individual's performance may be. In addition, there is a special 'spot bonus' provided as a reward for exceptional success in delivering one particular target covered in the performance contract.

Centralising capital investment and procurement

BP's capital investment decisions have become highly centralised. The head-quarters decides the allocation of capital investment in line with the company's overall strategy. The strategy for BP's capital investment is biased towards the upstream as BP believes it is the portion of the value chain that generates the highest return. BP's capital investment is predominantly based in 'politically secure countries of the OECD', with more than 70 per cent of capital employed in the United States and Europe: 'It is a balance we like. From that secure base, we can choose whether to grow within OECD, so long as we are competitive enough, or to take up some of the best opportunities that are coming up in the rest of the world' (John Browne, BP/Amoco, 1999a). Each year, the headquarters announces the amount of capital available for investment and the business streams and business units make proposals to compete for the capital. An investment committee holds a rigorous selection process and makes the final decision. The selection is based on the strategic direction of the whole company. BP calls this process the 'beauty contest'.

Along with the centralisation of capital investment in line with the strategic direction of the company, BP has been centralising procurement to reduce costs. In 1996, BP announced that it intended to save $1 billion per year from its annual procurement expenditure of $15 billion (*Financial Times*, 15 April 1998). Procurement in BP was renamed 'supply chain management'. The procurement process was restructured to increase communications between procurement and technical staff within the company, to rationalise the supplier base and develop closer interactions with suppliers who were able to meet BP's global needs and standards. The strategy is captured in the 'STARS' framework:

- *Supply chain management* Clarify BP's role in each supply chain in which it is involved.
- *Transparency* Understand the breakdown of costs for BP and the suppliers and the value to BP of each purchase, and measure the performance of suppliers.
- *Aggregation* Standardise and rationalise the supplier base and reduce unit costs by co-ordinating expenditures across business units through regional or global deals.
- *Relationships* The management of the relationships with suppliers is based on performance improvement, technology development and the market reality.
- *Sector strategies* Maximise value to BP and ensure security of supply by understanding the market drivers, market structure, and competitive situation as well as the buyer and supplier power.

Based on this framework of supply chain management, performance is monitored using five criteria: safety, relationships with suppliers, security of supply, supplier performance and price. Each of the criterion is measured in the performance contract.

The centralisation of procurement has been greatly facilitated by the advancement in information technology. BP has built a central data warehouse to collate information about BP's buyers and suppliers. BP business units and functions across the world within the BP system can log on to the system to find out if a potential supplier is doing business elsewhere within the group or another supplier offers better terms. Suppliers can log on the system to make online offers in response to a BP request. Bid prices are plotted over time and a supplier is selected on the basis of price and performance. The procurement managers use the information to aggregate purchases and negotiate better terms.

Technology

The BP Technology Council leads the scientific, technical and engineering activities throughout the BP group company. It distributes and co-ordinates programmes to business streams, each of which undertakes research, technology and engineering activities. About 30,000 technical staff work within business units and around 1,000 staff work in central technical facilities and organisations based in places such as London, Chicago and Houston. The council promotes cross-business initiatives and the transfer of best practice between businesses. In addition, the Technology Advisory Council, which consists of eminent academics and industrialists, provides advice to senior management on the state of technology within BP and helps identify current trends and future developments in technology.

Information technology management

E-ENABLED HUMAN RESOURCES

In December 1999, BP signed a global $600 million contract for five years with Exult, a California-based human resource (HR) business process management services provider for Fortune 500 companies (BP Press Release, 9 December, 1999). Under Exult's 'e-HR' services delivery model, the company assumes management, ownership and accountability for BP's global HR administrative and transactional process. This includes compensation, benefits, payroll, organisational development, performance management, training, employee development, recruiting/staffing/resourcing, expatriate administration, domestic relocation, employee relations, policy and legal compliance, employee data and record management, and vendor sourcing. These processes are managed in Exult's two client service centres in the United States and United Kingdom. BP retains the HR policy, strategy and professional resources. The integration of BP's internal HR operations, transactions and administration was expected to be implemented first in the United Kingdom and the United States and expanded to continental Europe, Canada, and other operating locations. The integrated HR system reduces HR management costs and enables nearly 100,000 BP employees in more than 100 countries all over the world to have web-enabled transparent and simple access to the work and life information they require. For example, a single salary payment system linked globally by the internet is being developed from the previous seven different systems. The new system speeds up communications and improves the service the HR department provides. When offered a new posting, employees fill in an online form with personal details and the proposed benefits such as housing allowance will be presented in less than a minute, compared with weeks under the previous salary payment system. Under the integrated online HR management system, BP has cut its HR staff by 60 per cent and is able to achieve annual savings of $100 million (*Business Week*, 3 December 2001).

E-ENABLED KNOWLEDGE-SHARING

BP has constructed a web-based employee directory called Connect. It contains personal home pages for BP employees including their photograph, work address, phone number, employment-related experience, and personal interests. It is intended to enable BP employees world-wide to communicate with each other on a more 'personal' basis and to share working experience: 'A common way of communicating creates a common culture' (John Leggate, BP Digital Director, quoted in *Business Week*, 3 December 2001).

Moreover, sharing knowledge through the company intranet can bring savings in business operations. For example, a BP exploration geologist in Norway discovered a more efficient way to find oil by changing the position of the drill heads, which reduces the number of misses. The description of this new process was then posted on the company intranet. Within 24 hours, a BP engineer working in Trinidad contacted the BP geologist in Norway, asking for more details. After a quick exchange of messages, the engineering team in Trinidad was able to save five days of drilling and $600,000 by applying the new drilling process (*Business Week*, 3 December 2001).

E-COMMERCE ACTIVITIES

- In January 2000, BP Marine, Shell Marine Products, Fuel and Marine Marketing LLC signed an agreement to develop a marine industry-backed portal on the internet called OceanConnect.com. The website is for auction and e-mail-enabled transactions for the purchase and sale of marine fuels.
- In February 2000, BP took an equity investment in ChemConnect and chose ChemConnect's World Chemical Exchange as its preferred third party platform for internet-based chemical trading. The World Chemical Exchange is the world largest and fastest growing chemicals and plastics online exchange with more than 4,000 member companies all over the world. It provides a platform for manufacturers, buyers, and intermediaries to find trading partners, negotiate pricing, and complete transactions online. Other equity investors in ChemConnect include the Dow Chemical Company, Eastman Chemical Company, Rohm and Haas, Anderson Consulting, and Chemical Week Ventures.
- In March 2000, BP, Royal Dutch/Shell, TotalFinaElf, Deutsche Bank. Goldman Sachs, Morgan Stanley Dean Witter, and SG Investment Banking announced they would set up an electronic market via the internet for over-the-counter energy and commodity trading. None of the companies has a

controlling interest. The new exchange called Intercontinental Echange aims to handle bids and offers for petroleum and precious metals.

- In March 2000, BP announced that it was acquiring a 3 per cent interest in Altra Energy Technologies, which provides a real-time, anonymous electronic marketplace where customers trade online natural gas, crude oil, natural gas liquids and power. Meanwhile, BP joined up with Excelergy Corporation to provide web-based customer information and transaction management technology to the deregulating retail energy market. The combination of partnership with Altra and Excelergy created a 'wholesale-to-retail' solution for energy customers across the United States.

- In April 2000, BP, Royal Dutch/Shell, Cargill and Clarksons announced that they were creating LevelSeas.com to provide freight management services covering market intelligence, online chartering, pre- and post- fixture activities and risk management tools including freight derivatives. It aims to service the freight needs of international businesses that rely on ocean transportation as a critical link in their global commodity supply chain.

- In April 2000, a group of fourteen world-leading energy and petrochemical companies including BP announced the launch of an independent industry procurement exchange using the CommerceOne Marketsite platform. The exchange conducts procurement activities related to goods and services used in oil and gas exploration and production, refining, petrochemicals and marketing. The collective annual procurement spending of the fourteen companies amounts to $125 billion, 40 per cent of which is spent in North and South America, 40 per cent in Europe and Africa, and 20 per cent in Asia Pacific and the Middle East. In addition to BP, the other thirteen partners are Royal Dutch/Shell, Conoco, The Dow Chemical, Equilon Enterprise, Mitsubishi Corporation, Motiva Enterprise, Occidental Petroleum, Phillips Petroleum, Repsol-YPF, Statoil, Tosco, TotalFinaElf, and Unocal.

Royal Dutch/Shell

Organisational structure

Because of the way in which it was formed (see below), the Royal Dutch/Shell Group of companies has an extremely complex organisational structure. It consists of three main parts: the parent companies, the group holding companies and shell companies (Figure 3.3). The group holding companies and Shell companies are collectively referred to as the 'Group'.

PARENT COMPANIES

The Royal Dutch/Shell Group of companies was created out of an alliance made in 1907 between Royal Dutch Petroleum Company (Royal Dutch) incorporated in the Netherlands in June 1890 and the Shell Transport and Trading Company (Shell Transport) incorporated in England in October 1897.[3] The Royal Dutch

Petroleum Company and Shell Transport and Trading Company are the parent companies of the group. According to the alliance agreement, the two companies merged their interests on a 60:40 basis while remaining separate and distinct entities (Figure 3.3). The shares of the parent companies are traded on a number of stock exchanges across the world including Netherlands, the United Kingdom, and the United States. They own, directly or indirectly, shares in the companies of the group and receive dividends from the group of companies. The two companies share, among other things, in the aggregate assets, dividends and interest received from group companies in the proportion of 60:40. Furthermore, the two companies share in the same proportion all the taxes on the dividends and interests.

GROUP HOLDING COMPANIES

The group holding companies (GHC) are Shell Petroleum NV, based in the Netherlands and the Shell Petroleum Company Ltd, based in the United Kingdom (Figure 3.3). The parent companies own the GHC and are entitled to nominate directors to the GHC. The GHC hold shares in the operating and

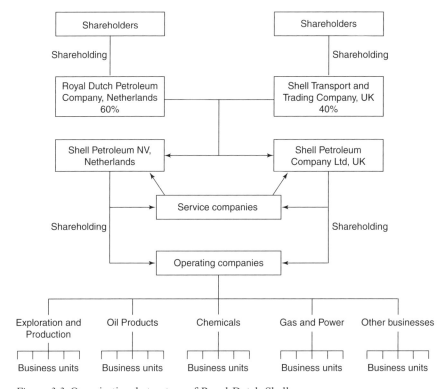

Figure 3.3 Organisational structure of Royal Dutch Shell.

Source: Royal Dutch Shell (2001a).

service companies, both directly and indirectly, through intermediate holding companies – the 'sub-holding companies' (Royal Dutch/Shell, 2001a: 2).

Shell companies (Shell) include service, operating, and sub-holding companies, in which the GHCs hold an interest, either directly or indirectly.

Service companies   Service companies are legal entities. They provide professional advice and services in areas such as law, finance, human resources, information technology and external affairs. They provide technical guidance, advice and services to operating companies and help the committee of managing directors with overall group strategy and policies. The thirteen Shell service companies include Shell International Petroleum Company Ltd, Shell Global Solutions International BV, Shell Internationale Research Maatschappij BV, Shell International Exploration and Production BV, Shell EP International BV, Shell Chemicals Ltd, Shell International Chemicals BV, Shell International Gas Ltd, Shell International Ltd, Shell International BV, Shell Hydrogen BV, Shell IT International BV, and Shell International Ltd.

The service companies provide their services through group and business service organisations. Service organisations may be located within service companies or within operating companies. They operate like business units but on a cost-recovery basis.[4] Shell businesses are required to use certain internal service organisations on matters that affect group strategic interests. Otherwise, they are free to choose whether to use internal or external service providers based on considerations such as cost and quality.

- Group service organisations provide services to all group businesses. Shell Finance Services provides financial advice and services, and operates group-level finance processes. Shell IT provides information technology advice and services, and operates the group's information technology infrastructure. Shell People Services provides human resource advice and services, and operates group-level human resources processes. LEAP provides advice and services on leadership and performance improvement. IP Services provides advice and services on patents, trademarks, intellectual property agreements and protection. Shell Pension Funds manages investments and administers pension funds for a number of Shell companies. Shell Aircraft advises on aircraft operations and operates a small aircraft fleet. Other group service organisations include Security Services, Legal Services, Health Services, Social Investment Advice and Real Estate Services.
- Business service organisations provide services within a single business stream, which usually include management advisory services.

Operating companies   Shell has operating companies in more than 135 countries around the world. They are legal entities and are organised into five business streams: exploration and production business, oil products business, chemical business, Gas and power business and other group businesses. Each business stream comprises business units and functions organised into zones, regions or global product lines.

- The exploration and production business (E&P) is organised into four regions: East Asia and Australasia; Europe and North America; the Middle East, South Asia and Russia; South America and sub-Saharan Africa. Each region consists of business units based on individual operating companies. Business service organisations include Shell Technology E&P, E&P business development, E&P business finance and human resources. They are based either in The Hague or Houston.
- The gas and power business is organised into five regions: East Asia and Australasia; Europe; North America; the Middle East, South Asia and Russia; South America and Africa. Business units (usually based on operating companies) operate in each of the region. Business service organisations including business support, global business and human resources are based in London.
- The oil products business is organised into zones and global product line. Zones include business units engaged in the manufacturing, supply, distribution, commercial and retail business sectors in Europe; Asia and the Middle East; Central and South America, Caribbean and Africa; Canada and the United States. Many business units are based on more than one operating company. Global product lines consist of business units in LPG (liquid petroleum gas), aviation fuels and marine fuels. In addition, innovation and research is based in Shell Global Solutions. Business services related to strategy, portfolio and environment, human resources, marketing and finance are provided through service organisations based in London, The Hague, Houston and Singapore.
- The chemicals business is organised into seven product business units including feed-stocks, intermediates and polymers, each of which covers one or more different chemical products, several business units of international joint ventures, and a number of core process organisations related to customer service, operations and procurement. 'Enabling organisations' (Royal Dutch/Shell, 2001a: 19) provide support in human resources, finance and business systems, as well as in technology, portfolio, and sustainable development.
- Other group businesses include Shell Capital, Shell Hydrogen, Shell Internet Works and Shell Consumer.

Governing relationships

The boards of the parent companies

The parent companies own the group. Each is a separate public company individually accountable to its shareholders for its investment in the group.

Royal Dutch   The Board of Management consists of at least two Managing Directors, under the supervision of a Supervisory Board consisting of at least five members. Managing Directors and Members of the Supervisory Board are nominated by the meeting of holders of priority shares and appointed by the general meeting of shareholders. These nominations for appointment may also be made by one or more holders of ordinary shares representing in the aggregate at least 1% of the issued share capital, if approved by the meeting of holders of priority shares. Each nomination must contain the names of at least two qualified persons. Shareholders cast all their votes to one of the two qualified persons. Managing Directors hold office until they retire unless relieved earlier from office by the general meeting of shareholders. Each year, one of the members of the Supervisory Board retires by rotation but is eligible for re-election. A member of the Supervisory Board retires after having served on the Supervisory Board for a period of ten years, or retires effectively on the first day of July following the initial 1 April on which the member is 70 years of age. If a vacancy occurs on the Board of Management when there are still at least two Managing Directors in office, or on the Supervisory Board when there are still at least five members in office, the Board of Management will notify the chairman of the meeting of holders of priority shares. The meeting will consult the Supervisory Board and the Board of Management and decide whether the vacancy is to be filled. If it is resolved to fill the vacancy, the appointment will be made at the next general meeting of shareholders. If there are not at least two Managing Directors or at least five members of the Supervisory Board still in office, a general meeting of shareholders must be held within three months to fill the vacancy.

Shell Transport   The board of directors consists of not less than three and not more than twenty members. There are currently eleven directors in office, of whom three are Managing Directors. Managing Directors are appointed by the board from among the members of the board. One third of the Directors retires by rotation at each Annual General Meeting of shareholders. The Directors longest in office retire each year. If some Directors have been in office for an equal period of time, the Director(s) to retire will be chosen by lot unless they otherwise agree between themselves. Managing Directors are not subject to retirement by rotation and are not counted in calculating the number of Directors to retire each year. The Managing Directors will, in the future, offer themselves for re-election on a regular basis in line with the combined code of good corporate governance.

Group committees   The boards of the parent companies oversee group activities through joint committees, each of which includes board members from both Royal Dutch and Shell Transport. The Group Audit Committee considers and advises the boards of the parent companies on the group's public financial statements; the system of risk management and internal control; the reports and performance of internal and external auditors. The Social Responsibility Committee considers and advises the boards of parent companies on conduct with respect to the Shell general business principles, the health, safety and environment commitment and policy, and other major issues of public concern. The Remuneration and Succession Review Committee considers and advises on the performance of the Committee of Managing Directors, the remuneration and succession of senior executives and other human resource matters.

Committee of Managing Directors

The members of the Board of Management of Royal Dutch and the Managing Directors of Shell Transport are also members of the Presidium of the Board of Directors of the group holding companies. They are known as Group Managing Directors. The Committee of Managing Directors (CMD) is a joint committee of Group Managing Directors, which is appointed by the Boards of the GHC. The GHC boards control the Shell companies through exercising majority shareholder rights in appointing directors and monitoring the management of the Shell companies. When the GHC does not have a controlling interest in a Shell company, the GHC still try to influence how such companies are managed, particularly in protecting the reputation of the group. Less influence is exerted in Shell companies in which the GHC interest is less than 20 per cent. CMD provides strategic direction, develops long-term plans and appraises performance of the group businesses (Figure 3.4).

Each CMD member has specific areas of responsibility covering geographic regions (Regional Managing Directors), group businesses or functions such as human resources or finance. The major responsibilities of CMD are as follows:

- *Strategy* Developing and communicating group strategy, and advising the GHC on their portfolio of investments.
- *Organisation* Organising the group's portfolio into businesses consistent with Group strategy, appointment and appraisal of business CEOs, and development of human resources and other assets. The Management Development Committee, consisting of senior group executives, provides support to CMD on human resources matters.
- *Planning* Considering business plans including individual investment proposals and developing a group plan in line with group strategy.
- *Performance appraisal* Monitoring performance against the plan, risk management and internal control, compliance with group policies and standards; appraising the performance of the businesses and the group as a whole against their plans.

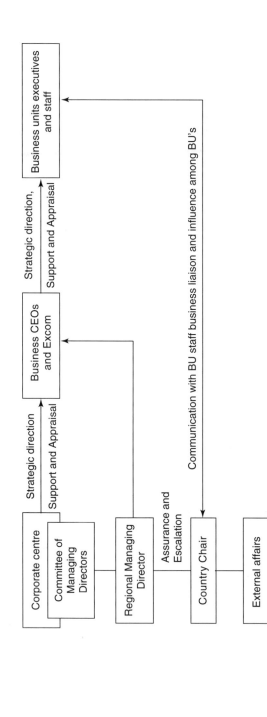

Figure 3.4 Governing relationships of Royal Dutch Shell.

Source: Royal Dutch Shell (2001a).

- *Risk management* Reviewing the group's system of risk management and internal control, including the framework of policies and standards.

The conference

The members of the boards of the parent companies and GHC meet regularly in 'conference' where CMD provides updates on group strategy, organisation, plans and performance, risk management and internal control. The conference is not a decision-making body. Each of the boards of the parent companies and GHC meet separately after the conference to make decisions they consider appropriate.

Corporate centre

Corporate centre is a service organisation providing support to CMD and functional leadership to group businesses. It also manages financial, tax and company affairs for the parent companies and GHC. It consists of eight directors and one Chief Information Officer (CIO) appointed by the CMD. The director of finance is responsible for financial strategy and investor relations. The Group Treasurer looks after dividend and finding issues, pension funds and insurance. The Group Controller is responsible for external reporting, financial accounting, risk management and internal control, governance, audit, and management information. The Head of Group Taxation takes care of tax issues including the tax implications of corporate restructuring. Human resources strategy, management succession and key appointments are under the control of Human Resources Director. The Planning, Environment and External Affairs Director looks after strategy and plans, internal and external communications, reputation management, external relations, sustainable development, health, safety and environment. The international director is responsible for regional and international matters, security and the role of country chair. The Legal Director manages legal matters and intellectual property. Finally, the CIO manages information and communications technology and systems. These function heads usually act as the chair or secretary of a number of cross-business forums such as HSE Advisors' Panel, Human Resources Council and the Sustainable Development Committee. These forums are endorsed by CMD for the purpose of sharing good practices and developing proposals for group policies, standards and guidelines.

Group business CEO and Excom

Each of the five business streams (exploration and production, oil products, chemicals, gas and power and other group businesses) within Shell's operating companies is headed by a chief executive officer (CEO), who provides strategic direction, support and appraisal for its various operations. CEOs are accountable to CMD for the performance of their businesses (Figure 3.4). Group business is organised into defined business units and/or service organisations. The creation of any new cross-border business units or service organisations must be endorsed by the group business CEOs, who ensure that the Head of Group Taxation is advised. Group business CEOs are required to seek the advice of the Group Controller as to whether their business units are appropriately defined and seek endorsement from CMD for organisational arrangements that present unusual circumstances or risks.

The CEO appoints the members of a business executive committee (Excom) on the advice of the Management Development Committee. The members of Excom are senior executives managing major business units and global business lines, or performing functions such as finance or human resources. They are accountable to the business CEO for the performance of their own area and support the CEO in his/her line accountability for the performance of the entire business. Moreover, each Excom member usually appoints several executives to help provide strategic direction, support and appraisal for their organisational area such as zone, region, global business line, market segment or function.

Business unit executives

The business unit is the lowest organisational level. Business unit executives align business unit targets and resources with the overall objectives of the business stream (Figure 3.4). They are accountable to and are appraised by the Group Business CEO, or by an appropriate zone, regional, global, functional or other executive, based on business performance. Business unit executives appraise the personal performance of business unit staff against targets.

Regional Managing Director and Country Chair

Regional Managing Director   Regional Managing Directors oversee Group strategy and plans for their geographic region, help cross-business co-ordination and give advice to CMD and business executives on the respective region (Figure 3.4). They are also consulted on proposals affecting their region before they are presented to CMD. The International Directorate supports the Regional Managing Directors, and liaises with the country chairs and the businesses on regional matters.

Country Chair   The Country Chair is appointed by the Regional Managing Directors in each country where Shell has activities and reports to a relevant Business Excom member (Figure 3.4). A senior Shell representative is appointed for countries where Shell does not have activities but Shell products are sold. In most countries, the Country Chair is also a business unit executive as well as a director of one or more Shell companies. The responsibilities of the Country Chair are as follows:

- managing Shell's reputation in the country;

- leading Shell's external affairs, including crisis management, security, and representation to government, media and business partners;
- ensuring the application of Shell general business principles in the country concerned;
- playing an active role in the attraction and development of human resources, senior management appointments, remuneration systems and labour relations;
- co-ordinating and promoting important issues and opportunities across various businesses in the country,
- reporting to the Regional Managing Director any significant concerns relating to the aforementioned issues that are unable to be resolved at the local level and advising the Regional Managing Director of any other information relating to the country that could potentially impact upon Shell's interests.

Each Country Chair leads a country co-ordination team consisting of representatives of all businesses with activities in the country. The team exchanges information and co-ordinates matters such as recruitment and crisis management. In essence, the Country Chair's job is to 'guard the group's reputation and interests' (Royal Dutch/Shell, 2001a: 7). Their responsibilities cover all Shell activities in the country, including any joint ventures. Any exception to the coverage must be approved by the Regional Managing Director. Each business has defined obligations to support the Country Chair. For example, they contribute to social investment and crisis management support, provide access to information on business principles, HSE, human resources and reputation, and participate in the country co-ordination team. Businesses consult the Country Chair on major business proposals with a potential impact on the reputation or strategic interests of Shell such as major divestments, staff reduction plans, or changes to legal entities.

Corporate headquarters' function

Formulating group business policies

Shell's business policies comprise Shell General Business Principles (SGBP), Health Safety and Environment Commitment and Policy (HSECP), Risk and Internal Control Policy (RICP). The function head for RICP is the Group Controller.

SHELL GENERAL BUSINESS PRINCIPLES

The SGBP outline the eight principles that have been adopted as policy by the GHC. Principle one defines the objectives of Shell companies as 'to engage efficiently, responsibly and profitably in the oil, gas, chemicals and other selected businesses and to participate in the search for and development of other sources of energy. Shell companies seek a high standard of performance and aim to maintain a long-term position in their respective competitive environments'. Principle two identifies five areas of responsibility for Shell companies: responsibilities to shareholders, to customers, to employees, to contractors, suppliers and joint venture partners, and to society. Principle three encompasses Shell's economic principles. Shell believes that profitability is essential to carrying out the responsibilities outlined in principle two and staying in business. Shell companies generally believe that a market economy can serve most efficiently the interests of the community. Criteria for investment decisions are not exclusively economic in nature but also include social and environmental considerations and an appraisal of the security of the investment. Principle four addresses business integrity. Direct or indirect offers, payment, soliciting and acceptance of bribes in any form are unacceptable. Employees must avoid conflicts of interest between their private financial activities and their role in the conduct of company business. All business transactions must be reflected accurately in the accounts of the company according to established procedures and subject to audit. Principle five specifies that Shell companies do not make payments to political parties, organisations or their representatives or take any part in party politics. Employees can engage in activities in the community, including standing for election to public office, where it is appropriate in the light of local circumstances. Principles six to nine address the issues of HSE, contribution to community, free competition within the framework of law, and open communication about Shell activities.

There are various institutional arrangements within Shell to support the process of SGBP. The Council for Sustainable Development, consisting of senior group executives, is responsible for integrating the economic, social and environmental aspects of Shell's activities. In addition, an issues-identification and management network and the group crisis team make sure that executives are informed of and act on issues that may arise. The function head for SGBP is the Planning, Environment and External Affairs Director. The International Directorate assists the function head to implement SGBP in each country through the Country Chair.

HEALTH, SAFETY AND ENVIRONMENT COMMITMENT AND POLICY

HSECP and a HSE management system have been adopted by the GHC. HSECP commits Shell to develop energy resources, products and services aiming to protect the environment and to use material and energy efficiently to provide products and services. Every Shell company is required to set targets for improvement and measures, appraises and reports performance. Moreover, Shell requires contractors and joint ventures to manage HSE in line with the Shell policies. HSE performance is included in the performance appraisal for all Shell staff and reward accordingly.

The function head is the Planning, Environment and External Affairs Director and is supported by the HSE Advisors' panel. The members of the Panel include

HSE advisors to business streams. The HSE Council consisting of senior group executives approves proposals from the HSE Advisors' Panel.

Internal control

GROUP AND BUSINESS POLICIES AND STANDARDS

The boards of the GHC are responsible for adopting a group policy for matters that are subject to external shareholder expectations and disclosures, and for implementing the policy across the group. A group standard is adopted either to clarify the implementation aspects of a group policy, or to set expectations for matters that are not subject to external disclosures but are still important enough to require common treatment across the group. The CMD endorses group standards, supported by the function head and the business streams. The business streams communicate with CMD for the implementation of the group standard. Business streams and service organisations operate within the boundaries of these policies and standards. Within these boundaries, they have extensive freedom to determine how business performance is to be achieved. The relevant group function head assists the process of getting support from businesses, endorsement from CMD and approval from GHC for group policies and standards. CMD advises businesses and Country Chairs whenever a group policy or standard is adopted. Businesses or Country Chairs then promote its implementation.

In addition, businesses adopt and implement business-specific policies or standards such as chemical marketing standards or deepwater oil production engineering standards and set up internal assurance mechanisms for the policies and standards.

IMPLEMENTING POLICIES AND STANDARDS

Annual assurance letter   The implementation of Group policies and standards in Shell businesses is monitored through the annual assurance letter process. There are two kinds of assurance letters submitted to the CMD: one is from each Country Chair and the other is from each business CEO. Each Country Chair submits to the relevant Regional Managing Director an annual assurance letter addressing the role of the country chair, the group policies and standards, and regulatory compliance issues, based on information provided by each business operating in the country. Each business CEO and service organisation submits an annual business assurance letter to the CMD, addressing group policies and standards as well as significant incidents or compliance issues on policies or standards. The business assurance letter is based on 'cascaded assurances' provided by each business unit or from a lower organisational level in the case of function service such as financial reporting. Each business unit bases its assurance on a structured self-appraisal, taking into account the results of independent appraisal. Each business stream prepares and implements assurance plans including self and independent appraisals. Business assurance committees review and endorse these plans and advise executives on actions.

The group function heads decide on the assurance requirements for their policy or standards. The group controller co-ordinates the assurance process, liaises with the function heads, and reassesses the scope of the assurance letters every year.

Joint ventures   Joint ventures that are controlled by Shell are expected to apply group policies and standards, and businesses provide assurance to the CMD through the annual assurance letter process. For all joint ventures that are not controlled by Shell – whether incorporated or not – businesses assess the particular situation and use whatever influence may be necessary to ensure that appropriate policies and standards are implemented. Factors to consider include: relevance, particular risks, stakeholders, and other sensitivities. Some subjects, such as business principles or health, safety and environment, apply to every joint venture. Others such as standards for sharing information on the Shell network are not always relevant. Business executives and ultimately business CEOs are accountable for carrying out and acting on this assessment. Moreover, the relevant Regional Managing Director maintains an overview of the application of policies or standards by joint ventures in the region under his/ her responsibility, particularly on matters such as business principles that could affect group reputation. International joint ventures that report all assurances through the business line should be agreed by the Regional Managing Director.

Strategic planning

Shell formulates business strategy on the basis of its understanding of the developments in energy market. Shell believes that hydrocarbons will remain the major world energy resources for at least the next thirty years with gas playing an ever-increasing role. Moreover, renewable energies will grow and hydrogen as a fuel has great potential in the long term (Royal Dutch Shell, 2001c). The strategy is to invest more in two business streams: exploration and production, and gas and power, with a focus on gas in particular. It is estimated that in 2001, capital investment in exploration and development, gas and power accounted for 46 per cent of Shell's total capital employed by businesses. The geographical direction for the business portfolio is to maintain leadership in Europe, increase Shell's presence in North America, invest in major developing countries such as China and India, and select specific projects for offshore development in Africa, the Middle East and the Caspian region. Through research and technology, Shell is to offer more environmentally-friendly products to customers and expand its hydrogen and renewable businesses.

MERGERS AND ACQUISITIONS AND DIVESTMENTS

Shell was not among the participants in the large-scale mergers and acquisitions after 1997, which fundamentally changed the competitive structure of the world's major oil and petrochemical industry (see Chapter 8). Shell's approach is to merge or acquire assets that provide a foundation for high growth, and fill its portfolio or skills gaps. The total amount of spending for acquisitions from 1998 to 2001 was 'only' $6 billion.

Exploration and production   Shell's exploration and production activities span over forty-eight countries around the world. The global portfolio, consisting of onshore and both deep and shallow offshore locations, is managed through assets exchange, acquisitions, and divestments. For example, in 2000, Shell exchanged its interests in the North Sea and in the Gulf of Mexico for Marathon's interest in Sakhalin Energy in Russia, and controlled a 55 per cent share of the development and operation of the Sakhalin project. In early March 2001, Shell's acquisition of Fletcher Challenge Energy was approved by the New Zealand Commerce Commission. However, the offer to acquire all of the shares in Australian Woodside Petroleum Ltd, in which Shell had a 34 per cent interest, was rejected by Woodside. In 2001 also, Shell Oil Company made a tender offer for all the outstanding shares of Barrett Resources in the United States at $55 per share in cash. In April 2000, Shell's 36% common interest in Altura, an associated company in the United States was sold. The group's share of Altura's production in 1999 represented approximately 54,000 barrels of oil equivalent per day. In Australia, the group's interest in the Barrow and Thevenard Island (Carnarvon Basin) concessions was divested. In the United Kingdom, the divestment of the group's interest in the Elgin and Franklin fields was concluded.

Gas and power   The gas and power businesses include the processing, selling and delivery of natural gas by long-distance pipeline and LNG (liquefied natural gas) by tanker; selling and delivering the liquid by-products of natural gas processing and gas to liquids conversion; marketing and trading of natural gas and electricity; wholesaling and retailing to industrial and domestic customers; and developing and operating independent power plants. The year 2000 witnessed many activities in the LNG business. Letters of intent were signed for selling up to two million tonnes of LNG a year to Japanese gas companies from 2004. The LNG will be supplied from an expansion of the Shell's North West Shelf LNG plant in Australia. Shell's interest in the Malaysia LNG Tiga plant was increased from 10 to 15 per cent. Shell and its partners in Nigeria and Oman agreed to look at expansion of their LNG projects. A bid was successful for capacity in the US Cove Point LNG terminal, which provides access to the growing US market. Agreements are also in place to develop a re-gasification terminal in Brazil and import projects are being developed in China and India. Moreover, Shell announced that four plants, each with a capacity of 75,000 barrels per day, could be built in the next decade by utilising Shell's leading gas to liquids technology.

InterGen   InterGen is a major international developer of private power projects in which Shell increased its equity interest from 50% to 68% during 2000. InterGen has twelve projects under construction and a total net operating capacity of 6.4 gigawatts (GW). The twelve power stations under construction are located in China, the United Kingdom, Turkey, Australia, Egypt, Mexico and the United States. Further power stations, with a total net capacity of 6.6GW, are under development in the United States, Brazil, Mexico, the United Kingdom and the Netherlands.

Oil products   The oil products business consists of sales and marketing of transportation fuels, lubricants, speciality products and technical services; refining, supply, trading and shipping of crude oil and petroleum products. Oil products services over 20 million customers a day through 46,000 service stations around the world, and more than 1 million industrial and commercial customers. The global refinery and retail portfolios are managed through acquisition and divestment activities. Investment in refining aims to reinforce their market position in higher-value-added areas, notably for transportation and specialty products, and to address environmental concerns through tighter product specifications. In 2000, the Sola refinery in Norway was closed and the Cressier refinery in Switzerland was sold. In the United States, Equilon's Wood River refinery was sold. Showa Shell in Japan announced that from 2001, as part of its strategic alliance with Japan Energy, Showa Shell would close a capacity of 50,000 barrels per day at its Yokkaichi refinery and that Japan Energy would stop refining operations at its Chita refinery.

Performance of retail networks is monitored closely to determine whether to expand or divest. For example, restructuring the retail portfolio involves the integration of retail sites acquired through swap and purchase arrangements into the Shell networks in Greece, Italy, Poland, the Czech Republic and countries in West and East Africa. Meanwhile, retail sites have recently been sold in mid-west Brazil and Southeastern Italy. In addition, Shell established a marketing joint venture with Sinopec in Jiangsu province of China in 2001, following Shell's investment in Sinopec's IPO in 2000. The joint venture provides 'a platform for the Shell brand and customer offerings' (Royal/Dutch Shell, 2001b: 27).

In marketing, environmentally friendlier products have recently been introduced, such as low-sulphur diesel, liquefied petroleum gas, biodegradable lubricants for marine leisure and lead-replacement fuel. The Shell/Ferrari Formula One partnership was renewed for another five years from 2000: '(T)op-level motor sport plays a vital role in the development and testing of high-quality, high-performance fuels and lubricants' (Royal Dutch/Shell, 2001b: 24). In trading, from January 2001, Shell Trading was established as a single global trading organisation to look after Shell's trading across the oil products, gas and power and chemicals businesses.

Chemicals   From 1998 to 2001, Shell reduced the number of chemical product businesses from twenty-one to thirteen, focusing the chemicals portfolio on selected businesses, and the number of sites was reduced from fifty-four to seventeen. Which businesses to retain and which to divest are determined on the basis of their historical performance, as well as their closeness of fit between any given business and Shell's other businesses. The chemical portfolio comprises 'a set of major linked petrochemical businesses in which group companies possess leading technologies and the proven capability to build and operate world-class plants' (Royal Dutch/Shell, 1999: 35). The long-term chemicals portfolio consists of eight product business areas including major cracker products, petrochemical building blocks and large-volume polymers, and four stand-alone companies or ventures – Basell, Infineum, CRI International and Saudi Arabia Petrochemical Company.

A major divestment programme started in 1999. In 2000, the polyethylene terephthalate business and the resins and versatics business were disposed of. The Kraton elastomers business was sold in February 2001 and the Carilon business was expected to stop operation during 2001. Along with the asset divestment, two world-class joint ventures were established in 2000. Basell, a 50:50 joint venture between Shell and BASF, was formed, creating one of the world largest polyolefins companies. The joint venture combined the assets of Montell and Targor, the polypropylene businesses of Shell and BASF respectively, and Elenac, the polyethylene joint venture formed in 1997 between Shell and BASF. In China a joint venture contract was signed with CNOOC Petrochemicals Investment Limited for a $4 billion petrochemical complex, in which Shell has a 50 per cent ownership share in Guangdong province. It is planned to be a world-scale petrochemicals operation, designed with the most advanced technologies, annually producing 800 kilotonnes of ethylene as well as propylene, polyethylene, polypropylene and other chemical products aimed mainly at the domestic Chinese market. The complex was expected to start up in 2005 after the partners made a final investment decision by the end of 2002.

Renewable energy   In 1997, Shell consolidated its activities in solar power, biomass (wood-based) power and forestry, into Shell Renewables. Shell Renewables now develops and operates wind farms and biomass power plants, manufactures and markets solar energy systems, and grows forests to supply markets with sustainably managed wood products. The Solar business manufactures solar photovoltaic cells in the Netherlands, Germany and Japan and produces modules in the Netherlands, Japan and India. A sales joint venture to market solar home systems was established with the national utility ESKOM of South Africa, 50 per cent of which is owned by Shell. In India, Sri Lanka and the Philippines, Shell has wholly-owned companies to market and supply solar home systems. The overall industry growth of solar energy is between 20–25 per cent a year, with the growth strongest in developed countries where the market is stimulated by strong government-supported programmes. Consolidation within the solar industry has created a small number of large players, which leads to reducing production costs. In early 2001, Shell and Siemens agreed to link their solar energy businesses and set up a joint venture, which would be owned 33 per cent by Shell, 34 per cent by Siemens, and 33 per cent by Eon Energie. The joint venture had an annual turnover of around $138 million on a pro forma basis and aims to become one of the world top five solar cell producers by 2007 with an annual manufacturing capacity of 100 megawatts. The joint venture would enable Shell to access better solar energy technology, including thin-film technology, and Siemens's extensive distribution network, covering more than 90 countries: 'This gives us a presence in the whole value chain and will allow us to take solar energy further into the mainstream' (Shell manager, quoted in *Financial Times*, 28 February 2001).

The wind energy industry is growing at more than 30 per cent a year. In 2000, Shell partnered with Powergen and developed the first UK offshore wind farm at Blyth, in which the Shell has a 33 per cent interest. The wind farm generates 4 megawatts electricity to supply 3,000 households. In Germany a 3 megawatt wind farm was opened on Shell's refinery site at Hamburg, supplying customers in Hamburg. In addition, Shell is engaged in the development of hydrogen as a future transportation fuel. A joint venture is being negotiated with International Fuel Cells to develop, manufacture and sell fuel processor devices. These devices will produce hydrogen from hydrocarbons and would greatly facilitate the introduction of clean, fuel-cell technology into the marketplace by allowing vehicles to refuel in the existing retail network. This would eliminate the requirement for investment in a new fuel distribution network. Shell is also active in the Californian Fuel Cell Initiative, a project designed to demonstrate the viability of fuel-cell vehicles in the marketplace. As part of this project, Shell is to help establish hydrogen vehicle refuelling facilities in California.

Managing the Shell brand

The Brand Council led by the Executive Vice President Marketing Oil Products oversees the management of the Shell brand. The Global Brand Standards defines the standards to protect and promotes the Shell brand.

Setting reward policy

The remuneration for senior management including Group Managing Directors and Directors of the parent companies is made up of three components: basic salary, annual bonus and long-term incentives.

Basic salary   The base salary scales for Managing Directors are set by reference to internal and external market surveys of companies of similar size and international scope. Base salaries are reviewed annually. Progression of an individual Managing Director's salary to the target position is usually over a three-year period from the time of appointment.

Annual bonus   The annual bonus is determined by the Group Remuneration and Succession Review Committee (REMCO), based on the extent of achievement of the Group performance targets covering financial, operational and social environmental objectives. The maximum bonus is 50 per cent of base salary and the payment of the bonus is non-pensionable.

Long-term incentives Since 1967, the group stock option plans have provided long-term incentives for Managing Directors. From 1998, options granted to the Managing Directors of Shell Transport are granted for ten years with a three-year vesting period. Moreover, 50 per cent of options granted to Managing Directors since 1998 have had performance conditions. The performance conditions are based on the total shareholder return over a three-year period, measured by the averaged weighted share price of Royal Dutch and Shell Transport over the ten-day period at the beginning and the end of the three-year period. This is compared with the equivalent data for other integrated oil companies. The REMCO determines the proportion of the share options subject to the performance conditions that will either become unconditional or lapse.

Centralising capital investment and procurement

During his tenure as Chairman of the CMD from 1998 to 2001, Sir Mark Moody-Stuart tackled the past lack of central control over capital spending in Shell. He closed down powerful national headquarters in the United Kingdom, the Netherlands, Germany and France and stripped Shell Oil in the United States of its autonomy over capital expenditure. Now investment proposals from Shell Companies involving unique circumstances or risks, or exceeding $100 million in value must be approved by the GHC. The GHC delegates authority to approve proposals not exceeding $100 million to each CMD member and to the Group Director of Finance. For investment proposals exceeding $20 million, authority for approval is delegated to certain senior business executives. A CMD member or the Director of Finance decides to which executives the authority is delegated. These authorities cannot be further delegated. Subject to this process, a relevant Shell Company makes the funds available and actions taken to implement the investment project. Moreover, these consideration levels also apply to the appraisal of the investment projects after they are implemented. Capital discipline was 'embedded in the organisation' under Sir Mark and will continue with 'a relentless focus' under Mr Phil Watts, Chairman of the CMD from July 2001 (*Financial Times*, 18 December 2000).

Shell has been implementing an e-procurement programme across its operating companies all over the world. It was expected that e-procurement would be in full operation by the end of 2002. E-procurement at Shell includes Online Bidding and ETrading. By July 2001, Online Bidding had been used in Shell more than 400 times for the procurement of suppliers and services, and for selling surplus stocks (Shell website, 2002). During an Online Bidding event, each approved supplier is able to see their position relative to other anonymous bidders, and the contract is usually awarded to the supplier offering the lowest price. An online auction typically lasts about an hour and finishes either when a set time limit is reached or when no further bids are submitted. The Online Bidding replaces the sealed-paper bids and offers a well thought out and properly constructed invitation to tender with clearly defined specifications and evaluation criteria. The transparency in the bidding reduces the cost of the contract.

ETrading is the process by which Shell's procurement transactions are carried out through Trade-Ranger, an industry-wide internet exchange that links the buyers' and suppliers' systems and provides comprehensive catalogues. Shell's management information system links the buying systems within its operating units to the Trade-Ranger, to which suppliers' selling systems are connected. The adoption of Trade-Ranger greatly simplifies the myriad of connections between buying and selling companies, and provides a simple platform connecting all transaction parties under common standards. This will lead to faster payments and reduction in transaction costs. The approved suppliers and Shell buyers are able to transact directly through Trade-Ranger rather than through the procurement department. The supplier and procurement department can adopt a more strategic and informed approach to managing the contract and their relationship. Compared with the conventional procurement process, E-Trading enables all procurement data to be collected and analysed in an easier and more transparent fashion, which leads to improvement in the quality and availability of up-to-date information, thereby reducing costs across the whole supply value chain.

Technology

Shell's R&D programmes are carried out through a world-wide network of laboratories, with major efforts concentrated in the Netherlands, the United Kingdom and the United States (Table 3.3). R&D expenses (including depreciation) for the years between 1996 to 2000 were $701 million, $662 million, $799 million, $505 million and $389 million, respectively.

EXPLORATION AND PRODUCTION

R&D for exploration and production aims to keep Shell at the forefront of technologies including: subsurface imaging and modelling to improve exploration success rates, increase hydrocarbon recovery and reduce lead times from discovery to production; improvement on the performance of oil and gas wells; reducing unit production costs, particularly in support of Shell's deep-water activities; developing the profitable use of unconventional resources and low mobility hydrocarbons; identifying best practices and implementing them speedily at all Shell's operating locations around the globe.

DOWNSTREAM GAS AND POWER

The focus of R&D has been on cost leadership and the creation of viable technical opportunities through researching on LNG, particularly LNG processing, safety, transport and storage. R&D programmes on further developing Shell's leading position in gas to liquids (GTL) conversion aim at improving catalysts and process technology to further reduce capital costs and improve process efficiency. GTL product development is also an important focus

Table 3.3 Principal research and technical service centres in the world: Royal Dutch Shell.

Research and technology centre	Location	R&D areas
Shell Research and Technology Centre	Louvain-la-Neuve, Belgium	Polymers, plastics, elastomers, resins and urethanes
Shell Global Solutions	Petit-Couronne, France	Lubricants, fuels, bitumen, automation and instrumentation
Shell Global Solutions (Deutschland)	Produkte-Anwengungs-und Entwicklungs-Laboratorium, Hamburg	Oil products
Shell Research and Technology Centre	Amsterdam, Netherlands	Chemicals and oil products and processes
Shell International Exploration and Production BV Research and Technical Service	Rijswijk, Netherlands	Oil and gas exploration and production
Shell Global Solutions	Thornton, UK	Fuel and lubricant technology, health, safety and environment solutions, analysis and measurement activities
Showa Shell Sekiyu, Atsugi Laboratory	Japan	Oil products, environmental studies, photo voltaic, new materials
Shell Global Solutions (Singapore)	Singapore	*
Bellaire Technology Centre	Houston, Texas	Oil and gas exploration and production
Westhollow Technology Centre	Houston, Texas	Oil and chemical products and processes, transportation
Calgary Research Centre (Alberta)	Canada	Oil and gas exploration and production, oil sands extraction and processing, and oil products and processes

Source: Royal Dutch Shell (2001c).

Note: *Not available.

of work. Furthermore, R&D efforts are focused on maintaining a leading edge in sustainable development across the downstream gas and Power technology portfolio.

OIL PRODUCTS

R&D programmes continue to emphasise the improvement of key products and their applications and the further advancement of process technologies including related technical services that provide group companies with a competitive advantage. High priority is given to product development, particularly related to health and the environment. Process research emphasises improvements in the reliability, availability and control of refinery processes and gas plants and supports the optimal exploitation of existing assets. A strategic programme targets the development of medium-term options in sustainable energy and sustainable mobility. The further development of the catalytic partial oxidation technology as part of this effort enables the operation of fuel cells with hydrocarbons instead of hydrogen.

CHEMICALS

R&D programmes aim to improve key products and technologies that provide Shell Chemicals with sustainable leadership positions in selected products. Improvements in manufacturing technology enable facilities to achieve increased feed-stock flexibility, product yield, energy efficiency or plant throughput, thereby lowering production costs. Technology in process intensification and manufacturing integration results in lower unit investment costs. R&D in chemicals is integrated into the business and new product concepts are introduced to enhance market positions.

Information technology management

The Group CFO heads the IT leadership team, which includes the Chief Information Officers of the business streams. The IT leadership team submits proposals to the IT Business Council consisting of senior group executives for approval. A group network security standard, the Trust Domain, supports the global business applications and information sharing, and controls the risks in the process of sharing knowledge.

Summary

During the 1990s, BP and Shell each implemented programmes of comprehensive institutional changes involving greatly enhanced central control and co-ordination mechanisms for all key aspects of company life. This transformation was truly revolutionary. At the heart of this change was the common adoption of the 'business unit' structure.

In BP, 150 business units are organised into four business streams from upstream exploration and production to downstream refining and marketing, gas and power, as well as chemicals. They are led by the Business CEO and the ExCo members of each business stream, who, in turn, are monitored by the Group CEO and the board of directors. The headquarters consists of the board of directors including the GCEO and his or her executive management team. The headquarters is supported by executives in functional areas such as finance and human resources. The headquarters formulates business policies including ethical conduct; employees; relationships; health, safety and environmental performance; control and finance. Under each of the five areas there are policy commitments and expectations. The business policies provide boundaries for business units to carry out their activities. The headquarters sets up internal control processes that apply to managers at various levels from line managers, BU leaders, function heads, regional presidents to BCEO and GCEO accountable to the business policies in the domain under their responsibilities. The headquarters is the 'brain' in determining strategic moves such as mergers and acquisitions, providing strategic direction for business development, and creating asset portfolios with high returns across the globe. Moreover, facilitated by investment in information technology, the headquarters is able to centralise capital investment and financial reporting as well as integrating the procurement process through e-businesses. The headquarters integrates the brands within the company under one global brand 'bp' and renovates the brand image and the value it carries. The headquarters, through performance contracts, monitors the performance of the subordinate business units to ensure the delivery of shareholder value. Meanwhile, the headquarters sets reward policies for executives and employees through bench-marking with peers in the same industry in order to make sure that the company can attract high-calibre personnel.

The structure of Royal Dutch/Shell is unique due to the historical alliance of Royal Dutch Petroleum in the Netherlands and the Shell Transporting and Trading Company in the United Kingdom on a 60:40 equity share basis. The two group holding companies under the parent companies – Shell Petroleum NV based in the Netherlands and the Shell Petroleum Company Ltd based in the United Kingdom. The parent companies appoint the directors in the GHCs. Under the two GHCs, operating companies in more than 135 countries, many of which are stand-alone business units, are organised into five business streams – exploration and production, gas and power, oil products, chemicals and other businesses including renewable energies, customer and financial services. The business headquarters is the Committee of the Managing Directors consisting of Managing Directors from both GHCs. The headquarters determines Shell's business policies comprising Shell General Business Principles, Health Safety and Environment Commitment and Policy, and Risk and Internal Control Policy. All Shell businesses including joint ventures are subject to these policies and principles. The headquarters exercises internal control through devising group and business policies and standards and by establishing the method through which relationships across the different layers of management are governed. The implementation of group policies and standards in Shell businesses is monitored through the process of issuing the annual assurance letter at various levels of the management team and through ensuring reward policies for executives and employees are set through bench-marking with peers in the same industry. The headquarters sets the strategic direction of the businesses and manages the Shell brand world-wide. The headquarters has centralised control over the rights of capital investment, which used to be in the hands of the powerful regional companies. The headquarters invests in R&D centres across the advanced countries to provide leading technologies for Shell's businesses. Moreover, by investing in information technology, the headquarters is able to integrate Shell's procurement process across the world.

In sum, the institutional revolution of the 1990s established the headquarters as the ultimate authority in commanding the company, and as the centre of planning and co-ordinating business activities. Its functions are to formulate business policies or business principles – the 'constitution' of the companies. Business units have autonomy to conduct their activities, but only within the boundaries of the centrally-determined policies and principles. The headquarters provides strategic direction for the growth of the whole company. It determines strategic moves such as mergers and acquisitions, the management of asset portfolios through asset acquisitions and divestment. The headquarters centralises capital investment and guarantees that all investment conforms to the strategic direction of the whole company. The headquarters invests in centralised brand management to promote the image of the company and unify tens of thousands of employees across the world. The headquarters sets up internal control processes and performance monitoring devices to ensure that business units operate in conformity with the strategic directions of the whole company and deliver performance targets. The headquarters determines the selection and appointment process to determine who will be the leaders of the company. Furthermore, the headquarters invests in and co-ordinates R&D activities across the business streams in order to sustain the company's leading position in technology. The headquarters invests in information technology to facilitate the centralisation of capital investment, financial reporting, human resources management as well as knowledge sharing within the company. The headquarters also invests in e-businesses to integrate global procurement process to reduce cost.

4 Government centralisation and corporatisation

CNPC and Sinopec from the 1950s to 1997

In the course of fifty years from 1949 to 1998, the institutional structure of China's oil and petrochemical industry experienced significant change (Table 4.1). Throughout the period of the command economy from the 1950s to 1970s, the Ministry of Petroleum was the 'commander' of the oil and petrochemical industry. It planned, organised, and administered the activities of the whole industry in the fashion of a military campaign. During the 1980s and 1990s, a series of significant experiments was carried out to transform the industry from government ministries to business corporations. In 1981, the oil industry became the country's first industrial sector to adopt the contract system across the whole industry (*hangye baogan*). The Ministry of Petroleum industry and the chemical industry were successively 'corporatised' into companies. The effort to construct large modern industrial corporations culminated in the nation-wide restructuring programme of 1998 and the subsequent flotation of the industry's core assets in the year 2000.

Government centralisation: 1950s–1970s

In December 1950, the State Council promulgated the 'Regulation on the Mining Industry in the People's Republic of China', which specified that the country's mineral resources were state assets and should be managed by the central government. In July 1955, the Ministry of Petroleum Industry (MPI) was established as the administrative body of the oil industry.

'Massive campaign' model

From 1950 to 1957, the total output of crude oil in China was less than 6 million tonnes (Table 4.2), and the country depended on oil imports. In order to become self-sufficient in crude oil supply for the country's industrialisation, the central government adopted a quasi-military 'massive campaign' (*da hui zhan*) model to explore and develop oil resources. The government provided the funds needed, and mobilised human and material resources nation-wide in a short period of time to the targeted area for exploration and development. The requisite massive human resources came from the People's Liberation Army (PLA). In 1952, Mao

Table 4.1 Chronology of the institutional change of China's oil and petrochemical industry: 1949–2001.

- 1 October 1949: the People's Republic of China was established. The central government set up the Ministry of Fuel Industry, responsible for the production and development of crude oil, coal, and electrical power.
- April 1950: the Bureau of Petroleum Administration was set up under the Ministry of Fuel Industry.
- 30 July 1955: the Ministry of Fuel Industry was abolished. The Ministry of Petroleum Industry, the Ministry of Coal Industry and the Ministry of Electrical Power were established.
- 22 June 1970: the Ministry of Coal Industry, the Ministry of Petroleum Industry and the Ministry of Chemical Industry merged into the Ministry of Fuel and Chemical Industry.
- 17 January 1975: the Ministry of Fuel and Chemical Industry was abolished and the Ministry of Petroleum and Chemical Industry and the Ministry of Coal Industry were established.
- 5 March 1978: the Ministry of Petroleum and Chemical Industry was abolished. The Ministry of Petroleum Industry and the Ministry of Chemical Industry were established.
- 1980: the State Energy Commission was established, responsible for administration over the Ministry of Petroleum Industry, the Ministry of Chemical Industry and the Ministry of Electrical Power.
- 1982: the State Energy Commission was abolished and the three ministries were placed under the administration of the State Council.
- 5 February 1982: China National Offshore Oil Corporation (CNOOC) was established.
- 12 July 1983: China National Petrochemical Corporation (Sinopec) was established.
- 17 September 1988: China National Petroleum and Natural Gas Corporation (CNPC) was established. Earlier in the same year, the Ministry of Petroleum Industry was abolished. The Ministry of Energy was established taking over governmental responsibility from the previous three ministries – the Ministry of Petroleum Industry, the Ministry of Coal Industry, the Ministry of Nuclear Industry – and responsible for electrical power industry from the Ministry of Hydro and Electrical Power.
- 1993: the Ministry of Energy was abolished.
- 24 January 1996: China National Star Petroleum Corporation (CNSPC) was established based on the exploration functions spun off from the Ministry of Geology and Mineral Resources.
- April 1998: the Ministry of Chemical Industry was abolished. The State Bureau of Petroleum and Chemical Industry was established taking over the governmental functions of the Ministry of Chemical industry and that of CNPC and Sinopec. It was under the administration of the State Economic and Trade Commission.
- 7 July 1998: CNPC and Sinopec were restructured into China National Petroleum and Natural Gas Group Company (CNPC) and China National Petrochemical Group Company (Sinopec Group).
- 5 November 1999: PetroChina Company Limited (PetroChina) was established based on the core assets of CNPC.
- 28 February 2000: China Petroleum and Chemical Corporation (Sinopec Corporation) was established based on the core assets of Sinopec Group.
- March 2000: Sinopec Group merged with CNSPC, which was renamed as Sinopec Star Petroleum Co. Ltd.
- 7 April 2000: PetroChina was floated on the Hong Kong and New York Stock Exchanges.
- 19 October 2000: Sinopec Corporation was floated on the Hong Kong, New York, and London Stock Exchanges.
- 28 February 2001: CNOOC was floated on the Hong Kong and New York Stock Exchanges.
- 2001: the State Bureau of Petroleum and Chemical Industry was abolished along with other bureaux of industrial administration.

Table 4.2 China's oil output, 1949–2000.

Year	Output (million tonnes)
1949	0.121
1950–52	0.942
The first five-year plan: 1953–57	4.998
1957	1.458
The second five-year plan: 1958–62	22.271
1962	5.746
1963	6.478
1964	8.481
1965	11.315
The third five-year plan: 1966–70	96.804
1966	14.542
1967	13.877
1968	15.992
1969	21.747
1970	30.646
The fourth five-year plan: 1971–75	280.609
1971	39.415
1972	45.672
1973	53.613
1974	64.850
1975	77.059
The fifth five-year plan: 1976–80	496.933
1976	87.156
1977	93.638
1978	104.049
1979	106.149
1980	105.941
The sixth five-year plan: 1981–85	548.978
1981	101.219
1982	102.205
1983	106.066
1984	114.601
1985	124.887
The seventh five-year plan: 1986–90	677.758
1986	130.670
1987	134.125
1988	137.028
1989	137.651
1990	138.284
The eighth five-year plan: 1991–95	722.100
1991	141.000
1992	142.000
1993	144.000
1994	146.100
1995	149.000

(Table 4.2 continued)

Table 4.2 (continued).

Year	Output (million tonnes)
The ninth five-year plan: 1996–2000	801.600
1996	158.500
1997	160.100
1998	160.200
1999	160.200
2000	162.600

Sources: CNPC and Sinopec (1949–90).
  BP Statistical Review of World Energy 2002 (1991–2000).

Zedong ordered the 57th Division of the 19th Army of the PLA to be reorganised into the 1st Division of Oil, the first 'oil corps' in China after 1949. From 1955 onwards, a number of oil fields were discovered and developed: Karamay Oilfield in Xinjiang, Yumen Oilfield in Gansu, Lenghu Oilfield in Qinghai, and Fuyu Oilfield. From the start, crude oil was regarded as a 'strategic material' and the oil industry was regarded as a 'strategic industry'.

After the Soviet withdrawal in the early 1960s, China's need to become self-sufficient in oil as fast as possible became more desperate than ever. In 1960, the government launched the biggest ever 'massive campaign' to develop oil resources in Daqing (Chapter 7), a remote area in the Northeast China. The government organised more than 500 manufacturing plants from all over the country to supply machines and equipment for Daqing and more than 200 research and design institutes to provide technology to Daqing. In three years, Daqing built up an annual production capacity of 6 million tones and enabled China to become self-sufficient in oil. Daqing was chosen by Mao Zedong as the model for the country's state-owned industries, representing 'selfless mass enthusiasm and frugal construction' (Nolan, 2001: 442). Over four decades, Daqing built up a production capacity to 56 million tonnes and maintained the output level at 50 million tonnes for twenty-five years. In 1964, a further campaign for developing oil-fields in East China resulted in the establishment of Shengli Oilfield in Shandong and Dagang Oilfield in Tianjin. In 1965, China for the first time became fully self-sufficient in oil supply. China's grave concern over energy security was greatly alleviated. In 1970, China exported 190,000 tonnes of crude oil and became a net oil exporter. There was great optimism in the industry about the country's long-term prospects as an oil exporter.

SELF-CONTAINED PRODUCTION UNITS

Many of China's oil fields are located in remote areas and were developed under arduous conditions. Like other large SOEs in China facilities and a huge welfare system were established many diversified businesses and a huge welfare system were established around the major oil production sites. Along with the construction of the oil fields, sectors related to oil production including technological services, engineering and construction, infrastructure and equipment were built up on site. Moreover, to fulfil the workers' living requirements, agricultural production, crop processing, housing construction, a heating system, hotels and restaurants were developed. To provide education and health care for workers and their families, schools, colleges and hospitals were set up. Over the years, a distinctive self-contained system emerged from a production region such as Daqing Petroleum Administrative Bureau (Daqing). For example, Daqing Oil Field Administrative Bureau had sixty-seven second-tier units (*erji danwei*) in five sectors covering core oil businesses, service companies, public infrastructure, diversified businesses and social functions (Figure 4.1). Among the total of 261,000 employees, only 39.5 per cent worked in the core oil businesses and 23 per cent worked in service companies related to the oil businesses. This self-contained

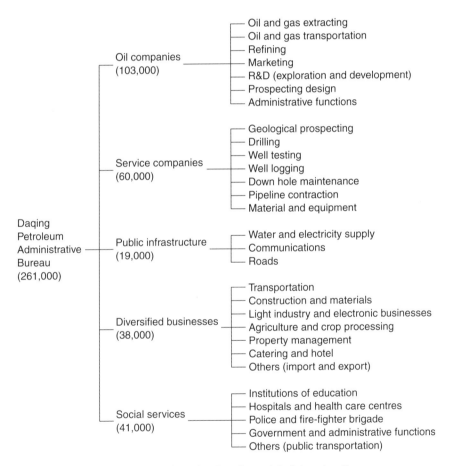

Figure 4.1 Organisation chart of Daqing Petroleum Administrative Bureau.

Note: Numbers in brackets are numbers of employees.

Source: Adapted and translated from Ding and Wang (1999: 54).

system, which is called *da er quan* ('big and comprehensive'), was run like a little country. This self-contained system also cascaded into a second-tier unit such as the No.1 Oil Extracting Plant under Daqing. The No.1 Oil Extracting Plant had thirty brigades in five sectors covering core oil businesses, service companies, public infrastructure, diversified businesses and social functions (Figure 4.2). It had 15,100 employees, 65 per cent of whom were engaged in core oil businesses and the rest worked in other four sectors. This smaller self-contained system was called *xiao er quan* ('small and comprehensive'), compared with the *da er quan* of Daqing. The same system could be found at whole industry level as well as in units that were even smaller than the second-tier units. This system posed enormous difficulties for the restructuring effort in 1999.

The 'massive campaign' model established an army of 'oil men' with a strong sense of responsibility for the collective and the country. They were highly

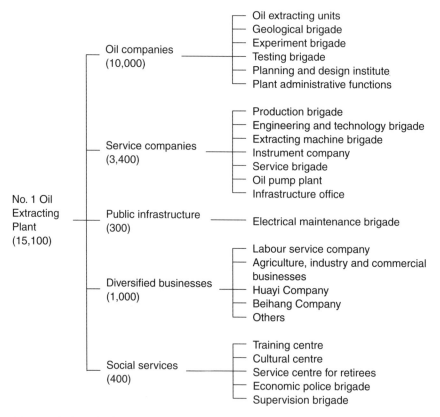

Figure 4.2 Organisation chart of No.1 Oil Extracting Plant of Daqing Petroleum Administrative Bureau.

Note: Numbers in brackets are numbers of employees.

Source: Adapted and translated from Ding and Wang (1999: 54).

disciplined and very skilful in organisation. They were able to mobilise fast to achieve their goals.

HEADQUARTERS

Under the 'massive campaign' model, the MPI was the administrative headquarters of China's oil industry. It made strategic decisions about the location of exploration and development. It planned the campaign, and organised human and material resources to support the it. It undertook and co-ordinated the production, transportation and marketing of oil and oil products based on the overall national plan set out by the State Planning Commission. It negotiated investment funds from the government and allocated them to its subordinate PAB all over the country. The various PAB were production units responsible for carrying out the production and investment plan.

Corporatisation and growing enterprise autonomy: 1980s–1997

'Big contract' model: 1981

China's oil industry faced serious difficulties at the beginning of the 1980s. After thirty years of development, resources in developed oil fields were depleting and government investment in oil exploration was shrinking. Oil output and investment in exploration had begun to decline. In 1981, the country's total oil output was 101 million tonnes, compared with 106 million tonnes in 1979 (Table 4.1). The investment fund available from the government for exploration and development was 1.7 billion yuan in 1981, only half of that in 1980. The major concern for the industry was how to raise funds to stabilise output in the developed oil fields and to explore and develop new oil resources. In 1981, the central government implemented the 'big contract' (*da bao gan*) system in the oil industry. Under the 'big contract' model, the MPI contracted with the central government for an annual production target of 100 million tonnes and a 'hand-over' to the state of 94.5 per cent of actual oil output. The MPI was allowed to export any excess oil above the production target and retain the revenue (in foreign exchange) from the difference between the government-set price and international market price. The retained revenue was earmarked as funds for introducing foreign advanced technology and equipment, and for importing pipelines and steel products exclusively for the oil industry. The oil produced above the contracted volume was also allowed to be sold at a higher price in the domestic market, the revenue from which were designated as oil exploration and development funds. The MPI then contracted with the subordinate PAB for their production target and the latter were allowed to retain the revenue from selling the amount of oil produced above the contracted production target.

The contract system provided a strong incentive for PAB to increase oil output. For example, the contracted oil production target for Shengli Oil-field in 1981 was 15.9 million tonnes and the actual oil output reached 16.11 million tonnes in the same year. In 1982, 340,000 tonnes were produced above the contracted target and the amount increased to 2.07 million tonnes in 1983. At the industry level, total production in 1981 was 101.22 million tonnes, exceeding the contracted target by 1.22 million tonnes. The industry raised 600 million yuan for exploration and development in 1981, equivalent to 25 per cent of the investment fund from the government in the same year. From 1981 to 1985, the industry raised a total of RMB12.6 billion for exploration and development (*China Petroleum*, November 1999: 20).

DUAL OIL PRICES

Under the contract system, the price for onshore oil followed a dual pricing system. The government set the price for the contracted oil. The price for oil produced in excess of the contracted quantity and for export followed the international market price. For example, in 1981, the government price for oil was about 100 yuan per tonne, compared with the price for exported oil of 600 yuan per tonne. From 1982, the MPI channelled a certain amount of crude oil allocated for export to domestic refineries for processing. The price of this amount of oil was fixed at a higher level than the government set price but below the international oil price, which was 545 yuan per tonne in 1982.

Upstream: CNPC

Corporatisation

In September 1988, the government abolished the Ministry of Petroleum Industry, the Ministry of Coal and the Ministry of Nuclear Industry and transformed the ministries into three corporations. The government administrative functions of the three ministries and the power sector of the Ministry of Water Resources and Power were merged into the Ministry of Energy. The MPI was restructured into China National Petroleum Corporation (CNPC). CNPC was a wholly state-owned oil company with legal person status and was designated by the state to manage the assets formerly under the MPI. CNPC was to engage in onshore oil and gas planning, exploration, development and production in China and offshore shallow water areas to a depth of less than five metres. In addition, the State Council granted CNPC the right to develop international co-operation in the onshore oil industry. However, CNPC was to continue with many of the functions formerly undertaken by the MPI, including formulating national quality standards for the oil industry and devising the policy for environmental regulation.

CNPC was a ministry-level corporation under the direct control of the State Council. It had an amalgamation of assets from its eighty-seven constituent enterprises, twenty-one of which were oil and gas production enterprises with legal person status. Major oil field PAB include Daqing, Shengli, Liaohe, Xinjiang and Tarim. In the 1990s, average total employment was more than 1.4 million. In 1997, CNPC produced 143.2 million tonnes of crude oil and

17.2 billion cubic metres of natural gas, accounting for 90 per cent of China's total oil output and 77 per cent of the country's total natural gas output. In addition, CNPC developed refining capacity but on a small scale. By 1997, it had twenty-four refining and petrochemical units under the supervision of various PABs and the total refining capacity was only 37 million tonnes.

The 'oil company' experiment

In early 1980s, the 'oil company' (*you gong si*) business model was proposed to reform the management system of China's oil industry. The objective was to break up the *da er quan* and *xiao er quan* system and establish oil companies focussing on core businesses of exploration, production and marketing. The offshore state-owned company, China National Offshore Oil Corporation (CNOOC), was the first among the corporations in China's oil industry to adopt the 'oil company' model when it was established in 1983 (Liu *et al.*, 1998: 13–19; Yan, 1998: 44–6).

For the onshore oil company CNPC, the reform plan to adopt the 'oil company' model included establishing CNPC as a united state-owned company engaging in international business development and operation, and transforming every subordinate PAB into an enterprise group with an 'oil company' as the core. The oil company covered production and business units in exploration, development, refining, transportation, marketing and geological R&D. Various businesses related to oil and gas operations such as drilling machinery manufacturing and maintenance, utilities and material supply were to be transformed into specialised service companies. Large-scale social services including schools, hospitals, public transportation services, property management and security services were to be restructured and gradually separated from the core businesses.

CNPC's experiment with the 'oil company' model started with the campaign to develop the Tarim oil field in 1989. The Tarim oil region is located in the Tarim Basin in northwestern China with a total area of 590 thousand acres, 60 per cent of which is the Taklimakan Desert. The geological reserves in the Tarim oil region were estimated by Chinese geologists to be 10.8 billion tonnes of oil and 8,400 billion cubic metres of gas (*China Daily Business Weekly*, 11 October 1998). Tarim was regarded as the strategic oil region for development to replace the depleting oil fields in Eastern China. However, the geological conditions of Tarim are extremely complex and the oil reservoir usually lies 4,500–6,000 metres beneath the earth's surface, which poses tremendous difficulties in exploration and development. After eight years of exploration and development, the proven geological reserves in Tarim only amounted to 215.38 million tonnes of oil and 124 billion cubic metres of gas by 1997 (CNPC, 1998). Exploration activities in Tarim attracted teams from global oil giants such as Exxon and BP but the discoveries have been disappointing. Some multinationals have withdrawn their operations in Tarim. The unfavourable geographical conditions and combined with high transportation cost produced a high overall cost for oil production in Tarim.

When the Tarim Petroleum Exploration and Development Headquarters (TPEDH) was established in April 1989 to explore and develop the Tarim oil region, CNPC headquarters decided to try a new management system with the objective of breaking away from the traditional 'massive campaign' model and establishing the 'oil company' model. TPEDH represented the state investment body and is under the direct leadership of CNPC headquarters. In contrast to the system of 'massive campaign' under which the oil-field PAB usually sets up all the oil service companies, TPEDH contracted other parties to undertake the oil service businesses, including material supplies, drilling, well testing, down-hole maintenance, oil field construction and pipeline construction. For example, the six contracted exploration companies in Tarim came from drilling companies in Xinjiang Oil Field PAB, Zhongyuan Oil Field PAB, Huabei Oil Field PAB, Daqing Oil Field PAB and Shengli Oil Field PAB (CNPC, 1998). TPEDH monitored and controlled the investment, construction, technological standard and schedule of the project contracted. Unlike the traditional oil field PAB that built up extensive supporting services related to oil businesses and social services for their employees, TPEDH out-sourced these services to local companies.

By 1997, most of the PAB of CNPC had restructured their organisations into four streams – oil and gas exploration and development, oil and gas fields construction and technological services, diversified businesses, and social services. This was illustrated in the organisational structure of Daqing PAB in 1997 (Figure 4.1). Moreover, Dagang Oil Field PAB and Jilin Oil Field PAB had been transformed into two enterprise groups with the 'oil company' as the focus of business operations.

The function of the headquarters

The structure of CNPC headquarters remained almost unchanged for over a decade after CNPC was established, except for the merging of the Construction Bureau into the Planning Bureau (Figure 4.3). The key functions of CNPC headquarters include the following:

PLANNING

Long-term planning   The development planning function of CNPC headquarters was closely related to the policies of the Chinese government. The overall development strategy for China's onshore oil industry in the 1990s, proposed by CNPC and approved by the State Council, could be summarised as 'stabilise East China, explore West China, simultaneously develop oil and gas, and expand international operations'. CNPC had twelve oil and gas production bases in the eastern part of China covering the extensive areas from east of Taihang Mountain to north of Yangzi River. This part of the country has been the major oil and gas production area since the 1960s. It contains two production regions – Songliao and Bohai Bay. The Songliao region has Daqing and Jilin oil fields.

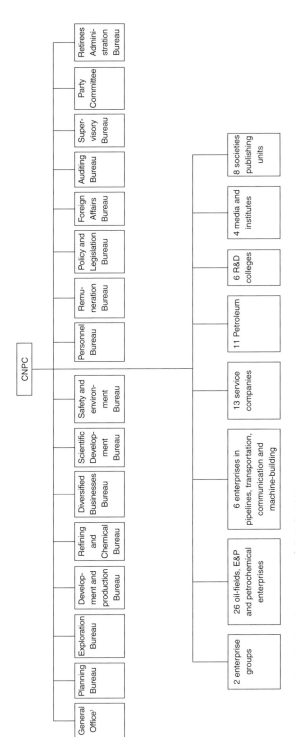

Figure 4.3 Organisational structure of CNPC, 1997.

Note: [1]Including Research Office.

Source: *China Petroleum Industry Yearbook 1998.*

Daqing is by far the biggest oil production base in China with an annual oil output of 50 million tonnes. The Bohai Bay region covers Shengli, Liaohe, Huabei, Dagang and Zhongyuan oil fields. However, production in most of these oil fields had been declining steadily, causing high costs. CNPC had seven oil and gas fields in the western provinces and autonomous regions such as Xinjiang, Shaanxi, Gansu, Ningxia, and Qinghai. Chinese geologists believe this region has vast oil and gas reserves. As the oil fields in the eastern part of China are depleting, the western region has gained increasing strategic importance in the development of China's oil and gas industry. Moreover, in line with government policy to improve the increasingly deteriorating environment and to promote gas as a substitute for coal and oil, CNPC devised strategies to develop the existing gas fields in Sichuan province, to reinforce the construction of gas fields in Shan-Gan-Ning region, to step up the exploration activities in the western part of China, to conserve reserves in the eastern gas fields, and to prevent waste in gas consumption. Furthermore, the development strategy of CNPC also related to China's desire for energy security. The strategy was to invest in some large and medium-sized projects with low risks and high return mainly in the China's neighbouring countries and in developing countries with rich hydrocarbon resources.

Business strategy planning   The Planning Bureau of the CNPC headquarters is responsible for devising long-term (ten-year) and medium-term (five-year) strategies and business development plans. These activities were guided by the overall development strategy set out by CNPC in consultation with the State Council. Planning projects in 1997 included strategies for oil resources, natural gas development, oil and gas pipelines, and downstream refining and petrochemicals development in the ninth five-year plan (1996–2000) and the year 2010 (CNPC, 1998). Even before the 1998 major restructuring (see Chapter 5, p. 102), CNPC had planned to develop as an integrated oil and petrochemicals company. In addition, the Planning Bureau arranged research plans for strategies on specific segments of the oil and gas industry (for example, oil and gas exploration and development) and on specific geographical regions (for example, Sichuan natural gas region).

Production planning   Another important planning function of CNPC head-quarters was to project the annual oil and gas demand and supply for the whole country, and draft the annual plan for oil and gas production, transportation and marketing for the whole industry. CNPC reported the demand and supply projections and production proposal to the State Planning Commission (SPC) and the State Economic and Trade Commission (SETC). The SPC then devised the country's annual plans for the overall balance of oil demand and supply, production, oil and gas allocation for processing, and oil import and export. Based on the state plan, The Planning Bureau worked out an annual, quarterly, and monthly plan for oil and gas production, transportation, and marketing, and implemented the plans at the constituent enterprises within CNPC. In addition, the Planning Bureau approved key large-scale projects, applying to the government for investment funds.

Investment planning   The power of CNPC headquarters in investment planning were exercised through approving key investment projects and allocating funds to finance the approved projects. The Planning Bureau was the main body responsible for this function. The principle for selecting projects for support was closely related to the company's development strategy, which was to increase investment in domestic and international exploration and development in the late 1990s. The centre controlled investment in overseas projects and the subordinate enterprises were not permitted to develop international operations.

RESOURCE ALLOCATION AND CO-ORDINATION

A very important function of CNPC headquarters was to co-ordinate with Sinopec (see Downstream: Sinopec, p. 90) for allocating crude oil to Sinopec's refineries. Before 1998, Sinopec had no upstream operation, but accounted for more than 80 per cent of China's total refining capacity. Approximately 60 per cent of the crude oil that Sinopec's refineries processed was supplied by CNPC. Based on the overall annual oil allocation plan devised by SPC, CNPC and Sinopec co-ordinated with each other for supply sources and transportation. The two corporations devised a detailed supply and transportation plan that was broken down into quarterly and monthly plans. They had regularly scheduled meetings to implement the plan in the relevant oil fields and refineries. However, the co-ordination between CNPC and Sinopec was fraught with difficulties. Sinopec's refineries preferred to buy oil from the nearest oil-fields, which CNPC did not always agree with. CNPC would have liked the oil allocation plan to be consistent with its own business strategy. For example, CNPC allocated oil produced in Tarim to Sinopec's refineries in central China. The objective was to help market the oil from remote western China and increase the oil output from that oil region. However, Sinopec's refineries in central China would prefer to buy oil supplied by oil fields in the Bohai oil region. In addition, the two-tier oil pricing system with multiple oil prices which developed in the 1990s (see Headquarters' function, p. 84 and p. 92) was manipulated by 'oil brokers' who could buy oil at the government-set low price through the 'back door' and sell it at a higher price to small local refineries. During the 1990s, refining businesses within CNPC also developed at a high speed. This sometimes led to the breakdown of the oil allocation plan set by the SPC and agreed to by both CNPC and Sinopec. Sinopec's refineries simply could not get a sufficient oil supply allocated to them. Moreover, when the international oil price was lower than the domestic oil price, Sinopec's refineries had a strong incentive to buy oil from the international market for processing. But crude oil import was restricted by the import quota system and subject to the annual total fixed amount set by the SPC. Meanwhile, the refineries were required stick to the oil allocation plan set out by the headquarters of Sinopec and CNPC respectively, necessitating the purchase of oil from CNPC at higher prices. This involved significant negotiation and co-ordination between Sinopec headquarters and its refineries, between CNPC headquarters and its oil fields, between Sinopec headquarters and CNPC headquarters. When disputes arose, the SETC was the mediator between CNPC and Sinopec.

MARKETING

Pricing   In 1995, the Chinese government began a new two-tier pricing scheme for crude oil. All domestic onshore crude oil was classified into one of the two categories, grade I oil and grade II Oil, each of which had different prices. For example, in 1995, there were two prices for grade I oil. Daqing oil and oil similar to Daqing oil produced by other enterprises was priced at 754 yuan per tonne; while Shengli oil and oil similar to Shengli oil produced by other enterprises was 684 yuan per tonne. In the same year, there were three different prices for grade II oil. Daqing oil and oil similar to Daqing oil produced by other enterprises was priced at 1,320 yuan per tonne; Shengli oil and oil similar to Shengli oil produced by other enterprises was 1,230 yuan per tonne; heavy oil produced by Liaohe and Gudao of Shengli was 1,160 yuan per tonne. The price for grade I oil was usually lower than the international market price, while the price of grade II oil was at or near the comparable international market prices. However, in 1998, international oil prices fell to levels at or below both grade I and grade II oil prices. Under the command-style production plan (*zhi ling xing ji hua*) set by SPC, CNPC directly supplied crude oil to Sinopec at the grade I oil prices. Oil produced between the guiding production plan (*zhi dao xing ji hua*) and the commanding production plan was sold at grade II oil prices. Oil produced above the guiding production plan was sold at the market price.

Imports and exports   The Ministry of Foreign Trade and Economic Co-operation (MOFTEC) was responsible for issuing import and export licences for crude oil and refined products. From the 1950s, China Chemical Import and Export Company (Sinochem), under the direct control of MOFTEC, monopolised the import and export businesses of the oil industry. In 1993, Sinochem went into partnership with CNPC and set up the China National United Oil Corporation (known as Chinaoil), taking on part of the import and export businesses of crude oil. Meanwhile, Sinochem worked with Sinopec and established the China International United Petroleum and Chemical Corporation (known as Unipec and now 70 per cent owned by Sinopec Corporation) managing part of the import and export businesses of refined products.

FOREIGN INVESTMENT AND OVERSEAS EXPANSION

Foreign investment in oil fields   China began to open its offshore territory to foreign oil companies for exploration and development in 1982 and CNOOC was given the exclusive rights to co-operate with foreign oil companies. Onshore territory was gradually opened up after 1985. CNPC was granted the exclusive rights to co-operate with foreign oil companies (most of them were multinationals) for onshore exploration and production. The International Exploration and Development Co-operation Bureau of CNPC headquarters was the body that planned and administered co-operation with foreign oil companies. It was responsible for inspecting and approving the letter of intent or agreement of co-operation between subordinate enterprises and foreign oil companies. The final decision-making power over the agreement lay with the leaders at the headquarters. However, the first formal international bidding did not happen until 1993, followed by two more rounds of bidding in 1994 and 1995. Bid areas offered to foreign oil companies have been 'limited to areas in which China would have technical and financial difficulties undertaking the operation on its own' (Choung and Terreson, 1998: 15, quoted in Nolan, 2001: 440). This is widely referred to as the policy of giving the multinational companies the 'hard bones' (Nolan, 2001: 440). By the end of 1998, CNPC had signed a total of forty-seven onshore oil contracts, with a total of $1.1 billion in foreign investment. Thirty Sino–foreign contracts were in operation, producing just 2.3 million tonnes of crude oil, with a total foreign investment of only $558 million (CNPC, 1998: 39).

Overseas investment The strategy to expand the oil and gas portfolio outside China was in line with government policy to enhance China's security of supply. Investment in overseas exploration and development began in the early 1990s. However, considerable progress was not achieved until 1997 when seven of the total of fourteen overseas project contracts were signed. Nevertheless, reserves and production from the overseas projects were on a very small scale. CNPC headquarters, through the International Exploration and Development Co-operation Bureau and Planning Bureau controlled the policy, planning and organisation of overseas exploration and development. It selected various enterprises for their special expertise in production and business management. By the end of 1997, CNPC had overseas recoverable reserves of 400 million tonnes, 63 per cent of which was under development. The total overseas reserves were equivalent to about 12 per cent of China's total recoverable reserves. In 1997, oil obtained from overseas production amounted to 970,000 tonnes, less than 1 per cent of China's total domestic output. In addition, 17 per cent of the oil from overseas production was transported back to China. The largest overseas projects were located in Sudan, Kazakhstan, Venezuela, Peru, and Iraq. Due to the international sanctions on Iraq, the two projects in that country with annual production capacity of 23 million tonnes could not be put into operation.

FINANCIAL CONTROL

Budget control There is no evidence to show that CNPC headquarters had stringent budget control measures over its constituent enterprises. At the end of 1997, each enterprise devised its own budget, which was submitted to the

Financial Bureau at the headquarters for 'inspection' (*shen cha*) and 'consolidation' (*hui zong*) into the annual budget for the whole company. The headquarters monitored budget execution in two ways. First, the Financial Bureau periodically analysed the major budget indicators of the whole corporation including revenue, costs, profits, capital expenditure and debt. The analysis was submitted to the CNPC leaders as a reference for making their decisions. Second, at the beginning of the budget year, the centre convened a company-wide meeting for budget examination. The principle for the examination was to check the increase in construction investment, reduce costs and expenditure, and rationalise the debt ratio and structure. However, it is unlikely that the centre was able to monitor effectively the real revenue and profit of its subordinate enterprises.

The 'big contract' system that began in 1981 and renewed under new terms in 1991 was still in practice near the end of 1990s. In addition to the contracted annual oil and gas output, in the late 1990s CNPC adopted a new business policy: the constituent enterprises were required to 'hand over' (*shang jiao*) targeted profits and fees charged for using reserves (*chuliang shiyong fei*); they were required to be responsible for their own profit or loss in business operations and for the balance of construction funds; the total amount of wages of an individual enterprise was pegged to its profit target and industrial value added (*gongye zengjia zhi*).[1] Typically, CNPC headquarters and the constituent enterprises had intense negotiations each year over the amount of hand-overs. For example, in 1998, Daqing was supposed to 'hand over' to CNPC headquarters 8.6 billion yuan. After prolonged negotiation, Daqing actually 'handed over' 10.4 billion yuan to the headquarters. This process was not easy since the production enterprises could retain the amount above their profit target agreed with the headquarters and set in the budget. Moreover, production enterprises invested heavily in developing diversified businesses and the major PABs each could have hundreds of diversified business companies. In 1997, Shengli PAB had 265 diversified business companies, Xinjiang PAB, 141, Liaohe PAB, 710 (CNPC, 1998). Daqing invested 100 million yuan into diversified businesses in the same year. This later caused tremendous difficulties for the headquarters to monitor the capital expenditure of its subordinate enterprises and huge problems in corporate governance. From 1991–5, the whole company of CNPC had a total amount of 6 billion yuan invested in more than 800 diversified business projects under subordinate enterprises, only 28.9 per cent of which were reported to make profits, 29 per cent were making a loss and 42.1 per cent could not be tracked.

Fund management   Funds for CNPC came from several channels including the government budget, state bank loans, domestic bond issue and overseas sources. In 1997, the planned funds for the whole company was 78.6 billion yuan. The central government budget allocated 11.4 billion yuan, of which 250 million yuan were for geological exploration. The State Development Bank provided 1.2 billion yuan in soft loans and 5.2 billion yuan in repayable loans. The State Construction Bank provided 4.3 billion yuan in loans. In the same year, CNPC for the first time issued bonds and raised 500 million yuan for developing the

Chang Qing and Xinjiang oil regions. In addition, funds in foreign exchange included loans from Japan Energy, Itochu, the World Bank, the Bank of China, and foreign governments. Most of these funds were sub-loaned to CNPC by institutions such as the Ministry of Finance and the Bank of China.

PERFORMANCE MONITORING

Under the 'big contract' system, the performance indicator for an oil enterprise was whether it achieved the contracted output level. In the 1990s, new performance indicators such as profits and industrial added value were introduced to evaluate an enterprise's performance. In line with the enterprise performance evaluation indicators announced by the government, CNPC headquarters devised its own evaluation measures, which were thenadministered by the Planning Bureau (CNPC, 1998: 46–9). There were ten performance indicators, each of which was weighted in the performance evaluation.

- *Enterprise profit and tax ratio of the industry* was the ratio of an enterprise's total profit and tax to the total profit and tax of the whole industry. The weight for evaluation was 8.
- *Oil and gas unit cost change ratio* was the change in unit costs between the beginning and the end of the year divided by the unit cost at the beginning of the year. The weight was 10.
- *Net profit/asset ratio* was to the ratio the total profit to the owner's average asset. The owner referred to the state. The weight was 10.
- *State assets value increase ratio* was the ratio of the value of state assets at the end of the year to the value of state assets at the beginning of the year. The weight was 12.
- *Reserve and production ratio* was the ratio of recoverable reserves found in the year to the oil and gas production volume in the same year. The weight was 12.
- *Labour productivity* was an enterprise's revenue increase divided by the total numbers of employees. The weight was 12.
- *Capital expenditure for every billion tonnes of recoverable reserves* was the total capital expenditure for oil and gas exploration divided by the increased geological reserves. The weight was 10.
- *Capital investment of production capacity for every million tonnes* was the total investment in oil and gas development divided by the increased oil and gas production capacity. The weight was 10.
- *Debt/asset* ratio was the enterprise's total debt divided by its total assets. The weight was 8.
- *Social contribution ratio* was the ratio of dividing the total amount of 'social contribution' to the average total assets. The social contribution included wage bills (salary, bonus, and allowances), medical and pension contributions, interest payments, VAT payments, net profit, product sales tax, and other taxes. The weight was 8.

Flotation of subordinate enterprises   From the 1990s, CNPC started to set up joint stock companies with limited liability and float them in the domestic stock market. By May 1998, four such companies had been floated. The initial approach was to float the diversified businesses under a PAB and subsequently inject core oil businesses into the company. Typically, the flotation was of a minority share in the floated company, with the majority share holding held by a PAB under CNPC. For example, Daming (Group) Company Ltd. of Shengli PAB was set up in 1992 as a company engaging in businesses covering construction materials production, electronics, chemicals, machinery maintenance, domestic and international trading. It was floated on the Shanghai Stock Exchange in 1993 and has since bought part of the oil extraction and development businesses of Shengli PAB. By 2001, Daming company had ten subsidiary companies in oil extracting, construction material production, electronics, chemicals, machinery building and maintenance, clothing-making, catering, domestic and international trading. Longchang Company Ltd of CNPC Pipeline Bureau was set up as a company engaging in diversified businesses in the pharmaceuticals, electronics, communications, and welding technology sectors. The company was floated on the Shenzhen Stock Exchange in 1993 and subsequently bought majority shares in three oil pipelines – Jiaozhou to Qingdao, Dongying to Huangdao, and Guangrao to Qilu Petrochemical Company. In May 1998, Liaohe Jinma Company Ltd grouped together the core oil production businesses from the Liaohe PAB and was floated on the Shenzhen Stock Exchange. This was the first oil enterprise to directly float its core production businesses on a Chinese stock exchange, and the Jinma shares were called the 'first shares of China's oil industry'. Liaohe PAB control 81.8 per cent of the floated company. Along with the flotation on the domestic stock exchanges, CNPC also set out to buy companies in the international capital market. In 1993, CNPC bought a majority ownership share (35.36 per cent) in Paragon, then the only oil company traded on the Hong Kong Stock Exchange, and restructured the company into CNPC (Hong Kong) Company Ltd in 1994. CNPC (Hong Kong) became the first company under CNPC that was traded on an overseas stock exchange. CNPC subsequently bought more shares in the company and by 1997, it controlled 92 per cent of CNPC (Hong Kong).

During the 1990s, the procurement system of CNPC became increasingly 'market-oriented'. Enterprises at different tiers within CNPC purchased material and equipment from the market and were permitted to import equipment autonomously. The centre had no control over the cost and quality of procurement. There were reports of serious accidents in oil fields caused by the use of products of low quality, including counterfeit products and equipment.

From 1997 onwards, CNPC started to centralise procurement at two levels: the headquarters and the first tier oil enterprises. Under the direct supervision of CNPC headquarters, the China Petroleum Material and Equipment Supplies Company (CPMES) was responsible for purchasing large-scale material and equipment such as steel, vehicles, construction equipment, and equipment exclusively for the oil industry. Import of technological equipment needed to be included in the overall plan for the introduction of new technology and required approval by the centre. The target was that from 1997, 80 per cent of CNPC's total procurement in terms of value should be purchased through the CPMES and the material supplies departments of each first tier oil enterprise. It was reported that of the total procurement bill of 48 billion yuan in 1997, 74 per cent was purchased through CPMES and the first tier oil enterprises (CNPC, 1998). This was a big step forward in centralising control over procurement.

R&D

CNPC's headquarters devised five-year plans for scientific development. Funds for R&D were allocated by the government following application to state key research programmes, CNPC headquarters and the oil enterprises themselves. By 1997, there were eight R&D institution directly under the centre and sixty-one R&D institutions under the first tier oil enterprises. In 1997, R&D funding amounted to 370 million yuan, 84 per cent of which was from the company itself and the rest was from the government. The Scientific Development Bureau was the administrator of the key research projects supported by the government and CNPC. It contracted out the key research projects to various R&D institutions in the company and was responsible for following up the progress of the research projects.

PERSONNEL

The President and Vice Presidents of CNPC were appointed by the State Council and the Chinese Communist Party (CCP) Department of Organisation. The party committee of CNPC headquarters had the power to select and appoint managers at enterprise level. However, the head of Daqing PAB was appointed directly by the State Council. Moreover, the party committee at the headquarters was responsible for organising and implementing the evaluation of managers at bureau (*ju ji*) and department (*chu ji*) level. Usually, the headquarters sent a team of managers to evaluate managers at the level of oil enterprises while each enterprise sent a team of managers to evaluate managers in units at a lower level.

SAFETY AND ENVIRONMENT

CNPC formulated regulations for safety and environment in China's oil industry. In 1997, following the management practice of international oil companies, CNPC devised and promulgated the 'Oil Industry Health, Safety and Environment Management System', which was intended to be the standard for

China's oil industry. The headquarters monitored the level of emission and pollution through a three-tier network of environment monitoring at the level of the centre, the oil enterprises and production units.

Downstream: Sinopec

Corporatisation

In 1983, the Chinese government approved the separation of the refining and petrochemical section from the Ministry of Petroleum Industry. The refining and petrochemical assets were grouped together with the chemical and synthetic fibre manufacturing enterprises from the Ministry of Chemical Industry and the Ministry of Textile Industry to create the China National Petrochemical Corporation (Sinopec). Sinopec was responsible for the administration and development of China's petrochemical industry. It was charged with the formulation of policies for producing refined oil products and petrochemicals, supervising the construction and operation of refining and petrochemical plants in China, and marketing refined oil products and petrochemicals.

Sinopec was a ministry-level corporation under the direct control of the State Council. The creation of Sinopec was intended to develop the downstream businesses, which are complementary to CNPC's upstream productions. In the 1990s, total employment remained around 650,000. In the mid-1990s, Sinopec had a total of thirty-six production enterprises. The main production enterprises included Shanghai Petrochemical Corporation, Yanshan Petrochemical, Zhenhai Refining and Chemical, Qilu Petrochemical, and Yangzi Petrochemical. When it was established, Sinopec owned more than 90 per cent of China's total refining capacity. The share had declined during the 1990s due to the vigorous growth of refineries owned by CNPC, various local governments and the Ministry of Chemical Industry. In 1996, Sinopec had a refining throughput of 118 million tonnes and an ethylene output of 2.5 million tonnes, accounting for more than 80 per cent of China's refining throughput and ethylene output (Sinopec, 1998).

The function of the headquarters

Figure 4.4 shows the structure of Sinopec headquarters in 1996.

PLANNING

Long-term planning   Sinopec was responsible for formulating policies for China's refining and petrochemical industry. It devised the sector's long-term goals and specific plans to achieve those goals. In the ninth five-year plan for the petrochemical industry, the goal was: 'To compete with [the world's leading large petrochemical companies] in technology, management, and efficiency as well as in product mix, quality, price and technological service, and not to lose ground in the intense competition with them. With the support of the government, the petrochemical industry must be revitalised and enabled to become one of the 'pillar industries' leading the growth of the national economy and upgrading of the national economic structure' (Sinopec, 1998: 27). The strategy for development was to pursue 'large economies of scale, advanced technology, a series of improved products, and stringent and fine management practice' (Sinopec, 1998: 26).

Planning business strategies   Business strategies were planned to ensure that by the year 2000, China's petrochemical industry matched international standards of production and technology. This meant, for example, ensuring that future refineries were designed to produce more than 5 million tonnes a year and new ethylene projects had a minimum capacity of 450,000 tonnes per annum (Nolan, 2001: 448). For the period from 1996 to 2010, Sinopec drew up a 'two-stage business development plan'. The target for the first stage was to increase the annual oil processing capacity to 200 million tonnes and the annual ethylene production capacity to 5 million tonnes by the year 2000. In the second stage, Sinopec would strive to expand its oil refining capacity to 300–350 million tonnes and the annual ethylene production capacity to 8–10 million tonnes by the year 2010 (Sinopec, 1998: 26).

Planning production   Another important planning function of Sinopec head-quarters was to forecast China's annual demand for refined products (gasoline, diesel, lighting oil, aviation fuel, naphtha oil, and fuel oil). Based on this information, Sinopec consolidated the information for demand and proposed to SPC the overall annual demand projections for the whole country. For the annual supply of refined products, Sinopec, CNPC, and those provincial governments that had refineries worked out their own production plans but were required to follow the crude oil allocation plan set by the SPC and the projection of annual demand for refined products. However, the final production plan was decided by SPC in consultation with Sinopec and CNPC. The SPC also determined the annual amount of imports of refined products. The SPC then devised the country's annual plans for the overall balance of demand and supply for refined products, production, and import and export. Based on the state plan, Sinopec controlled the crude oil allocation to its subordinate enterprises.

Planning investment   Sinopec headquarters planned investment in key project construction and technological upgrading for existing production facilities. The government determined a list of key projects for development in each five-year plan, which usually involved intense competition among different industrial sectors to get listed on the stock market. In line with the government's regulation, Sinopec headquarters set a certain ratio of funds available for a given project as the precondition to getting the project approved by the government. For key projects, Sinopec headquarters was the main component in the investment and the enterprises concerned were the legal persons responsible for project planning, construction, production, and debt repayment. In project management, Sinopec headquarters adopted a budget-based subcontracting system: the centre simply made sure that the expenditures were within the budget and that the enterprises concerned possessed the autonomy to execute the project.

RESOURCE ALLOCATION AND CO-ORDINATION

The Chinese government required that all crude oil produced by CNPC should supply refineries of Sinopec and local refineries except for crude oil needed by oil field production and for export. Based on SPC's plan for allocation, Sinopec and CNPC devised specific plans to allocate crude oil to refineries under Sinopec and local refineries for processing. Production enterprises under CNPC were not permitted to supply local refineries directly, which were usually supported by local governments. However, this policy was very difficult to implement in reality. As discussed in the function of the CNCP headquarters, p. 83, there was close co-ordination between Sinopec and CNPC in the allocation of crude oil.

MARKETING

Pricing   Under the two-tier pricing scheme for crude oil, Sinopec implemented a system of weighted average prices for crude oil to facilitate the equalisation of crude oil costs among its subordinate enterprises. Enterprises covered by this scheme paid surcharges for the difference in respect to their purchase of domestic onshore crude oil; meanwhile, they were entitled to reimbursement granted by Sinopec regarding the purchase of domestic onshore crude oil or crude oil from overseas. In 1996, Sinopec imposed a surcharge of 60 yuan per tonne and granted reimbursement of 80 yuan per tonne. The surcharge and reimbursement were 137 yuan per tonne and 127 yuan per tonne respectively in 1997. However, in the second half of 1997, international crude oil prices fell substantially. Sinopec revised the surcharge and reimbursement to 120 yuan per tonne and 100 yuan per tonne respectively. This system was suspended at the beginning of 1998.

The price of refined products was fixed by the government. For petrochemical products, the government relaxed its control over the years and most petrochemical products were sold at market prices. For example, Shanghai Petrochemical Corporation sold about 70 per cent, 79 per cent and 83 per cent of its sales volume outside government control in the years 1996, 1997 and 1998, respectively (SPCC, 1998).

Sales network   Sinopec headquarters sales management department supervised marketing, while regional sales companies were responsible for sales in any given region. Provincial oil companies carried out sales within their provincial and municipal territories. The sales department in Sinopec's subordinate enterprises marketed products produced by their own enterprises. Development companies set up by Sinopec in special economic zones engaged in domestic trading. Sales

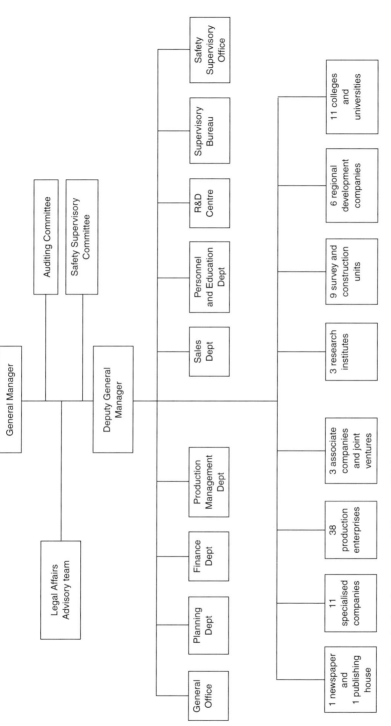

Figure 4.4 Organisational structure of Sinopec, 1996

Source: Sinopec.

of refined products were required to go through Sinopec's sales companies as the major sales channel, complemented by CNPC and local refineries. For petrochemical products, the sales department in enterprises directly supplied their customers. Petrochemical products' trading centres in different cities served as sales channels as well. A pilot study on the integration of production enterprises and sales companies was carried out in Fujian Province.

Import and export   MOFTEC was responsible for issuing import and export licences for crude oil and refined products. After the 1950s, China Chemical Import and Export Company (Sinochem), under the direct control of MOFTEC, monopolised the import and export businesses of the oil industry. In 1993, Sinochem and Sinopec as equity share partners established the China International United Petroleum and Chemical Corporation (known as Unipec and now 70 per cent owned by Sinopec Corporation) managing part of the import and export businesses of refined products. In 1994, SPC imposed a quota on imports of refined products and allocated the quota to provincial oil companies. In 1996, SPC ruled that refined products should only be imported by Sinopec headquarters and supplied to provincial oil companies at ex-plant price. Within Sinopec, technology imports for key projects had to obtain approval from the headquarters.

FINANCIAL CONTROL

Financial control is a critical function through which headquarters can exercise control over subordinate enterprises. However, this function was very weak in the case of Sinopec's headquarters and the subordinate enterprises had a high degree of financial autonomy. During the 1990s, Sinopec headquarters relaxed its control over fourteen management rights, including the right to retain profit. Under the 'two-level legal person' (*erji faren*) approach, each of Sinopec's subsidiaries was a profit centre and an independent legal entity, responsible for its own profit or loss. They each produced their own annual financial report, which was submitted to Sinopec headquarters. The headquarters consolidated the financial report from subordinate enterprises and produced the annual balance sheet for the whole company. Sinopec's subordinates were supposed to hand over around 25 per cent of post-tax profits to Sinopec headquarters, and retain 75 per cent themselves. In practice, at least until the restructuring of 1998/99, the subordinate enterprises may have retained substantially more than 25 per cent of their post-tax profits (Nolan, 2001). In 1996, Sinopec headquarters was estimated to have received only around one billion yuan in profits handed over from its subordinate enterprises, compared with a total of 5.5 billion in operating profits for the whole of Sinopec in that year (Sinopec, 1999: 12). Sinopec's own auditing report revealed that it was very difficult to collect profit and fees from enterprises in the late 1990s. Huge amounts of money were kept by subordinate enterprises through such mechanisms as retaining profits that were supposed to be handed over to the headquarters, cheating on tax payments, and false reporting of profits and losses.

From 1994 to 1996, the auditing department of the headquarters estimated that these types of funds totalled 6.5 billion yuan.

For subordinate companies floated on international markets, such as Shanghai Petrochemical Corporation and Zhenhai Refinery and Petrochemical Corporation, Sinopec received a stream of revenue from its privileges as a majority shareholder in the company concerned. The use of retained profits by internationally floated companies within Sinopec were said by Sinopec to be 'matters for the floated companies themselves to decide'. However, in practice there was still considerable negotiation between floated companies and the headquarters about the total amount of 'hand-overs', of which dividends were just one element.

Sinopec's subordinate enterprises were entitled to raise capital from the international market, but any big capital investment plan (above 200 million yuan) needed to be approved by the State Planning Commission through Sinopec headquarters.

PERFORMANCE MONITORING

From the mid-1990s, in line with the enterprise performance evaluation indicators announced by the government, Sinopec headquarters devised its own evaluation measures, which were administered by the Planning Bureau. There were eleven performance indicators including the ratios of profits to revenues, total assets to value-added, return on capital, capital to value-added, debt to assets, inventory turnover, social contribution, and social accumulation. However, the power of the headquarters to monitor the performance of its subordinate enterprises was very weak.

ASSET MANAGEMENT

Approval from Sinopec's headquarters was required for the asset rights transactions of its subordinate enterprises. Enterprises engaged in asset transactions were required to submit documents to the headquarters and get their assets appraised by institutions approved by headquarters. It was also required that the results of asset appraisal and the share-holding structure must be reported to and approved by the headquarters. It was required that restructuring whole enterprises or partial production facilities into stock-holding companies should be reported to and inspected by the headquarters.

Flotation of subordinate enterprises After the early 1990s, some subordinate enterprises under Sinopec were restructured into joint stock companies and listed on both domestic and international markets. Sinopec headquarters had the power to recommend subordinate enterprises to the government for listing. By the end of 1998, Sinopec had fourteen companies floated as A-share on the domestic market and four companies listed on international markets (Sinopec, 1999: 13). The total assets of the listed companies were 78.3 billion yuan, accounting for 20 per cent of Sinopec's total assets in 1997. Sinopec held 62 per cent of the total shares of the listed subordinate companies. From 1993 to June 1998, the sixteen listed companies raised a total amount of 21.8 billion yuan from stock market share issurance. The most significant listings were the four companies floated on international markets – Shanghai Petrochemical Corporation in 1993, Zhenhai in 1994 (chapter 7), Yizheng and Yanhua in 1997. Important production enterprises such as Qilu and Yangzi were floated on the Shanghai Stock Exchange in 1998.

Joint ventures with overseas partners   There was a rapid growth of joint ventures with overseas partners in Sinopec during the 1980s and 1990s, which were another path through which to bring in international capital. By 1996, Sinopec had 155 joint ventures and investment from overseas partners was promised to be $1.3 billion (Sinopec, 1998: 288). Sinopec headquarters encouraged subordinate enterprises to set up joint ventures. For key projects that were listed in the state's five-year plan and Sinopec itself, the headquarters participated in the negotiations and had the power to veto any given joint venture proposal. However, the headquarters and the respective subordinate enterprise (the future joint venture partner on China's side) usually had considerable interaction and the final decision usually reflected the ambitions of the enterprise. For projects that did not require support from the headquarters in terms of construction and production, the enterprises were allowed to freely set up joint ventures.

From the mid-1990s, the growth of joint ventures within Sinopec reached a new stage. Investment scale increased and foreign partners included the world's leading multinationals. For example, the joint venture of Yangzi and BASF producing polyethylene had a total investment of $2 billion. Yaraco, the joint venture between Sichuan Vinylon Plant and BP, had a total investment of $2.3 billion. Moreover, several ethylene plants each with an annual ethylene capacity of 6–800,000, together with associated petrochemical production facilities, were under negotiation with multinationals. By 1996, letters of intent of co-operation were signed between BP and Shanghai Petrochemical Company, BASF and Yangzi Petrochemical Company in Nanjing, Dow Chemical and Tianjin Petrochemical Company, and Phillips Petroleum Corporation and Lanzhou Chemical Company as well as that between Shell and CNOOC at Huizhou (see Table 8.7 in Chapter 8). Each of these joint ventures involved $2.5–4 billion dollars' investment and was intended to form an important part of the global business system of the global giants.

Mergers and acquisitions   From the mid-1990s, Sinopec headquarters organised a number of significant mergers. In a number of cases, the merger initiative came from the enterprises themselves and gained support from the centre. For example, Shanghai Petrochemicals Corporation increased its national acrylic fibre market share from one-third to one-half by 1998 through two acquisitions: the take-over of the Shanghai Jinyang Acrylic Fibre Plant in 1996 and the acquisition of Zhejiang Acrylic Fibre Plant in 1998. In 1997, Yanhua Corporation was created through the merger between Yanshan Refinery with Tianjin Hangu Petrochemicals Plant, China's largest lubricant producer. In addition, Sinopec headquarters arranged mergers in which the acquiring company took over all the debt of companies in financial distress. For example, in 1997, Qilu Petrochemical Company took over two companies in bankruptcy: Zibo Chemical Fibre Plant and Zibo Petrochemical Plant. The deal involved more than 3 billion yuan. Sinopec headquarters closely co-ordinated with the government for favourable policies related to mergers. The concept of 'mergers', for a long time, meant strong companies taking over debt-ridden plants or companies. This approach of 'the strong support the weak' (*yi qiang dai ruo*) was in sharp contrast to the pattern of international mergers in which 'the strong merge with the strong' (*qiang qiang lian he*) in the 1990s.

The most notable merger organised by Sinopec and supported by the State Council was the Donglian Experiment. In the autumn of 1997, the Chinese State Council decided to merge four petrochemical enterprises located in Nanjing into a single new company, Donglian. Li Yizhong, the Executive Vice-President of Sinopec was charged with the task of executing the merger. The merger was highly significant in that it brought together four enterprises – Yizheng Chemical Fibre, Yangzi Petrochemical, Nanjing Chemical and Jinling Petrochemical Company – previously under three different administrative departments, Sinopec (Jinling and Yangzi), the National Textile Council (Yizheng) and Jiangsu Provincial Government (Nanjing Petrochemical Company). Moreover, each of the enterprises was one of the largest (by value of sales) in the country in their respective sector: Jinling was the fourth largest oil processing enterprise. Yangzi and Nanjing were the first and the twelfth largest chemical materials enterprises respectively, and Yizheng was the second largest chemical fibre enterprise (SSB, ZDQN, 1996). The merger provoked intense debate in China. Opponents held that the merger was intended to 'kill' the autonomy of the individual enterprises and would be detrimental to China's enterprise reform. Moreover, it was argued that mergers through government administrative measures would be unable to create desirable synergies. Proponents argued that the merger was a move in the right direction by trying to create large enterprises that could compete with powerful multinational companies as China's market became increasingly open. Donglian began operation in early 1998. Only three months later, the State Council announced a major restructuring programme involving the nation-wide reorganisation of China's entire oil and petrochemical industry (Chapter 5). Donglian was to be merged back into the new integrated Sinopec. In August 1998, the merger between BP and Amoco initiated the massive consolidation process among the world' leading oil and petrochemical companies, which provoked intense debate in China about industrial policy (Chapter 8).

Short-lived as it was, the Donglian experiment was highly significant in the institutional reform of China's oil and petrochemical industry. It was directly supported by the State Council. The objective was to 'prove that state-owned enterprises under the administration of different government departments and industries can be merged and united, to demonstrate that mergers can create value through optimising resource allocation and eliminating superfluous investment and construction, and to make an inroad to the domestic and international competition' (Li Yizhong, quoted in *Caijing*, November 2000).

PROCUREMENT

From the mid-1990s, the headquarters began the attempt to centralise procurement across the company but the effort proved futile. Subordinate enterprises made their own procurement decisions through their own material procurement departments. For engineering construction projects, the sub-contracting system barely touched upon the issue of the procurement of materials and equipment under the control of the headquarters.

R&D

In the early 1990s, Sinopec headquarters formulated the 'eight-year plan for scientific development from 1993 to 2000'. Three R&D institutes in Beijing, Shanghai and Fushun were under the direct administration of Sinopec headquarters. In addition, each subordinate large enterprise had an R&D centre. The headquarters determined the scientific and technological projects that were of strategic importance to the growth of the whole industry. The headquarters organised large enterprises such as Jinshan, Yanhua, and Yangzi to carry out these R&D projects based on the principle of sharing costs and research results. For projects with the headquarters' investment, the headquarters had the intellectual property rights over the research results, which could be transferred to enterprises within Sinopec at favourable terms. For technology transfer to enterprises outside of Sinopec, the headquarters approved the terms and fees for transfer.

However, the control over R&D resources at the level of headquarters was weak and each enterprise funded their own R&D projects. Investment in R&D projects sponsored by the headquarters accounted for 30 per cent of the consolidated R&D investment. To raise funds for R&D, the headquarters began to collect R&D fees from subordinate enterprises on a monthly basis. However, it was difficult to collect the R&D fees. The headquarters needed to remind repeatedly the subordinate enterprises of the submission date.

PERSONNEL

As with CNPC, the President and Vice Presidents of Sinopec are appointed by the State Council and the CCP Organisation Department. In principle, Sinopec is responsible for appointing all managers at the enterprise level. However the Chairmen of large subordinate enterprises, such as SPCC, are appointed directly by the State Council and the CCP Organisation Department. An important result of success in running a subordinate enterprise is promotion to the headquarters. Moreover, the party committee at the headquarters organises 'evaluation teams' (*kao cha zu*) to examine the leaders of the subordinate enterprises.

SAFETY AND ENVIRONMENT

Sinopec formulated regulations for safety and the environment for China's petrochemical industry. The headquarters monitored the level of emissions and pollution through setting a maximum target of pollutant emission at its constituent enterprises. The Clean Production Centre at the headquarters was responsible for promoting approaches of clean production and technology, providing consulting services for subordinate enterprises, and organising training in clean production and technology. However, the headquarters' monitoring capacity was rather weak.

The 'holding company' experiment

In the mid-1990s, China's policy makers took the important industrial policy decisions to adopt the 'holding company' experiment to precede further institutional reforms in key industrial sectors. In 1994, the State Council chose Sinopec, China Aviation Industry Corporation (AVIC) and China Non-ferrous Metal Industry Corporation as the pilot companies for the experiment. In January 1997, the State Council formally designated Sinopec as the model for others to study in experimenting with the national holding company system. The goal was to create truly independent holding companies that cast off their former 'ministerial' functions, and became genuinely independent business entities.

The State Council appointed Sinopec to be the 'state investment institution'(*guojia touzi ren*), managing all the state-owned properties within Sinopec. The State Council delegated supervisors to Sinopec, who set up a supervisory committee and were entrusted to supervise the management of the state-owned assets within the company guided by the 'Regulations on the management and supervision of properties in state-owned enterprises'. Sinopec did not have board of directors. The President of Sinopec was the representative legal person who assumed responsibility for managing the whole company. The President and Vice Presidents were appointed by the State Council. Sinopec was empowered to reform the organisational structure and petrochemical product mix in its subordinate enterprises. Meanwhile, Sinopec retained the administrative responsibilities such as allocation of crude oil and refined products.

In the 1990s, reforms in the oil and petrochemicals sector, which emphasised increased autonomy for enterprises at the level of the production unit, greatly enhanced the sense of independence in Sinopec's large constituent enterprises. This was further encouraged by ambiguity and hesitation in central government policy towards the sector. From the mid-1990s, Sinopec faced increased competitive pressure from the world's leading petrochemical companies in the Chinese market. One top official pointed out that, due to the fact that the individual enterprises were incapable of competing with the multinationals, they would be 'easily defeated one by one' in the competition. The problematic relationship between enterprise autonomy and corporate centralisation needed to be tackled. It was recognised explicitly that the headquarters urgently needed to centralise control over resources, assets, capital, technology, engineering construction, machinery manufacturing, domestic marketing and international trade. However, the task of centralising these rights in the hands of Sinopec headquarters was formidable. Moreover, the headquarters believed that it was essential to unify upstream and downstream if Sinopec was to truly compete with the multinationals: 'The situation of separation of exploration, processing and sales cannot continue to exist in China, or China will be at a disadvantage compared to the multinational companies' (senior official at Sinopec, January 1997, quoted in Nolan, 2001: 465). They believed that turning Sinopec into a real 'economic' entity required vertical integration and genuine centralisation of key functions, especially financial control. However, as Sinopec started to implement the Sinopec Holding Company experiment, an even more profound institutional change in China's oil and petrochemical industry was about to take place, as we shall see in the following chapter.

Summary

During the period from their establishment in the 1980s to industry restructuring in 1998, the headquarters of CNPC and Sinopec were each responsible for both government and business functions. CNPC and Sinopec still carried government administrative responsibilities for the industry such as formulating technological standards and devising environmental regulations. The most important function for the two companies was implementing government plans related to resource allocation and production and co-ordinating between them over the plans' implementation. They were assigned responsibility for generating revenue handed over to the government treasury. However, they did not have rights over product pricing and marketing and capital investment above 500 million yuan (CNPC) and 200 million yuan (Sinopec), which were tightly controlled by the central government. During the same period, the enterprise reform in China emphasised strongly the enlargement of enterprise autonomy at the level of production units, and casting off the shackles of government planning. The subordinate enterprises within CNPC and Sinopec were able to retain a greatly increased share of profits. They had the autonomy to make investments not only in core businesses but also in diversified businesses. They were able to finance expansion through bank loans and bonds and were responsible for debt repayment. They were listed in the domestic and international capital markets, which reduced the ownership rights of CNPC and Sinopec over them. They negotiated and set up joint ventures with multinational companies. In the case of Sinopec, strong subordinate enterprises initiated mergers and acquisitions in order to increase their market share for specific products. The functions of CNPC and Sinopec headquarters in financial control, performance monitoring, procurement, and R&D were very weak. This put CNPC and Sinopec into an awkward position. In executing government functions, the headquarters of CNPC and Sinopec were simply an extension of government administration. In exercising business functions, the headquarters of CNPC and Sinopec did not have autonomy in product pricing, capital investment, and marketing. Moreover, they did not have effective control over their subordinate enterprises, even in the most important aspect of financial affairs and performance monitoring. During the 1990s, as China further liberalised its economy, the tension between the headquarters of CNPC and Sinopec and their respective subordinate enterprises became increasingly marked.

5 Restructuring for vertical integration and flotation

CNPC and Sinopec in 1998 and 1999

By 1997, the structure of China's oil and petrochemical industry was divided into four sectors, each of which was designated a major company in charge of its own businesses. CNPC and CNOOC had dominant positions in onshore exploration and production, and offshore exploration and production, respectively. Sinopec was the principal refiner and petrochemical producer. Sinochem was responsible for the import and export of crude oil and chemical products. Petroleum sales companies at provincial and county levels were in charge of selling petroleum products, especially retailing, in the domestic market. In 1998, the Chinese government decisively supported the creation of two new vertically integrated oil and petrochemical companies, the new CNPC and Sinopec. In the following year, CNPC and Sinopec each undertook a fundamental internal restructuring. The core productive assets were separated from the non-core businesses. The core businesses were then grouped together into a joint-stock company for international listing. From industrial reorganisation to company restructuring, the whole process was completed in less than two years and involved intense debate. This was a dramatic and immensely significant step in the evolution of China's industrial policy.

Major restructuring: 1998

Disintegrated industry structure

Before 1998, the structure of the oil industry was characterised by three 'divisions': between onshore exploration and production (E&P) and offshore E&P; between upstream business and downstream business; between domestic trading and international trading. Each of the five major players engaged in one of the business areas.

The five majors were CNPC, CNOOC, Sinopec, China National Star Petroleum Corporation (CNSPC), and Sinochem. CNPC and CNOOC were dominant players undertaking onshore and offshore E&P, respectively. In addition, CNSPC engaged in E&P in both onshore and offshore areas specified by the government and had the freedom to expand into the downstream oil business.

In the refining and petrochemical sectors, Sinopec was the principal player. Sinopec owned more than 90 per cent of China's refining capacity. The share declined to 80 per cent in 1997 due to the vigorous growth of refineries owned by CNPC, local government, and Ministry of Chemical Industry (MCI). Sinopec's share in China's total refining capacity declined further because of the establishment of Donglian in September 1997 (Chapter 4). However, Sinopec was still the major state refiner. In petrochemical production, the Ministry of Chemical Industry supervised the production of most finished chemicals, while Sinopec mainly engaged in the production of chemical feed-stocks such as olefins and aromatics.

In the trading sector, Sinochem, under the administration of the Ministry of Foreign Economic Affairs and Trade, was responsible for the import and export of crude oil and chemical products. In the domestic market, petroleum sales companies at provincial and county levels were in charge of sale of petroleum products, especially retailing.

However, CNPC, Sinopec, CNOOC and CNSPC each had strong ambitions and had made serious efforts to expand upstream and downstream. The Chinese government had virtually encouraged CNPC to develop its downstream businesses, refining in particular. CNOOC had been under negotiation with Royal Dutch/Shell for a major petrochemical complex in Huizhou, Guangdong Province. Upstream and downstream, companies competed for funding from the government as well as for right to set prices for crude oil, refined products, and petrochemicals. One company's gain in investment capital from the government was often at the cost of another company's resources for further development. In the end, the government had to be responsible for all the losses incurred.

Government restructuring

In March 1998, the Chinese government started a major reform programme aimed at restructuring and streamlining the government's functions. This restructuring plan involved the 'major restructuring' of the country's entire oil and petrochemical industry from upstream oil and gas exploration and production, refining and marketing, to downstream petrochemicals.

The government reform reduced the number of government ministries and state commissions to 29 from 40 (Figure 5.1). In addition to three newly established ministries and one new state commission, twenty-five of the original forty ministries and state commissions were retained. The remaining fifteen were restructured and transferred into seven newly created 'state bureaux', which included coal, oil and petrochemicals, metallurgical products, machine-building, textile, domestic trade, and light industry. These state bureaux were affiliated to the State Economic and Trade Commission (SETC). For the energy sector, the most notable change was the abolition of the Ministries of Coal Industry, Chemical Industry (MCI), and Power Industry. State bureaux were set up for coal and chemical industries respectively and the Department of Power was created for the power industry under the SETC.

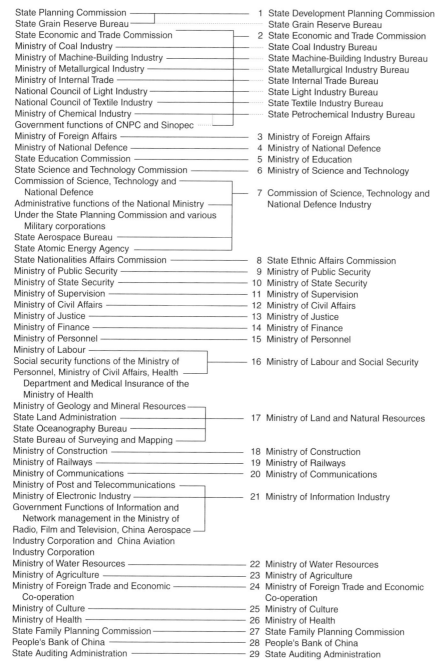

Old organisations | New organisations

State Planning Commission — 1 State Development Planning Commission
State Grain Reserve Bureau ——— State Grain Reserve Bureau
State Economic and Trade Commission ——— 2 State Economic and Trade Commission
Ministry of Coal Industry ——— State Coal Industry Bureau
Ministry of Machine-Building Industry ——— State Machine-Building Industry Bureau
Ministry of Metallurgical Industry ——— State Metallurgical Industry Bureau
Ministry of Internal Trade ——— State Internal Trade Bureau
National Council of Light Industry ——— State Light Industry Bureau
National Council of Textile Industry ——— State Textile Industry Bureau
Ministry of Chemical Industry ——— State Petrochemical Industry Bureau
Government functions of CNPC and Sinopec ———
Ministry of Foreign Affairs ——— 3 Ministry of Foreign Affairs
Ministry of National Defence ——— 4 Ministry of National Defence
State Education Commission ——— 5 Ministry of Education
State Science and Technology Commission ——— 6 Ministry of Science and Technology
Commission of Science, Technology and
   National Defence ——— 7 Commission of Science, Technology and
Administrative functions of the National Ministry ——— National Defence Industry
Under the State Planning Commission and various
   Military corporations
State Aerospace Bureau ———
State Atomic Energy Agency ———
State Nationalities Affairs Commission ——— 8 State Ethnic Affairs Commission
Ministry of Public Security ——— 9 Ministry of Public Security
Ministry of State Security ——— 10 Ministry of State Security
Ministry of Supervision ——— 11 Ministry of Supervision
Ministry of Civil Affairs ——— 12 Ministry of Civil Affairs
Ministry of Justice ——— 13 Ministry of Justice
Ministry of Finance ——— 14 Ministry of Finance
Ministry of Personnel ——— 15 Ministry of Personnel
Ministry of Labour ———
Social security functions of the Ministry of ——— 16 Ministry of Labour and Social Security
Personnel, Ministry of Civil Affairs, Health ———
   Department and Medical Insurance of the
   Ministry of Health
Ministry of Geology and Mineral Resources ———
State Land Administration ——— 17 Ministry of Land and Natural Resources
State Oceanography Bureau ———
State Bureau of Surveying and Mapping ———
Ministry of Construction ——— 18 Ministry of Construction
Ministry of Railways ——— 19 Ministry of Railways
Ministry of Communications ——— 20 Ministry of Communications
Ministry of Post and Telecommunications ———
Ministry of Electronic Industry ——— 21 Ministry of Information Industry
Government Functions of Information and
   Network management in the Ministry of
Radio, Film and Television, China Aerospace ———
Industry Corporation and China Aviation
Industry Corporation
Ministry of Water Resources ——— 22 Ministry of Water Resources
Ministry of Agriculture ——— 23 Ministry of Agriculture
Ministry of Foreign Trade and Economic ——— 24 Ministry of Foreign Trade and Economic
   Co-operation ——— Co-operation
Ministry of Culture ——— 25 Ministry of Culture
Ministry of Health ——— 26 Ministry of Health
State Family Planning Commission ——— 27 State Family Planning Commission
People's Bank of China ——— 28 People's Bank of China
State Auditing Administration ——— 29 State Auditing Administration

Figure 5.1 Organisational changes for central government ministries, 1998.

For the oil and petrochemical industry, the State Bureau of Petroleum and Chemical Industry (SBPCI) was established as an administrative body to take over the government function of the MCI, CNPC and Sinopec. The SBPCI had one general office and five departments responsible for planning and development, industrial policy and legislation, enterprise reform and finance, and personnel (Figure 5.2). In addition, the SBPCI administered several other bodies such as the Chemical Overseas Co-operation Centre and the Sub-Council of the Chemical Industry, which acted as service institutions facilitating overseas business. The SBPCI reported to the SETC and was headed by Li Yongwu, the former Vice-minister of the MCI. The main responsibilities of the SPCIB were industrial planning and devising overall development strategies for the oil and petrochemical industry. It also promoted the continued restructuring of the 7,500 state-owned enterprises under CNPC and Sinopec. Another main responsibility was to formulate re-employment programmes for workers made redundant as a result of the restructuring measures.

Before 1997, the Ministry of Geology and Mineral Resources (MGMR) conducted limited exploration activities both onshore and offshore but turned the fields it discovered over to CNPC for development. At the end of 1996, its exploration functions were spun off from the ministry and turned into China's third upstream state oil company, named China National Star Petroleum Co-operation (CNSPC). Under the government reform programme, the MGMR was merged into the new Ministry of Land and Natural Resources. Thus it disappeared from the petroleum industry's organisational structure.

The new CNPC and Sinopec

The restructuring programme for the oil and petrochemical industry created two new, vertically integrated oil and petrochemical groups – the new CNPC and Sinopec (Table 3.3). With sales revenue at $25–30 billion each, both of the two groups would have been listed in the world's top 100 enterprises.

The assets of Sinopec and CNPC were reorganised along geographical lines, with those located in eastern and southern China coming under the management of Sinopec and those in northern and western China coming under CNPC. Under the reorganisation scheme, Sinopec transferred nineteen petrochemical enterprises to CNPC, of which fourteen were engaged in production and five in marketing. The transferred enterprises included Daqing General Petrochemical, Fushun Petrochemical, Dalian Petrochemical, Dalian West Pacific Petrochemical, Lanzhou Chemical Industrial, and Jinzhou Petrochemical. CNPC transferred to Sinopec twelve enterprises including eleven enterprises engaged in oil exploration and production, and Zhongyuan Petrochemical. Refineries and olefins plants formerly under the Ministry of Chemical Industry were transferred to either Sinopec or CNPC depending on the location of these refineries.

The new CNPC was led by Ma Fucai, former CNPC Vice President and Director of CNPC's Daqing PAB. It had assets worth 470 billion yuan ($57.8billion). CNPC managed oil, gas, and petrochemical facilities in twelve

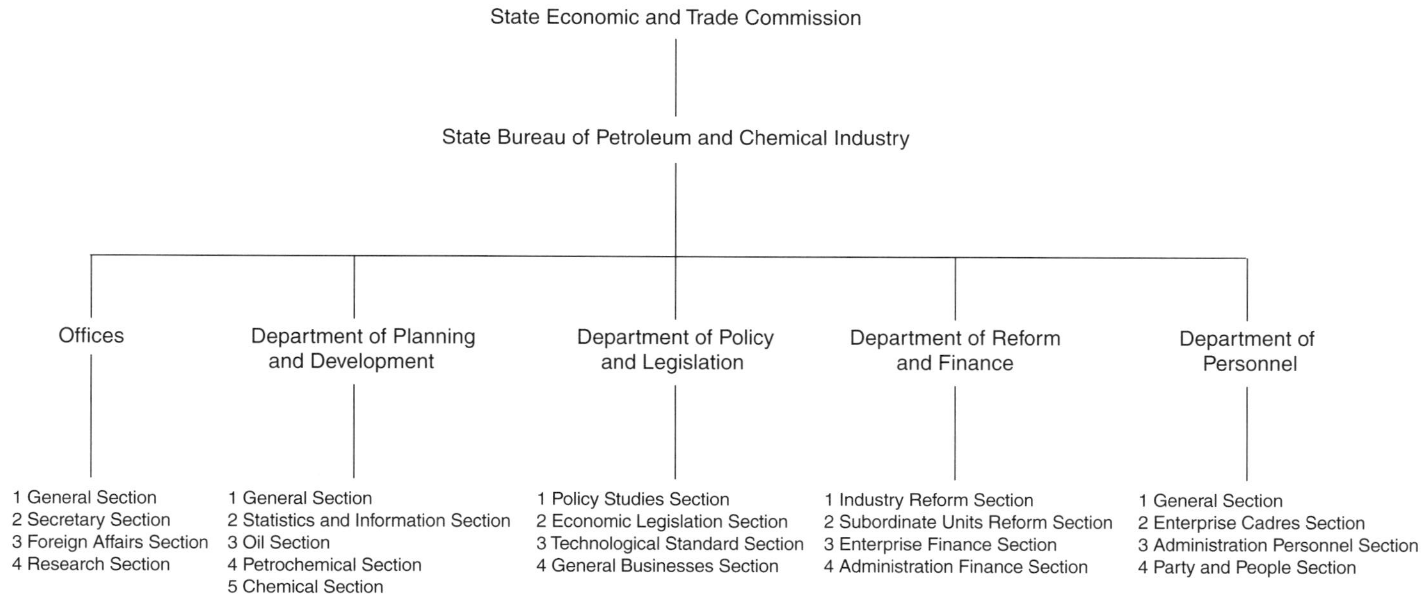

State Economic and Trade Commission

State Bureau of Petroleum and Chemical Industry

Offices	Department of Planning and Development	Department of Policy and Legislation	Department of Reform and Finance	Department of Personnel
1 General Section	1 General Section	1 Policy Studies Section	1 Industry Reform Section	1 General Section
2 Secretary Section	2 Statistics and Information Section	2 Economic Legislation Section	2 Subordinate Units Reform Section	2 Enterprise Cadres Section
3 Foreign Affairs Section	3 Oil Section	3 Technological Standard Section	3 Enterprise Finance Section	3 Administration Personnel Section
4 Research Section	4 Petrochemical Section	4 General Businesses Section	4 Administration Finance Section	4 Party and People Section
	5 Chemical Section			

Figure 5.2 Organisational structure of the State Bureau of Petroleum and Chemical Industry (SBPCI).

Note: Sec. = Section, Admin. = Administration.

provinces, regions and municipalities[1], including oil and gas producing complexes such as Daqing, Liaohe, Xinjiang, Tarim, and Sichuan. The new CNPC was strong in upstream oil and gas exploration and production. It accounted for 74 per cent of the total recoverable oil reserves in China, 67 per cent of onshore crude production capacity, and 40 per cent of China's refining capacity.

The new Sinopec was headed by Li Yizhong, the former President of Donglian and also the former Executive Vice President of Sinopec. It had assets of worth 381 billion yuan ($45.9 billion). It controlled oil and gas fields, oil refineries, and petrochemical companies in nineteen provinces, autonomous regions, and municipalities.[2] Among the eighty-nine subsidiaries, twenty-five were petro-chemical producers, including China's major petrochemical enterprises such as Shanghai Petrochemical, Beijing Yanshan Petrochemical, Yangzi Petrochemical, Tianjin Petrochemical, and Qilu Petrochemical. The company accounted for about 60 per cent of China's total refining capacity and about 30 per cent of the onshore crude production capacity.

Also transferred to Sinopec and CNPC were local sales companies under the two companies' territory (Table 5.1). CNPC and Sinopec were allowed to expand their marketing activities, especially retail business, into each other's territory. Moreover, the two companies were empowered by the State Council to make their own investment decisions, including forming joint ventures with foreign companies and raising funds to finance growth. Apart from the integration of production and marketing, Sinopec and CNPC also ran scientific research institutions, information centres, plant construction companies, and colleges and universities.

The restructuring of China's oil and petrochemical industry resulted in CNPC and Sinopec holding the dominant position in the onshore oil production and refining capacity, respectively. However, CNOOC and CNSPC and the three state oil trading companies – Sinochem, Unipec, and Chinaoil – continued to operate.

VERTICAL INTEGRATION

Through vertical integration, the new Sinopec and CNPC were integrated companies with operations across the whole value chain from upstream oil and gas exploration and development to downstream refining and petrochemical production. CNPC now had direct access to the market for refined products and could create its brand name through mass advertising. With new oil-producing assets, Sinopec had secured access to, and reliable supplies of, crude oil. Moreover, the downstream assets from Sinopec transferred to CNPC would contribute greatly to CNPC's effort to enhance its marketing skills. Both companies now had complementary assets and capabilities in R&D across the whole value chain. This could enable both companies to combine their strengths in R&D in upstream and downstream technologies. In production, now there would be more incentives for oil production units to ship their crude oil, and for refiners to sell their chemical feed-stocks, to nearby companies that were in the same business group.

Table 5.1 New CNPC and Sinopec after 1998 restructuring.

New CNPC		New Sinopec	
Oil and gas reserves and production		*Oil andagas reserves and production*	
Oil reserves	4.1 billion tonnes	Oil reserves	1.2 billion tonnes
Gas reserves	76 billion cubic metres	Gas reserves	4.3 billion cubic metres
Oil production	107 million tonnes	Oil production	36.3 million tonnes
Gas production	14.8 billion cubic metres	Gas production	2.4 billion cubic metres

Major oil and gas production units	*Major oil and gas production units*
Daqing Petroleum Administration Bureau	Shengli Petroleum Administration Bureau
Jilin Petroleum Group Company Ltd	Zhongyuan Petroleum Administration
Liaohe Petroleum Exploration Bureau	Bureau
Dagang Oil Field Group Company Ltd	Henan Petroleum Administration Bureau
Huabei Petroleum Administration Bureau	Jianghan Petroleum Administration Bureau
Xinjiang Petroleum Administration	Jiangsu Petroleum Administration Bureau
Bureau	Dianqiangui Petroleum Administration
Sichuan Petroleum Administration Bureau	Bureau
Qinhai Petroleum Administration Bureau	
Changqing Petroleum Administration	
Bureau	
Yumen Petroleum Administration Bureau	
Tuha Petroleum E&D Headquarters	
Tarim Petroleum E&D Headquarters	
Jidong Petroleum E&D Company	

Refining units and capacity (tonnes/year)		*Refining units and capacity (tonnes/year)*	
Jilin Refinery	300	Yanshan Petrochemical Corp.	9,500
Huhhot Refinery	1,000	Tianjin Petrochemical Corp.	6,000
Liaohe Oil Field Asphalt Plant	2,500	Shijiazhuang Refinery	2,500
Daqing Chemical Synergist Plant	3,500	Cangzhou Refinery	1,500
Sichuan Nanchong Refinery	150	Gaoqiao Petrochemical Corp.	7,500
Dushanzi Refinery	6,000	Shanghai Petrochemical Co. Ltd	5,300
Golmud Refinery	1,000	Jinling Petrochemical Corp.	7,000
Karamay Refinery	3,300	Yangzi Petrochemical Corp.	6,000
Yumen Refinery	4,000	Anqing Petrochemical Plant	2,800
Zepu Refinery	150	Jiujiang Refinery	2,500
Shaanxi Majiatan Refinery	100	Zhenhai Refining and Chemical	
Shaanxi Majialing Refinery	300	Co. Ltd	8,000
Yanchang Refinery	100	Fujian Refinery	4,000
Qinghai Refinery	1,350	Qilu Petrochemical Corp.	8,000
Xianyang Refinery	2,500	Jinan Refinery	4,000
Mudanjiang Petrochemical		Luoyang Petrochemical Plant	5,000
Works	350	Lyoyang Experimental Plant	200
Jilin Chemical Industry Group	4,500	Wuhan Petrochemical Plant	2,500
Fuyu Refinery	200	Jingmen Petrochemical Plant	5,000
Tumen Yanbian Petrochemical		Baling Petrochemical Corp.	5,000
Works	200	Maoming Petrochemical Corp.	8,500
Nong'an Petrochemical Works	150	Guangzhou Petrochemical Corp.	5,200

(Table 5.1 continued)

Table 5.1 (continued).

New CNPC		New Sinopec	
Dandong Petrochemical Works	300	Refinery of Henan Oil Field	120
Shenyang Xinming Wax Chemical	100	Shengli Heavyoil Plant	2,500
Works		Shengli Refinery	150
Qiqiha'er Chemical Works	350	Dagang Refinery	3,000
Heilongjiang Petrochemical Works	500	Huabei Chemical Pharmaceutical	
Acheng Petrochemical Works	100	Plant	200
Daqing Petrochemical Corporation	6,000	Jianghan Oil Field Refinery	300
Linyuan Refinery	2,500	Nanyang Refinery	620
Harbin Refinery	1,500	Zhongyuan Refinery	1,300
Qianguo Refinery	2,500	Beihai Refinery	500
Fushun Petrochemical Corporation	9,200	Hangzhou Refinery	300
Anshan Refinery	2,500	Baoding Petrochemical Works	500
Liaoyang Chemical Fibre		Qingdao Petrochemical Works	2,500
Corporation	4,000	Zhongjie Petrochemical Works	150
Jinzhou Petrochemical Corporation	5,500	Nandagang Petrochemical Works	100
Jinxi Petrochemical Corporation	5,000	Taizhou Petrochemical Works	300
Dalian Petrochemical Corporation	7,100	Wuxi Petrochemical Works	150
Lanzhou Refining and Chemical	5,500	Qingjiang Petrochemical Works	200
Corporation		Yangzhou Petrochemical Works	150
Urumqi Petrochemical Plant	2,500	Jianhu Petrochemical Experimental	
Total	87,800	Plant	100
		Yangchen LPG Plant	100
		Binzhou Petrochemical Works	400
		Ji'nan No.2 Petrochemical Works	300
		Kenli Refinery	400
		Linyi Petrochemical Works	200
		Guangrao Petrochemical Works	300
		Shouguang Petrochemical Works	150
		Changyi Petrochemical Works	150
		Dongming Petrochemical Works	300
		Lijin Refinery	150
		Boxing Petrochemical Works	100
		Boxing Oil and Grease Chemical	
		Works	100
		Yan'an Refinery	1,500
		Yongoing Refinery	300
		Xi'an Petrochemical Works	150
		Zhanjiang Refinery	1,500
		Total	125,240

Sales companies	*Sales companies*
Helongjiang Provincial Petroleum Company	Beijing City Petroleum Companay
Lilin Provincial Petroleum Company	Tianjin City Petroleum Company
Liaoning Provincial Petroleum Company	Shanghai City Petroleum Company
Dalian City Petroleum Company	Hebei Provincial Petroleum Company
Shenyang City Petroleum Company	Henan Provincial Petroleum Company
Inner Mongolia Petroleum Company	Shaanxi Provincial Petroleum Company
Shanxi Provincial Petroleum Company	Shandong Provincial Petroleum Company
Xi'an City Petroleum Company	Anhui Provincial Petroleum Company
Gansu Provincial Petroleum Company	Jiangxi Provincial Petroleum Company

Table 5.1 (continued).

New CNPC	New Sinopec
Ningxia Petroleum CompanyXingjiang Petroleum Company	Hubei Provincial Petroleum Company
	Hunan Provincial Petroleum Company
Qinghai Provincial Petroleum Company	Jiangsu Provincial Petroleum Company
Sichuan Provincial Petroleum Company	Zhejiang Provincial Petroleum Company
Chongqing City Petroleum Company	Fujian Provincial Petroleum Company
Tibet Petroleum Company	Guangdong Provincial Petroleum Company
	Guangxi Petroleum Company
	Yunnan Provincial Petroleum Company
	Guizhou Provincial Petroleum Company
	Hainan Provincial Petroleum Company

Source: *Oil and Gas Journal*, 10 August 1998, and author's own research.

Moreover, efficiency could be enhanced by rationalising the production capacity and process. In line with the SETC arrangement to achieve a balance of supply and demand in the domestic market for refined oil products, Sinopec and CNPC reached an agreement to push up the prices of refined oil products in September 1998. The crude oil processed in Sinopec in the fourth quarter of 1998 was 11 per cent less than in the same period of 1997. A few refineries were closed down to rationalise the capacity (*China Chemical Reporter*, 16 September 1998: 6), including Yueyang Petrochemical General Plant, Changling Refinery, Cangzhou Refinery. Jinling Petrochemical Co., Anqing Petrochemical General Plant, Jiujiang Petrochemical General Plant and Gaoqiao Petrochemical Corporation each closed down an atmospheric distillation unit. Tianjin, Wuhan, Maoming, Guangzhou Petrochemical Corporation all operated at below full capacity operation in oil refining. In crude oil resource allocation, oil field enterprises had also decreased the supply of crude oil to small local refineries, and Sinopec centrally allocated crude oil to its refineries. However, under the government co-ordination, Sinopec continued to prioritise processing domestic onshore crude oil, despite the fact that the price of domestic crude oil was higher than that of the imported oil.

ECONOMIES OF SCALE

Size and other structural considerations bestow significant economic advantages on petroleum companies because the oil industry business requires gigantic investment to ensure petroleum can be found, produced, refined, processed, and distributed. The industry is characterised by few competitors due to the high barrier to entry and limited rights to own or access to reserves. After restructuring, CNPC and Sinopec accounted for around 90 per cent of crude oil production in China, and they were responsible for over 75 per cent of natural gas output. Combined oil refining capacity amounted to over 95 per cent of the Chinese total. The two companies also accounted for 90 per cent of the country's ethylene cracking capacity. In the petrochemical sector, Sinopec had thirty-two petrochemical enterprises and CNPC controlled thirty-five. For petrochemical products, the proportion accounted for by Sinopec and CNPC were 56 per cent and 33 per cent for ethylene; 55 per cent and 34 per cent for polyethylene; 57 per cent and 23 per cent for polypropylene; and 39 per cent and 21 per cent for synthetic resin (*Asian Chemical News*, 7 September, 1998).

The dominant position of CNPC and Sinopec in the domestic market would enable the two companies to compete more effectively in a more open and competitive domestic market. Moreover, it would provide them with the financial resources to expand into the world market to gain access to cheaper exploration and production opportunities. In a capital-intensive sector such as the oil industry, it is vital to have the financial strength to achieve growth.

COST REDUCTION

The creation of new CNPC and Sinopec was a response to the need to reduce costs through economies of scale and scope. China's oil and petrochemical industry suffered huge profit declines due to the large fall in world oil prices in the late 1990s and the financial crisis in Southeast Asia. The gap between the domestic and world oil prices resulted in rampant oil smuggling into China, which severely hurt the profit of the domestic producers and caused a huge stockpile of products. On the other hand, the economic downturn in Southeast Asia resulted in a sharp decline in the demand for petroleum and chemical products in the region. Moreover, due to the currency depreciation, producers in Southeast Asia became more competitive in terms of the prices of their products in the world market, including China. This seriously hurt the sales and profits of Chinese enterprises and affected their competitiveness in the domestic market. In the first six months of 1998, Sinopec's sales of refined oil products and chemical fibres fell by 10 billion yuan ($1.2 billion) compared with the same period in 1997.

The reorganisation enabled both CNPC and Sinopec to reduce their operating and management costs. In 1999, Sinopec, which operates the Shengli and Zhongyuan oil fields and some other oilfields in South China, was able to cut high-cost oil output by 1.2 million tonnes and cancel construction plans for 440,000 tonnes of low-efficiency production capacity. CNPC, which oversees most of the country's major oil fields, took stringent measures to supervise investment decisions and production management to cut its operating costs. Crude oil exploration costs and oil processing costs were cut by 5 per cent in 1999. In the same year, some high-cost oil wells were closed, leading to a fall in output to 106.6 million tonnes of oil, 780,000 tonnes less than in 1998. Moreover, the group planned to lay off 100,000 employees by the end of 2000 (*China Daily Business Weekly*, 14 February, 1998: 8).

Restructuring for flotation: 1999

For both CNPC and Sinopec, the 1998 restructuring was just the first step towards constructing a market-oriented company with profitability as the target.

Both companies realised that their principal competitive rivals were not each other but rather, the global oil companies within China. Meanwhile, they needed to expand into the world market to seek business opportunities, especially in securing greater access to oil and gas resources. They needed the financial resources and management capabilities to transform themselves into globally competitive oil and petrochemical companies. From 1999, CNPC and Sinopec implemented a major internal restructuring programme in an attempt to establish the internal structure of a modern large corporation. The core of this restructuring was to divide core businesses and non-core businesses in their subordinate companies. On the basis of this separation, the core businesses in each of the subordinate enterprises were set up as branch companies (*fen gong si*). CNPC and Sinopec grouped these branch companies together to list them in the international market.

Core businesses

The massive task of separating core and non-core businesses was carried out in the fifty-four enterprises under CNPC, among which thirteen were oil and gas enterprises, fifteen refining enterprises, twenty-one marketing companies, one pipeline and transportation company, two R&D institutions, and two other companies.[3] Within Sinopec, sixty-two enterprises undertook the process of separating core businesses from non-core businesses, among which six were oil and gas enterprises, twenty-four refining and petrochemical enterprises, twenty-two sales enterprises, one pipeline enterprise, one import and export company, and five R&D institutions.

The division of core and non-core businesses of CNPC is presented in Table 5.2.

OIL AND GAS ENTERPRISES

Core businesses refer to businesses in oil and gas exploration and development, oil and gas storage and transportation, refining and chemicals, oil and gas marketing, research in exploration and development, engineering, planning, production maintenance, and electricity and water supply in oil extraction plants. Non-core businesses refer to technical services for core businesses, businesses providing support for production, diversified businesses and social functions.

REFINING AND PETROCHEMICAL ENTERPRISES

The category of core businesses includes key refining and chemical production, key supporting manufacturing facilities, oil and gas storage and transportation (including railways and ports exclusively for this purpose), chemicals marketing, R&D related to production, quality control, and daily manufacturing maintenance. Non-core businesses included chemical complex construction and installation, transportation, supporting businesses for manufacturing, diversified businesses, and social functions.

Table 5.2 Division of core and non-core businesses in CNPC, 1999.

Units category	Core businesses	Non-core businesses
Oil and gas enterprises	• Oil and gas exploration and production • Oil and gas storage and transportation • Refining and chemicals • Oil and gas marketing • Exploration and development, engineering and planning • Manufacturing maintenance • Electricity and water supply in oil extraction plants	• Technical services for core businesses: seismic exploration, drilling, well-testing, well-logging, downhole operation, oil-field construction • Manufacturing support and diversified businesses: machinery manufacturing and maintenance, transportation, water supply, electricity generation and supply, communication, material supply, construction materials, light industry and electronics, non-petroleum chemicals (diversified enterprises), intermediary agents, financial institutions, agriculture, food and tourism and hospitality and housekeeping services, etc. • Social functions: education, medical care, social security, retired employee administration, police and prosecution and courts, fire-fighting brigade, governmental departments, community offices, property management, etc.
Refining enterprises	• Key refining and chemical production • Key supporting manufacturing equipment • Oil and gas storage and transportation (including railways and ports for this exclusive use) • Chemical products marketing	• Chemical complex construction and installation • Transportation • Overhaul • Manufacturing support, diversified social functions
Marketing enterprises	Storage, transportation and sales of crude oil, natural gas and petroleum products	Diversified businesses and social functions
Pipelines and transportation enterprises	Transportation and storage of oil and gas	Pipeline construction, non-petroleum industrial production, diversified businesses and social functions
R&D institutions	Exploration and development research and refining research	Diversified businesses and social functions

MARKETING ENTERPRISES AND OTHERS

Diversified businesses and social functions were separated from the core businesses of storage, transportation and sales of oil, gas and petroleum products. Pipelines and transportation enterprises solely engage in the business of oil and gas storage and transportation. The businesses of pipeline design and construction, 'diversified businesses' and social functions are non-core businesses.

BRANCH COMPANIES

The branch companies of core businesses in each of the existing enterprises were not given legal person status. Taxes and contracts implementation continued to be administered by the present enterprise. The management team of the present enterprise hold concurrent posts in branch companies. The number of employees in the newly established branches was stringently controlled. It was planned to have between sixty and 100 management teams, around six to eight functional departments, and around three to five executive positions. In addition, Party organisations were set up simultaneously with the establishment of these branch companies.

Non-core businesses

There were four categories of non-core businesses (see Table 5.2).

SERVICE ENTERPRISES

These included enterprises that provide engineering and technical services to core businesses such as seismic exploration, drilling, well testing, well logging, downhole operation, oil field construction and refining and chemical complex construction. It was expected that technical service companies would be set up to carry out service projects for core businesses and, in the meantime, compete for international projects.

SUPPORTING BUSINESSES

These included enterprises that provide services for both core and non-core businesses such as water supply, electricity generation and supply, communication services, material supply, and transportation services.

DIVERSIFIED COMPANIES

Diversified companies are those under the direct control of CNPC and Sinopec as well as those controlled by the subordinate enterprises under CNPC and Sinopec. Multiple ownership structures such as share-holding and stock co-operatives were encouraged in diversified companies. Assets with low efficiency were expected to improve themselves through leasing, auction, or employee buy out. Employees were strongly encouraged to set up their own businesses or look for jobs elsewhere.

SOCIAL FUNCTIONS

Social functions included schools and colleges, hospitals and health centres, and security services. The assets, finance and personnel of those entities that could not be completely separated at the time, were to be managed separately and have independent accounts. The costs were to be shared proportionally by core and non-core businesses.

It was anticipated that CNPC and Sinopec would each group together their core businesses (all the branch companies) into a joint stock company and list them on the international market. However, the approach towards further reorganisation of the service enterprises was far from clear. At the end of 1999, the Chinese government announced that the social functions in state-owned enterprises should be transferred to the administration of local governments. However, implementation of this policy was a complicated task. It involved difficult negotiation and co-ordination with local government at various levels, which were not always willing to 'accept' these social functions from the two companies.

Summary

The reorganisation of China's oil and petrochemical industry in 1998 demonstrated that the headquarters of CNPC and Sinopec had won the struggle to become 'the headquarters' to lead the industry's development with the full support from the Chinese government. Through the 1998 reorganisation, CNPC and Sinopec each became an integrated oil and petrochemical company. The subsequent restructuring for flotation in 1999 and 2000 established the 'one-tier' legal person system (*yiji faren zhi*). It dashed the hopes for independence held by the subordinate enterprises, which had been encouraged by the preceding reforms. CNPC and Sinopec Group each created a 'child company' – PetroChina and Sinopec – that amalgamated the core businesses and floated in the international market. This was an immense step in the evolution of China's industrial policy.

6   Corporate structure and headquarters' function

PetroChina and Sinopec

On 5 November 1999, CNPC grouped together its core businesses and created PetroChina as a joint stock company with limited liability. On 25 February 2000, China Petroleum and Chemical Corporation, known as Sinopec, was established on basis of the core businesses from the old Sinopec, now known as Sinopec Group.

In April 2000, PetroChina was listed on the New York and Hong Kong stock exchanges. The initial public offering (IPO) accounted for 10 per cent of the company's total shares, and raised $2.89 billion. Among the shares issued, 32.1 per cent were bought by strategic and corporate investors including BP Amoco, Sing Hung Kai, Hong Kong Cheung Kong Enterprises, and Hutchison Whampoa. After this global listing, CNPC held a 90 per cent of PetroChina's total equity. Six months later, in October 2000, Sinopec was listed on the stock exchanges in New York, Hong Kong and London. The IPO accounted for 21.21 per cent of the company's total shares, and raised $3.73 billion. After the global flotation, 56.06 per cent of Sinopec's equity was controlled by its parent company Sinopec Group. Before the global listing, Sinopec Group had debts amounting to $3 billion owed to the State Development Bank, China Construction Bank, Bank of China and China Industrial and Commercial Bank. Sinopec Group signed a 'debt for equity swap' (*zai zhuan gu*) agreement with the State Development Bank and three asset management companies, Cinda, Orient and Huarong,[1] transferring the Sinopec Group's debt into equity shares owned by the four institutions. After the global listing, the four institutions owned 22.73 per cent of Sinopec's equity. The remaining 21.21 per cent of Sinopec's equity was owned by overseas investors including the three largest global oil companies Exxon Mobil, Shell and BP. Exxon Mobil, Shell and BP promised to purchase 20 per cent, 14 per cent and 13.5 per cent respectively of Sinopec's IPO, involving share purchases of up to $1 billion, $430 million and $400 million respectively. ABB Lummus, the petrochemical plant design and construction company, also agreed to purchase $100 million worth of shares. Other overseas corporate investors include Henderson Investment Ltd, Hong Kong and China Gas Company, Cheung Kong Enterprises and Hutchison Whampoa. Both Cheung Kong and Hutchison Whampoa are part of the group of companies owned by Li Ka-shing, whose business empire is based in Hong Kong, and includes Canada's Husky oil company.

PetroChina

In 2000, PetroChina achieved an impressive performance that caused analysts to 'revise their forecasts for PetroChina' (*Financial Times*, 27 April, 2001). Compared with 1999, PetroChina's business performance in 2000 took a great leap forward in almost every aspect. Total revenue was $29.2 billion, a 37 per cent increase from 1999, and net profit was $6.7 billion, more than double that of 1999. The chemicals and natural gas segments were turned around from losses to positive earnings. Impressive as it was for a company trading in the international market just one year, Ma Fucai, PetroChina's chairman remained cautious: 'For the operating profit of the company, 80 per cent was contributed by the rising crude oil and by refined oil prices' (quoted in *Financial Times*, 23 April, 2001). PetroChina's average oil price rose from $16.9 per barrel in 1999 to $27.2 per barrel in 2000, an increase of 61 per cent.

Businesses

EXPLORATION AND PRODUCTION

PetroChina is the largest producer of oil and gas in China. By the end of 2000, it had 11.0 billion barrels of proved reserves (both developed and undeveloped) of crude oil, 32.5 trillion cubic feet of natural gas located in the northern and western parts of China. Fifty per cent of the crude oil reserves are from Daqing oil field and one-third of the natural gas reserves are from Tarim. In 2000, the total output of crude oil was of 2.10 million barrels per day, which accounted for 67 per cent of China's total production. The total output of natural gas was 505.3 billion cubic feet. The breakdown of oil sales showed that 71 per cent of crude oil was processed by PetroChina's own refineries, 18 per cent went to refineries of Sinopec, 6 per cent was bought by regional refineries, and 5 per cent exported.

As with every oil and gas company, reserve replacement[2] is a critical and continuing issue. PetroChina's crude oil reserves account for an overwhelming percentage of 73 of its total crude oil reserves. As much as 89 per cent of the proved crude oil reserves have already been developed. PetroChina's largest producing region, Daqing, is in the secondary recovery stage. Polymer flooding has been applied to about 14 per cent of Daqing's production. Despite PetroChina's goal of increasing natural gas as a source of overall reserve replacement, the shortfall in reserve replacement will become increasingly difficult to replace onshore. To achieve its long-term return and growth, PetroChina has to consider options to guarantee that it has adequate reserves. The options include CNPC's acquisition of international assets. According to an agreement concluded before PetroChina's flotation, CNPC granted PetroChina the option to purchase, at any time, all of CNPC's interests in one or more overseas projects. Another option is to swap reserves or form joint ventures with international majors to explore and develop oil and gas resources.

In the year 2000, PetroChina owned twenty-four refineries located in the northeastern and northwestern part of China. The major refineries were Fushun Petrochemical, Dalian Petrochemical, Daqing Petrochemical and Lanzhou refinery. In addition, PetroChina held a 67.29 per cent interest in Jilin Chemical Industrial Company listed on the New York, Hong Kong and Shenzhen stock exchanges, an 80.95 per cent interest in Jinzhou Petrochemical Company listed on the Shenzhen Stock Exchange. However, none of the refineries had a primary distillation capacity exceeding 10 million tonnes. Major refined products are diesel, gasoline, fuel oil, naphtha, jet fuel, lubricants, asphalt, and paraffin. In 2000, the refineries processed 547 million barrels of crude oil, accounting for 36 per cent of total domestic production. Approximately 92.5 per cent of the crude oil was supplied by PetroChina's exploration and production division and 44.2 million tonnes of gasoline, diesel and jet fuel was produced.

PetroChina's position in marketing is not as strong as Sinopec's. This sector has become increasingly important in the oil and gas industry under the customer-oriented business philosophy with the rationale of controlling the final consumer market at the end of the value chain. PetroChina's refining and marketing division was created on the basis of previously separate businesses, including refineries owned by PetroChina, and those received from Sinopec during the 1998 reorganisation. PetroChina has been integrating these refineries through upgrading those with relatively large capacity and closing down those that are small and inefficient. Since 2000, PetroChina has begun upgrading and expanding two refining hubs in Dalian and Lanzhou up to an annual capacity of 20 million tonnes, each involving an investment of $1.2-$1.3 billion.

Since 1999, there has begun a process of integrating the three-tier distribution system. The number of distribution layers and wholesale distribution outlets has been reduced significantly. In 2000, PetroChina had 989 regional wholesale distribution outlets in China, most of which were located in coastal areas, along railways and along the Yangtze River, where economic prosperity results in high demand for petroleum products.

In storage and transportation, by 2000, PetroChina had 8,748 kilometres of crude oil pipelines with an average daily throughput of 2.2 million barrels, and 984 kilometres of petroleum product pipelines, with an average daily throughput of 17,807 tonnes. Crude oil storage facilities had a total capacity of 10.9 million cubic metres and the capacity of 342 petroleum product storage facilities totals 7.0 million cubic metres. Most of these facilities are in the northeastern and northwestern part of China. Many of them are obsolete. PetroChina plans to acquire and construct transport and storage facilities in the eastern and southern part of China to help to improve its distribution infrastructure nationwide. A refined product pipeline system of 1,207 kilometres is under construction. It will have an annual throughput capacity of 5 million tonnes of refined products transported from Lanzhou to Chengdu and Chongqing, where demand for refined products is estimated to significantly exceed supply.

In retail marketing, in the year 2000, PetroChina had 11,350 service stations,[3] compared with 20,259 service stations operated by Sinopec, 45,000 by Exxon Mobil, 46,000 by Royal Dutch/Shell and 27,545 by BP. Average daily sales volume of gasoline and diesel was a minuscule 2.7 tonnes per service station. Most of CNPC's service stations were located in the northeastern and northwestern part of China. Sinopec had an 89 per cent market share for refined products in eastern and southern regions, which have the highest income in China. In 2000, PetroChina expanded its sales and market share in the eastern and southern regions of China by increasing the number of service stations and expanding storage facilities. PetroChina sold 2,250 million tonnes of gasoline and diesel in these regions, which accounted for 5 per cent of its total sales of gasoline and diesel.

NATURAL GAS

For environmental reasons, the Chinese government is encouraging industrial and residential use of natural gas. A preferential value-added tax (VAT) of 13 per cent has been adopted for gas production as compared with a 17 per cent VAT for oil production. Large cities such as Beijing and Shanghai have taken measures to increase gas consumption to reduce air pollution. The increased use of natural gas by power stations and households in China will result in a change in customer mix. In 2000, chemical plants accounted for approximately 50 per cent of PetroChina's gas sales.

PetroChina is the largest natural gas transporter and producer in China. It has an aggregate length of 11,617 kilometers of gas pipelines, of which 10,525 kilometres are operated by PetroChina's natural gas segment. In 2000, natural gas production was 1.38 billion cubic feet per day, compared with Sinopec Corporation at 0.22 billion cubic feet per day. However, natural gas production volume was less than 20 per cent of that of the global giants. PetroChina is working with Shell on developing natural gas resources in its Changqing oil and gas region.

PetroChina has a dominant market share of 70 per cent in domestic transmission infrastructure and is expanding transmission pipelines to transport natural gas to major markets along the Yangtze River and regions in eastern China. These projects are known as Zhongxian-Wuhan project, Qinghai-Lanzhou project and West to East natural gas transmission project (*xi qi dong shu*). The Zhongxian County to Wuhan City project is intended to link the Sichuan gas region with Hubei Province and Hunan Province with a designed annual throughput capacity of 105.9 billion cubic feet. The Qinghai-Lanzhou project is intended to capture the market in the Xining and Lanzhou regions. The West to East project is the most ambitious of the three, with a total investment of 120 billion yuan (approximately $16.9 billion). It is designed to transport natural gas from Xinjiang and Changqing to Shaanxi Province, Henan, Anhui, Shanghai and other areas in the Yangtze River Delta, with a total length of approximately 4,200 kilometers.

PetroChina has a production sharing contract with Shell Exploration (China) Ltd to jointly develop natural gas resources in Changbei in the Changqing oil and gas region. For the West to East natural gas pipeline construction project, PetroChina received tenders from nineteen international oil and gas companies including BP, Shell and Exxon Mobil. The negotiation process was protracted and the initial commencing date of September 2001 was postponed. In September 2001, BP withdrew its bid out of the concern for the 'commercial viability' of the project. At the end of 2001, PetroChina and Shell signed a temporary agreement under which they would take ownership shares of 55 per cent to 45 per cent respectively for a period of 45 years. The project began construction in July 2002. Meanwhile, the working framework agreement was signed. This specified that PetroChina and Sinopec would have 50 per cent and 5 per cent the equity shares in the project, respectively. The remaining 45 per cent equity share was equally divided among three international consortia: Shell International Natural Gas Company and Hong Kong China Gas Company; Exxon Mobil Natural Gas Pipeline Company (China) and Hong Kong China Lighting and Power Company; Gazprom and the Russian Natural Gas Construction and Transmission Company.

PETROCHEMICALS

In the year 2000, PetroChina had seventeen chemical plants among which Daqing Petrochemical and Jilin Chemical are the leading producers. In 2000, its income from chemical operations was $8 million, a significant improvement on the loss of $206 million in 1999. Ethylene production reached 1.5 million tonnes, accounting for 32 per cent of China's total production. The chemicals division has operated with huge inefficiency characterised by raw material losses and high energy consumption, which are the key factors contributing to high production costs. In 2000, the average energy consumption of the ethylene production facilities was 872 kilograms of standard oil per ton, significantly higher than the world average of 500 to 690 kilograms of standard oil per ton. The average ethylene percentage loss was 1.3 per cent, compared to the world average of 1.0 per cent (PetroChina, 2001).

R&D

Apart from the two research institutes directly under the headquarters, each of PetroChina's subsidiaries and branch companies has its own R&D department and technology centre. They focus on independently developing specific technology for their respective companies. They also work on R&D projects co-ordinated by the headquarters. In 2000, 22,300 employees were working in R&D functions and the R&D spending was US$212 million. Technology in exploration and production lags behind the world level. For example, oil field development equipment is equivalent to world level of the late 1980s and exploration equipment is equivalent to world level of the early 1990s. Oil extracting machinery and oil and gas treatment equipment are either imported altogether or assembled in China. Key electronic instruments and software for exploration and production are imported. China's industrial experts pointed out that China's capability of technological innovation in upstream oil and gas industry is still at the level of a 'third world' company, which is a major constraint on the indigenous forms' competitiveness and efficiency (*China Petroleum*, January 1999: 49).

Corporate structure

The board of directors of PetroChina consists of thirteen directors, three of whom are independent non-executive directors. Five of the directors are currently affiliated with CNPC. The chairman of the board of directors is Ma Fucai, who is also the President of CNPC. In 2000, Franco Bernabè, former CEO of ENI, Chairman of France Bernabè Group and Vice Chairman of H3G was appointed as independent non-executive director and Chairman of PetroChina's Audit Committee. From 1992 to 1998, Mr Bernabè was the chief executive officer of Italy's ENI, leading the restructuring programme of ENI Group. The board of directors currently has four management committees to supervise issues such as financial reporting, performance evaluation, executive compensation, business strategy, and health, safety and environment (Figure 6.1).

According to China's Company Law, a joint stock company with limited liability must set up a supervisory committee. The supervisory committee of PetroChina consists of seven supervisors, six of whom are elected by shareholders and one by employees. The supervisors representing the shareholders are elected at the general shareholder meeting while the supervisor representing employees is elected by PetroChina's employees. The supervisory committee is responsible for monitoring financial matters and overseeing the actions of the board of directors and senior management personnel in carrying out their duties.

In 2000, PetroChina had four business divisions: exploration and production division consisting of fourteen enterprises, headed by Luo Yingjun; the refining and marketing division consisting of twenty-eight enterprises, headed by Lin Qingshan; the chemicals division consisting of seventeen enterprises, headed by Zhang Xinzhi; the natural gas division consisting of two enterprises, headed by Shi Xinquan (Figure 6.1). Also led by the senior management are two research institutes, the Planning and Engineering Institute and the Exploration and Development Institute, and one trading company, China National United Oil Corporation (Figure 6.1). None of these senior executives holds a position in CNPC.

At first sight, the organisational structure of PetroChina is not very different from that of an international integrated oil and gas company. However, if one takes a closer look, two important issues appear: (1) PetroChina's relationship with its parent CNPC and (2) the integration of powerful subsidiaries like Daqing (Chapter 7).

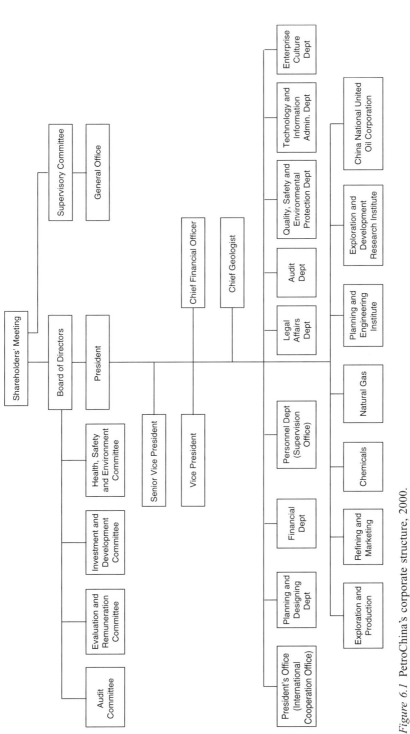

Figure 6.1 PetroChina's corporate structure, 2000.

Source: PetroChina.

The relationship with CNPC

Prior to its global offering, PetroChina reached various agreements with CNPC regarding competition, supply of products and services. According to the non-competition agreement between CNPC and PetroChina, as long as CNPC holds not less than 30 per cent of PetroChina's shares, CNPC will not engage in any businesses within or outside China that directly or indirectly competes with businesses in which PetroChina is involved. Moreover, when CNPC encounters business opportunities that are in competition with PetroChina, CNPC must notify PetroChina of these business opportunities immediately. In addition, CNPC must make its best effort to offer such opportunities to PetroChina on terms and conditions acceptable to PetroChina. Furthermore, CNPC grants PetroChina the option to purchase at any time all of CNPC's assets outside China.

During CNPC's internal reorganisation in 1999, CNPC retained the non-core businesses, many of which are essential for PetroChina to obtain products and services not currently available from other sources. According to the Comprehensive Products and Services Agreement between PetroChina and CNPC, CNPC provides PetroChina with oil field construction and technical services, production services, supply of material services, social services, and financial services. PetroChina will pay for the services at either State-administered price or market prices. If the services are not available from other independent companies, PetroChina will pay CNPC the actual cost of the service plus an additional margin of no more than 15 per cent for certain construction and technical services and a margin of 3 per cent for other types of services.

The agreements indicate that the parent, CNPC, gives support to the 'child', PetroChina. However, CNPC is the controlling shareholder of PetroChina and it draws its principal income from PetroChina's dividend payment. In 2000, CNPC received approximately $3.1 billion as a dividend payment from PetroChina,[4] accounting for 53 per cent of its net profit. CNPC has the non-core businesses as well as social functions employing more than 800,000 people, most of which are hugely loss-making. CNPC is reorganising these non-core businesses and may influence PetroChina's decision on the level of dividend payment in order to support CNPC's financial situation. Moreover, as a controlling shareholder, CNPC holds the dominant position in the shareholders' meeting, which may give it the power to intervene in important issues from business strategy to the appointment of senior executive management.

Sinopec

The year 2000 was the first year of Sinopec's international listing. Compared with that of 1999, business performance in 2000 improved considerably. Total revenues were $39.7 billion, a 37 per cent increase from 1999, and net profit was $2.3 billion, almost four times of that in 1999. Most of Sinopec's revenue increase came from the marketing and distribution of its refined products 'at a time of unusually robust prices' (*Financial Times*, 17 April, 2001).

Businesses

EXPLORATION AND PRODUCTION

Sinopec has six oil and gas producing fields in China, among which Shengli is the second largest oil field next to PetroChina's Daqing. Shengli's production in 2000 was 530,000 boe (barrel of oil equivalent), which accounted for 74 per cent of Sinopec's total annual production. By the end of 2000, Sinopec had 3 billion barrels of proved reserves (both developed and undeveloped) of crude oil, 999 billion cubic feet of natural gas. In 2000, the total output of crude oil was of 676,000 barrels per day, which accounted for 22 per cent of the total production in China. The total output of natural gas was 2.2 billion cubic feet. Over 85 per cent of the total production of crude oil and natural gas was supplied to Sinopec's own refineries and petrochemical plants.

In March 2000, China National Star Petroleum Company was merged into Sinopec Group Company and renamed Sinopec National Star. In June 2001, Sinopec announced that it would list A-shares on the Shanghai Stock Exchange and planned to raise 10.35 billion yuan, of which 6.44 billion would fund the acquisition of Sinopec National Star from its parent. The acquisition of Sinopec National Star, which has proven oil and gas reserves of about 622 million boe, would increase Sinopec's upstream production by 10 per cent.

REFINING AND MARKETING

- *Refining* Sinopec is the largest refiner in China, accounting for 52 per cent of the total domestic throughput in 2000. Of the 105.5 million tonnes of crude oil processed in 2000, 26 per cent was from Sinopec's exploration and production division, 20 per cent from PetroChina and CNOOC and 54 per cent from foreign sources such as the Middle East, West Africa, and Southeast Asia. A total amount of 75 million tonnes of gasoline, diesel and jet fuel, kerosene, lubricant, LPG and fuel oil was produced. Sinopec owns twenty-five refineries located mainly in the eastern and southern parts of China with the highest income in the country. Four refineries – Maoming, Zhenhai, Qilu and Jinling – have an annual primary distillation capacity exceeding 10 million tonnes and eight other refineries have an annual primary distillation capacity of 5–8 million tonnes.
- *Wholesale* Sinopec has about 1,000 storage facilities with a total storage capacity of 13 million cubic metres operated by its wholesale distribution centres in nineteen provinces. In 2000, Sinopec sold a total of 67 million tonnes of gasoline, diesel, jet fuel and kerosene, 64 per cent of which was sold through wholesale channels. Among the 43 million tonnes of wholesale sales, 68 per cent was sold through Sinopec's distribution centres to

customers mainly from the public transportation, tourism, and agricultural industries; 23 per cent was sold to special customers including the military, the national reserves, railways, and airlines, marine, and utility industries; and 9 per cent was sold to independent distributors.

- *Retail* Sinopec realised that once China had joined the WTO, its retail marketing sector would face even more fierce competition from the multinationals that have advanced technology and logistics expertise in managing distribution networks. Sinopec has been aggressively expanding retail service stations across its principal market in the eastern and southern parts of China. In 2000, Sinopec acquired 8,000 service stations, built 600 service stations and renovated 500 existing service stations. The total number of service stations owned and operated by Sinopec amounted to 20,259 in 2000. In addition, Sinopec operated 2,700 service stations owned by Sinopec Group. Sinopec sold 24 million tonnes of gasoline and diesel in 2000, constituting 40 per cent of the domestic market.

  Prior to the reorganisation of 1998, China's refining sector was separated from the marketing and distribution sector. Refineries had considerable independence in production and sales. This poses tremendous problems for Sinopec in rationalising production capacity across different products and locations in response to fluctuations in market demand. Sinopec has began to integrate the refining and distribution sectors. It intends to manage the refineries as a single production system instead of independent production centres.

PETROCHEMICALS AND MARKETING

Sinopec is the largest petrochemical producer in China. It has seventeen petrochemical plants located in the eastern and southern parts of China, among which Yanhua, Shanghai, Qilu, and Yangzi each has over 400,000 tonnes of ethylene production capacity per annum. Sinopec produced 2.2 million tonnes of ethylene in 2000, accounting for 46 per cent of China's total production, compared with 32 per cent for PetroChina and 15 per cent for the Sinopec Group. However, most of the petrochemical plants need to be upgraded and revamped to reduce energy consumption and improve product quality. Moreover, the product mix needs to be adjusted, Sinopec needs to increase the production of specialised chemicals and highly differentiated products.

In 2000, the sales of petrochemicals were $6.8 billion, contributing 17 per cent to the total operating revenue. Marketing of petrochemical products is through two channels: direct sales to customers who are mainly large and medium sized manufacturing enterprises, and sales to distributors nation-wide. In 2000, Sinopec produced 20 million tonnes of petrochemical products, 60 per cent of which was sold directly to customers and 40 per cent to distributors. Sinopec markets its petrochemical products through its annual sales conferences, at which most of the sales are arranged under one-year sales contracts. Sinopec needs to establish stable and long-term supply relationships with its customers, and to establish a unified national sales network.

R&D

Sinopec's headquarters has six R&D institutes. Four institutes focus on R&D in refining and petrochemicals, one focusses on upstream exploration and production, and one focusses on production safety and occupational health. Moreover, there are over 100 R&D departments in Sinopec's subsidiaries. They focus on developing specific technologies for their respective companies independently. They also work on R&D projects co-ordinated by the headquarters. In 2000, there were 35,000 employees working in these R&D functions and Sinopec's R&D spending was $200 million.

Corporate structure

Sinopec's board of directors consists of ten directors, three of whom are independent non-executive directors and one is an employee representative director. Two of the directors are currently affiliated to Sinopec Group. The Chairman of the Board of Directors is Li Yizhong, who is also the President of Sinopec. The Board of Directors currently has three management committees to supervise issues such as financial reporting, executive compensation, and business strategy (Figure 6.2).

The Supervisory Committee of Sinopec consists of eight supervisors, seven of whom are elected by shareholders and one by employees. In addition, Sinopec has one independent supervisor. In 2000, seven of the supervisors concurrently hold positions with Sinopec Group. The Supervisory Committee is responsible for monitoring financial matters and overseeing the actions of the Board of Directors and the senior management personnel in carrying out their duties. Resolutions must be approved by two-thirds or more of the supervisors to be effective.

Sinopec has four business departments: the Oil-field Exploration and Production Department consisting of six enterprises, the Refinery Department consisting of twenty-four enterprises, the Chemical Department consisting of seventeen enterprises, and Sales Company leading sales branches in subsidiaries (Figure 6.2). Also led by the senior management are six research institutes, and one trading company, China International United Petroleum and Chemicals Corporation (Figure 6.2).

Relationship with Sinopec Group

Before international flotation, Sinopec Group transferred to Sinopec six oil-fields and twenty-four refining and petrochemical enterprises. Sinopec Group retained eight refining and petrochemical enterprises: Nanjing Chemical Industry Company, Nanjing Chemical Plant, Zhongyuan Petrochemical, Sichuan Vinylon Plant, Qingjiang Petrochemical, Baoding Petrochemical, Maoming Petrochemical Ethylene Industrial Company, and Tianjin Petrochemical United Chemical Company. Of the twenty-four refining and petrochemical enterprises transferred to Sinopec, Sinopec Group retained some individual production plants, including

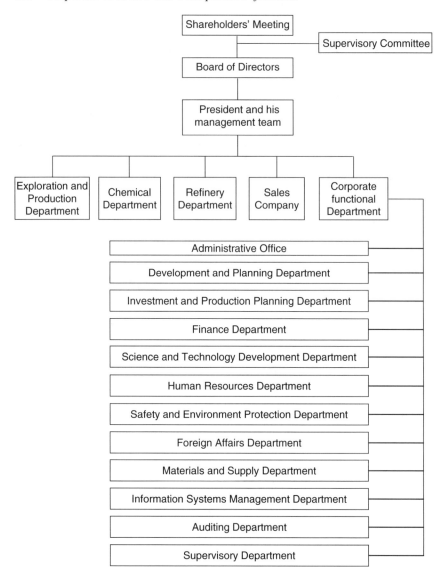

Figure 6.2 Sinopec's corporate structure, 2000.

Source: Sinopec.

three refining plants, nine chemical plants, two catalyst plants, one plastic plant and one plastic film plant. In addition, Sinopec Group has two polyester plants in Tianjin and Luoyang that are currently under construction. These plants produce ethylene, PE, PP, Polyester and Caprolactam.

Sinopec has reached various agreements with Sinopec Group regarding competition, supply of products and services. According to the non-competition agreement between Sinopec and Sinopec Group, as long as Sinopec Group holds no less than 30 per cent of Sinopec's shares, Sinopec Group will not engage in any businesses within or outside China that are directly or indirectly in competition with businesses in which Sinopec is involved. When Sinopec Group wishes to enter into new businesses related to Sinopec's primary businesses, Sinopec Group will grant Sinopec the right of first refusal. Upon notification from Sinopec Group, Sinopec has thirty days to decide either to accept the business opportunity or allow Sinopec Group to pursue the opportunity. Sinopec Group must offer any such business opportunities on terms that are acceptable to Sinopec. Moreover, Sinopec Group grants Sinopec a five-year option to acquire any of the existing businesses retained by Sinopec Goup and a five-year option to acquire any new businesses acquired or developed by the parent in the future.

Among the non-core businesses retained by Sinopec Group, many supply services for Sinopec. According to the agreement for mutual provision of products and ancillary services between Sinopec group and Sinopec, Sinopec Group provides Sinopec with construction and services, production services, storage and transportation services, a supply of material services, financial services and information advisory services. Sinopec will pay for the services at government-administered prices, government-guided prices or market prices. If prices for services are not available from other independent companies, Sinopec will pay the parent the actual cost of the service plus an additional margin not exceeding 6 per cent of such cost.

Sinopec Group also retained social services employing more than 600,000 people, most of which are hugely loss-making. Sinopec signed a three-year community service agreement (from the beginning of 2000) with Sinopec Group. Sinopec Group will provide Sinopec's employees with community services including primary and secondary schools, hospitals and medical centres, environmental protection services and public transport facilities.

Sinopec Group has three main means to generate funds and finance the losses produced by the non-core businesses: revenues generated by business operations retained by Sinopec Group; financial support from government agencies through preferential policies; and dividends received from Sinopec. As Sinopec's controlling shareholder, Sinopec Group may influence Sinopec's determination of its dividend payment in favour of Sinopec Group's financial situation. Moreover, Sinopec Group holds the dominant position in the shareholders' meeting, which implies that Sinopec Group may have the power to intervene in important issues from business strategy to the appointment of senior executive management personnel.

Corporate centralisation: PetroChina and Sinopec

PetroChina and Sinopec have been striving to centralise control at the corporate level over production, product pricing, financial affairs, marketing, capital investment, and procurement, facilitated by investing in information technology systems in the company.

Both companies have obtained rights in production and in product pricing from the government. Within the company, PetroChina and Sinopec each is improving their financial reporting system by integrating the reporting format and approach over different production units. Each company is integrating their refineries and distribution system. Each company is taking back the right of large-scale capital investment from their subordinate enterprises. Each company has set up an e-commerce platform for procurement and trading.

Planning

CRUDE OIL

Each year, SDPC requires each of the three companies, PetroChina, Sinopec and CNOOC, to submit their projected domestic consumption and their estimated production volumes for the following year. Based on these estimates and the forecast of international crude oil prices, SDPC sets the annual production targets for the three companies and determines the permitted levels of crude oil imports and exports nation-wide. SETC then allocates the crude oil import and export quota to PetroChina and Sinopec. However, the actual production volumes are determined by the companies themselves and do not necessarily follow the submitted estimates.

NATURAL GAS

SDPC publishes the annual production targets for natural gas producers based on estimates of domestic consumption submitted by PetroChina, Sinopec and CNOOC. SDPC also formulates the annual gas supply guidance plan that requires the companies to distribute the specified amount of natural gas to named fertiliser producers. However, the actual production volumes are determined by the companies themselves.

REFINED PRODUCTS AND PETROCHEMICALS

There are limited or no government controls on refined products except for a certain amount of gasoline and diesel. For gasoline and diesel, SDPC allocates to PetroChina and Sinopec a quota of minimum supplies that must be made available to meet the requirement of the special customers. There was no government control on petrochemical production volumes after 1994.

Marketing

PRICING

- *Crude oil* The restructuring pegged China's oil prices to Singapore FOB oil prices in June 1998. This was perceived as a significant step in the integration of China's petroleum industry with that of the world. From June 1998, SDPC published monthly a list of benchmark prices for a number of crude oil grades, based on the average daily Singapore FOB prices for the previous month plus the import duty of 16 yuan per tonne. On top of these benchmark crude oil prices, PetroChina and Sinopec negotiated a premium (5 per cent) relative to the benchmark price. When disputes arise between PetroChina and Sinopec, the SDPC co-ordinates and makes the final decision on the crude oil prices. From March 2001, the SDPC stopped publishing the monthly crude oil benchmark prices. PetroChina and Sinopec agreed to adhere to the same benchmarking system as before. The benchmark prices are now determined by PetroChina and Sinopec instead of the SDPC.

- *Natural gas* There are three components included in the price of natural gas: wellhead price, pipeline transportation tariff and purification fee. For natural gas sold within the government guidance plan, the SDPC fixes well head prices. For natural gas sold above the government-formulated gas supply plan, the SDPC publishes the median guidance wellhead price with a 10 per cent upward and downward adjustment by the natural gas producer. PetroChina and Sinopec negotiate the actual wellhead price with commercial gas users and municipal governments within the adjustment range. PetroChina and Sinopec ask the SDPC for examination and approval of the pipeline transportation tariff based on the capital investment made in the pipeline, the depreciation period for the pipeline, and the end user's ability to pay. PetroChina and Sinopec set the purification fees based on the cost of gas purification, which must be approved by the SDPC. The government proposed replacing the well head prices with the well head guidance prices and setting prices based on a ratio between the thermal value and the price of composite alternative energy. Sales of natural gas to fertiliser producers would be set by the government at a discount to the market price. These proposals had not been adopted by March 2001. If they were adopted in the future, it would enable PetroChina and Sinopec to negotiate natural gas prices with customers based on market demand and supply with reference to such pricing ratios.

- *Refined products* PetroChina and Sinopec set the wholesale price of gasoline and diesel. The SDPC required the prices to be at least 5.5 per cent lower than the retail prices. Before June 2000, both PetroChina and Sinopec had the freedom to set ex-plant prices every two months. They are also allowed to set wholesale and retail prices for refined products within 5 per cent of the guidance prices published by the SDPC. If PetroChina and Sinopec needed to adjust the retail prices within less than two months, they had to obtain approval from the SDPC and report to the SDPC their retail prices for each province ten days before the pricing changes took effect. The prices set by CNPC and Sinopec also applied to service stations owned by foreign companies and the private sector. No price discrimination was allowed between urban and rural areas within any given province. In fact, the SDPC only revised the retail guidance prices four times between June

1998 and May 2000, despite frequent joint applications from PetroChina and Sinopec for price adjustment to reflect market demand and supply. Prices for special customers such as agriculture, civil aviation, railways, transportation, the armed forces, the police and the national strategic reserves were set by SDPC, which were higher than the ex-plant prices, but lower than the retail prices. Products sold to foreign invested enterprises (FIEs) were based on FOB prices, and for these, FIEs could get an export rebate.

From June 2000, the SDPC started to determine and publish the retail guidance prices for gasoline and diesel on a monthly basis. However, the government has no restrictions on how the companies set the prices for sales of gasoline and diesel between PetroChina and Sinopec, or among the production and business units under PetroChina or Sinopec. Prices for kerosene, heavy oil and wholesale LPG are determined by the companies with reference to the government-formulated retail guidance prices for gasoline. The companies are permitted to set freely the prices for sales of lubricants, asphalt and paraffin wax.

- *Petrochemicals* For petrochemical products, PetroChina and Sinopec determine the prices of all of their petrochemical products except that the prices for urea and synthetic resins for producing agricultural film are determined by the SDPC. Imports of major petrochemicals such as synthetic fibres and synthetic resins account for 30–40 per cent of the domestic demand. Prices of these products in China fluctuate with international prices, especially prices in the Southeast Asian market. Sinopec and PetroChina determine and adjust prices based on the domestic demand and supply, international prices, tariffs, and transportation costs.

DISTRIBUTION: RETAIL AND WHOLESALE

Before 1998, the distribution system for refined oil products in China was divided into provincial, municipal and county levels under the administration of the Ministry of Commerce. They were collectively called 'local petroleum companies' (*difang shiyou gongsi*). In the 1998 reorganisation, these local petroleum companies were merged into either CNPC or Sinopec. CNPC and Sinopec acted as the first-tier wholesalers to supervise the business operations of the second-tier wholesalers, the provincial petroleum companies. The provincial petroleum companies administered the retail service stations. Refiners were allowed to sell their products only to the first-tie wholesalers.

For refined products, only PetroChina and Sinopec have the right to conduct gasoline and diesel wholesale businesses in China. Only domestic companies including Sino–foreign joint ventures, are permitted to engage in retail of gasoline and diesel. Domestic companies can engage in sales and distribution of petrochemicals. Foreign companies are permitted to participate in sales and distribution of petrochemicals only to the extent that the products are produced in China by a facility owned by the foreign companies.

The SETC is responsible for setting import and export quotas for crude oil and refined products. In addition, the MOFTEC issues import and export licences for crude oil and refined products to oil and gas companies once they have obtained import or export quotas from the SETC. PetroChina holds quota and conducts import and export businesses through the China National United Oil Corporation that holds licences. Sinopec has taken back the rights of crude oil import and export from its subordinate companies such as Zhenhai (Chapter 7) and centralised the import and export businesses at Unipec.

Foreign investments

EXPLORATION AND PRODUCTION

Only CNPC and Sinopec have the right to co-operate with foreign companies in onshore crude oil and natural gas exploration and production in China. CNOOC and Sinopec (through its subsidiary Sinopec National Star) have the right to co-operate with foreign companies in offshore crude oil and natural gas exploration and production. MOFTEC approves the production sharing contracts and Sino-foreign equity and co-operative joint venture contracts. Under the Regulations of the People's Republic of China (PRC) on Exploration of Onshore Petroleum Resources in Co-operation with Foreign Enterprises, PetroChina does not have the right to co-operate directly with foreign oil and gas companies on the basis of a production sharing contract. CNPC, however, will sign a PSC with foreign partners and assign to PetroChina all the commercial and operational rights and obligations under the PSC.

Transportation and petrochemicals   PetroChina and Sinopec can establish joint ventures with minority foreign shareholdings in pipeline transportation, oil storage and oil jetties. However, PetroChina's west to east gas transmission project has been granted preferential policies by the government so that there is no limitation on foreign shareholdings. For refineries, ethylene and PVC resins production, joint ventures with foreign participation must be majority-owned by Chinese people.

Procurement

E-COMMERCE

Both PetroChina and Sinopec are moving quickly to set up platforms for online procurement. In August 2000, PetroChina, CNPC and Hutchison Whampoa signed a memorandum of understanding with the intent to establish a business to business online trading platform for oil and gas products. The online trading platform began operation in July 2001. PetroChina has an annual procurement bill of 50 billion yuan, 20 per cent of which is expected to be procured through the online trading platform. If realised, this could save 5 per cent of the total procurement cost. Sinopec's e-commerce system began operation in September 2000. The system consists of two platforms: one for petrochemical product marketing and the other for material procurement. By the end of 2000, the petrochemical product marketing system had 460 registered members and provided over 1,000 petrochemical products in seven major categories such as synthetic resins, synthetic fibres and synthetic rubbers. With over 700 customers, total online trade value was 15.7 billion yuan from August 2000 to the end of 2001 (Sinopec website, 2002). The material procurement system is intended to unify and standardise Sinopec's procurement process to reduce costs. By the end of 2001, this system has over 1,800 registered suppliers, offering 80,000 products for procurement. Total material procurement value through the e-commerce system from August 2000 to the end of 2001 was 8.1 billion yuan (Sinopec website, 2002).

Financial control

CAPITAL INVESTMENT

PetroChina and Sinopec are able to make capital investment in oil and gas exploration and development free of government approval. However, for investment in other projects, the two companies must obtain approval from the government authorities. New investment projects exceeding 50 million yuan must be approved by the SDPC and investment in renovation and expansion projects exceeding 50 million yuan must be approved by the SETC. In addition, borrowing from foreign banks and foreign governments for financing capital investment must be approved by the SDPC and the State Administration of Foreign Exchange.

Within the company, PetroChina and Sinopec each has been eliminating the practice of permitting individual plants to make investment decisions. The decision power has been centralised to the corporate level in order to achieve consistency between investment and overall corporate strategy. All investment decisions over 50 million yuan in exploration and development, and 30 million yuan in petrochemicals, must obtain approval from the headquarters.

FINANCIAL REPORTING SYSTEM

From June 2000, PetroChina started a three-stage strategy to develop a new financial management information system. The first stage is to set up a uniform financial reporting system. By October 2001, PetroChina had unified the accounting policy across the whole company, standardised the coding system and reporting process, and clarified management responsibility at various tiers of the headquarters, business divisions and branch companies. The second stage is to centralise the financial systems in oil fields, refineries and marketing and distribution companies. The third stage is to integrate the whole financial management information system within the entire company. This is a huge task, and one that is highly significant for the establishment of a modern enterprise system in China's large corporations.

Information technology system

PETROCHINA

PetroChina's information system is fragmented. Individual department, subsidiaries, branches, oil fields and plants have developed information systems for their own use. The systems do not have integrated application sub-systems to process and control different categories of financial and operating data. Automated data provision between corporate headquarters and subsidiaries is very limited. PetroChina has reported that it is working with Pricewaterhouse-Coopers Consultants (Shanghai) to formulate information technology development plans in constructing an integrated enterprise resource planning (ERP) system and electronic business system (PetroChina, 2001: 72). In 2001, PetroChina planned to spend 165 million yuan for constructing an information technology system (PetroChina, 2001: 71).

THE ERP SYSTEM OF SINOPEC

To facilitate corporate centralisation, Sinopec is developing a complete ERP system that will integrate information between corporate headquarters, business segments and production plants. The ERP system includes data and a platform for financial information, raw materials, equipment management, a production plan, and marketing and distribution data for the entire company. Sinopec planned to spend 360 million yuan in 2001 to continue the construction of the ERP system (Sinopec, 2001: 84). The ERP system is expected to be fully established by 2004.

Performance monitoring

PetroChina and Sinopec both have pioneered the implementation of performance contracts with their senior and middle managers. Performance contracts consist of key performance indicators (KPIs) such as net income, return on capital and cost reduction targets. PetroChina has signed performance contracts with more than 300 senior and middle managers and Sinopec has signed performance contracts with its 480 senior and middle managers. The compensation of these managers is linked with their achievement of the contracted performance targets. The compensation structure of the senior and middle managers in PetroChina and Sinopec is similar. It has three components: basic salary, performance bonuses and stock appreciation rights (SARs). According to the law, companies are not permitted to repurchase and hold their own shares for offering stock options. SARs entitle the recipients to receive cash payments when the company's share price rises above the exercise price granted in the SAR. For example, the exercise price of the SAR with Sinopec is the initial public offering price of the company's H-share at HK$1.61 per share (Sinopec, 2001).

The weight of each of the three components varies with the Chairman, President, Vice Presidents and Department General Managers. For example, the total remuneration of the Chairman of PetroChina consists of 30 per cent basic salary and 70 per cent SARs. The remuneration of the President and the Vice Presidents consists of 25 per cent basic salary, 60 per cent SARs and 15 per cent performance bonus. The remuneration for Department General Managers consists of a 25 per cent basic salary, 50 per cent SARs and 25 per cent performance bonus.

Summary

The restructuring of China's oil and petrochemical industry in 1998 established CNPC and Sinopec Group respectively as 'the firm' for developing China's oil and petrochemical industry. The further restructuring and flotation of core businesses was intended to eliminate the autonomy of strong subordinate enterprises. The headquarters of PetroChina and Sinopec both realised that centralisation of capital investment and financial control was essential in constructing competitive large multi-plant corporations. It was also crucial to implement the company's policies and monitor the subsidiaries' performance. Both PetroChina and Sinopec began to adopt the performance contract system above the level of middle manager. They are establishing integrated information technology systems to facilitate this centralising process. However, PetroChina and Sinopec face complicated and difficult tasks on two fronts. First, they need to establish their credibility as business entities that are independent of their parents in the market and create shareholder value. Second, they must work hard in the organisational integration process to ensure the central control of the headquarters over their subsidiaries. Neither of these is an easy task.

Where is the headquarters?

We have seen the institutional evolution of China's oil and petrochemical industry from the 1950s to the year 2000. In the course of five decades, the industry experienced three major stages of development in relation to the function of the headquarters. During the first stage from the 1950s to the 1970s, China's oil industry developed in the fashion of a military 'massive campaign'. The objective was to develop oil production as fast as possible to support national economic development. After the former Soviet Union's withdrawal of assistance, the pressing need was to become self-sufficient in oil supply. Under the leadership of the State Council, the Ministry of Petroleum Industry was the administrative headquarters of China's oil industry. It made strategic decisions as to the location for exploration and development. It planned the campaign and organised human and material resources nation-wide to support the campaign. It undertook and co-ordinated the production, transportation and marketing of oil and oil products based on the overall national plan formulated by the State Planning Commission. It negotiated investment funds from the government and allocated them to its subordinate petroleum administrative bureaux all over the country. The various PAB were production units responsible for carrying out the production and investment plan. The legacy of the 'massive campaign' model is an army of 'oil men' with a strong sense of responsibility for the collective and the country. They are highly disciplined and very skilful in organisation. They are able to mobilise fast to achieve their goals.

China began to liberalise its post-Mao economy in the late 1970s. In the second stage of development from the 1980s to 1997, China's oil and petrochemical industry experienced significant institutional change. In 1983, China Petrochemical Corporation was created on the merger of assets from the refining and petrochemical section of the Ministry of Petroleum Industry and some of the chemical and synthetic fibre manufacturing enterprises under the Ministry of Chemical Industry and the Ministry of Textile Industry. The Ministry of Petroleum Industry was transformed into China National Petroleum Corporation in 1988. The function of the headquarters of CNPC and Sinopec in this period were two-fold: government functions and the business functions. Created as state-owned companies, CNPC and Sinopec still carried government administrative responsibilities for the industry such as formulating technological standards and devising environmental regulations. The most important function of organising production was controlled by the government. The headquarters of the two companies carried out the government's plans related to resource allocation and production, and there was mutual co-operation to ensure the implementation of the plans. CNPC and Sinopec were entrusted by the State Council to manage the state's assets and were made responsible for generating revenue to hand over to the government treasury. Moreover, in carrying out business functions, they did not have the rights over product pricing, marketing and capital investment above 500 million yuan (CNPC) and 200 millian yuan (Sinopec). These business decision-making rights were tightly controlled by the central government. In this sense, CNPC and Sinopec were 'administrative entities' rather than 'economic entities'. During the same period, enterprise reform in China stressed the enhancement of enterprise autonomy at the level of the production unit. The subordinate enterprises of CNPC and Sinopec were able to retain a greatly increased share of profits. They had the autonomy to make investments not only in core businesses but also in diversified businesses. They were able to finance expansion through bank loans and bonds and were responsible for debt repayment. They were listed in the domestic and international capital markets, which reduced the ownership rights of CNPC and Sinopec over them. They negotiated and set up joint ventures with multinational companies. In the case of Sinopec, strong subordinate enterprises initiated mergers and acquisitions in order to increase their market share of particular products. The functions of the CNPC and Sinopec headquarters in financial control, performance monitoring, procurement, and R&D were weak. This put CNPC and Sinopec into an awkward situation. In executing government functions, the headquarters of CNPC and Sinopec were simply an extension of various government administrative responsibilities. In exercising business functions, the headquarters of CNPC and Sinopec did not have the rights to fix product prices, to decide capital investment above a certain amount, and to market their product. At the same time, they did not have effective control over their subordinate enterprises even in the most important aspect of financial affairs and performance monitoring. Their exercised their control over subordinate enterprises mainly through the appointment of senior manager in subordinate enterprises.

During the 1990s, as China further liberalised its economy, growing autonomy at the enterprise level caused tension between the headquarters and the subordinate enterprises. Under CNPC, Daqing, the largest oil-field in China with an annual production volume of 50 million tonnes, became increasingly ambitious for development as an independent entity across the value chain from upstream to downstream (Chapter 7). Under Sinopec, Zhenhai, the second largest refinery in China with an annual primary distillation capacity of 8.5 million tonnes in 1997, also aspired to become the largest refiner in East Asia and to expand its existing petrochemical businesses through mergers and acquisitions (Chapter 7). The question that arose was: 'where is the headquarters?'

The reorganisation of China's oil and petrochemical industry in 1998 demonstrated that the headquarters of CNPC and Sinopec respectively had won the struggle to become 'the headquarters' leading the industry's development with the support of the Chinese government. Through the 1998 reorganisation, CNPC and Sinopec each became an integrated oil and petrochemical company. The subsequent restructuring for flotation in 1999 and 2000 established the 'one-tier' legal person system and dashed the aspirations for independence of the subordinate enterprises. CNPC and Sinopec Group each created a 'child company' – PetroChina and Sinopec – that amalgamated the core businesses and was floated on the international market. PetroChina and Sinopec have obtained from the government rights over product pricing, production, and investment in core businesses. They are centralising their control over their branch companies in respect to capital investment, finance, and marketing. They are investing in the establishment of integrated information technology systems within the company to facilitate the centralisation process. They have begun to monitor the performance of managers through KPI-based performance contracts. The task of centralisation is formidable, considering the enormous autonomy the subordinate enterprises had come to enjoy by the 1990s.

However, the question of 'where is the headquarters?' still remains. PetroChina and Sinopec are independent legal persons able to conduct their own business but the degree of independence remains unclear. CNPC has non-core businesses as well as social services employing more than 800,000 people, most of which are hugely loss-making. The non-core businesses and social services of Sinopec Group employ over 600,000 people and none of them made a profit in 1999. As the controlling shareholder of their respective 'child companies', CNPC and Sinopec Group may influence the determination of the level of dividend payment in favour of their own financial situation. They may have the power to intervene on important issues from business strategy to the appointment of senior executive management. On the other hand, PetroChina and Sinopec may struggle to obtain more resources for their own development. For the respective 'mother companies', PetroChina and Sinoipec Group are just one (albeit a highly important) part of their business interests. Each of them is seeking to develop other majority-owned floated companies in the oil and petrochemical sector, as well as in other sectors. In late 2001, PetroChina announced it would establish a department in charge of the company's expansion into the international exploration and development market. However, Ma Fucai, Chairman of PetroChina and President of CNPC, stressed the strategy of overall development of CNPC:

> We will construct PetroChina into a 'lean' company with high efficiency, standardised operation, and international competitiveness. Meanwhile, for the other enterprises existing in CNPC, we will build up a group of competitive regional service companies and specialised technology companies that are able to operate independently and are responsible for their own profit and loss. We must sustain increases in domestic oil and gas production; meanwhile, we must accelerate overseas oil development.
>
> (quoted in *China Petroleum*, February 2001)

In sum, the institutional structure of China's oil and petrochemical industry remains uncertain.

The next chapter will examine two cases at Daqing under PetroChina and Zhenhai under Sinopec, and analyse their relationship with the headquarters of CNPC and Sinopec, respectively.

7 From production unit to autonomous enterprise and back to production unit
Daqing and Zhenhai

The institutional transformation of China's oil and petrochemical industry has affected the position of individual production enterprises in many ways. This chapter examines cases at Daqing and Zhenhai. Daqing, developed from the late 1950s, is the largest oil production region in China and Zhenhai, developed from the early 1970s, is China's second largest refinery in the late 1990s. Each of the enterprises developed a strong sense of corporate identity and high ambitions. Each of the two companies struggled for business autonomy during the 1990s. As a result of the restructuring and flotation of PetroChina and Sinopec, the position of each of the enterprises changed drastically from an increasingly autonomous enterprise into a production unit within a large corporate entity.

Daqing

Daqing Petroleum Administration Bureau (known as Daqing Oilfield or simply 'Daqing') is 150 kilometres to the northwest of Harbin, the capital city of Heilongjiang Province in northeastern China. A well-constructed motorway connects Daqing with Harbin and Binzhou Railway runs right through the middle of the oil production region. The oil region covers an area of 10,000 square kilometres, 138 kilometres from north to the south and 73 kilometres from the east to the west. In the late 1990s, there were nineteen oil fields in Daqing producing 50 million tonnes of crude oil per annum.

Exploration activities started in Daqing in 1955 and oil was discovered in 1959. At the beginning of 1960s, the 'massive campaign' was launched to develop oil fields in Daqing. Under the leadership of the Ministry of Petroleum Industry, more than 40,000 people were mobilised nation-wide to Daqing in three months. More than 500 manufacturing plants were organised nation-wide to supply machines and equipment for Daqing and more than 200 research and design institutes to provide technology to Daqing (He, 1999). In three years, Daqing built up crude oil production capacity of 6 million tonnes. This enabled China to become self-sufficient in oil supply at a time when China faced enormous economic difficulties. The discovery and production of oil in Daqing greatly enhanced China's confidence for industrialisation. Daqing was selected by Mao Zedong as the model for the state-owned enterprises in China and was regarded as a 'flagship' among New China's industrial sectors.

Not only does Daqing have political importance, it also has been the biggest oil field in China in terms of proven reserves and annual output. Annual production of crude oil in Daqing remained stable at 50 million tonnes for twenty-four years after 1976. By 1999, its proved crude oil reserves were 5983.3 million barrels, accounting for 55.6% of CNPC's total proved oil reserves. In each year from 1988 to 1998, Daqing's annual production represented approximately 50% of CNPC's total annual output. In 1997, it generated revenues of 50 billion yuan and post-tax profits of 6.5 billion yuan, accounting for 30 per cent of CNPC's total revenue and 63 per cent of CNPC's post-tax profit (CNPC, 1998).

Ambition

Over the years since its establishment, Daqing developed a powerful sense of corporate identity associated with being the number one enterprise in China. People working there are immensely proud of its history. They are proud of being 'Daqing people' (*Daqing ren*). Daqing was developed from scratch under extremely difficult conditions. The first generation of workers endured unimaginable hardships in order to achieve the goal of national self-sufficiency in crude oil and developing the nation's industry. Successive generations strived hard and managed to sustain annual production at a stable level of 50 million tonnes. In 1996, Daqing was ranked China's largest state-owned enterprise in terms of revenue. Its revenue of $5.3 billion was far ahead of the second-ranked enterprise, the China Northeast Electricity Corporation Group (SSB, 1997: 277). Daqing is deeply proud of being the 'pillar' of China's industrialisation and of its enormous long-term contribution to the national finances.

Daqing had legal person status in early the 1990s. By the late 1990s, it had grown into a large and diversified company. Like most large state-owned companies in China, Daqing has a huge system of social functions such as education, medical care, and security services. It provides its employees with a 'cradle to grave' welfare system. It primarily engaged in oil and gas exploration and production activities, with relatively small downstream oil refining and petrochemical production activities. Daqing had a group of service companies providing services in exploration, development, drilling and oil-field construction. Daqing's research and development system included two colleges and three research institutes, which had developed new recovery technologies to sustain production. Daqing had established crude oil pipelines of an aggregated length of more than 900 kilometres, linking it to the ports of Dalian and Qinghuangdao in Bohai Bay. In 1996, under the leadership of its 'visionary' leader Ding Guiming, Daqing carried out a restructuring programme with the ambition of developing Daqing into a multinational integrated oil company that could compete with leading multinational oil companies. Instead of just being an 'oil field', Daqing aspired to become an 'enterprise' with the autonomy to expand into the world market. Daqing strongly believed that their development was closely linked to the nation's industrial development and ultimately to the national interest (Ding Guiming, interview, December 1999).

Struggle for autonomy and independence

The 'big contract' system adopted in 1981 increased China's oil production. However, China's oil enterprises started to suffer increasing losses from the middle of the seventh five-year plan (1986–90). The year 1988 saw aggregate losses for the whole industry. Problems such as insufficient investment in exploration and development, huge levels of debt, inadequate R/P ratio (reserve to production ratio) became increasingly serious.

During the ten years from 1988 to 1998, the average cost of crude oil increased approximately by 600 yuan per tonne with an average annual rate of increase of 22 per cent. In 1998, CNPC's crude oil cost was estimated at $11.6 per barrel, compared with the international oil prices of $9 per barrel at its lowest point. Though domestic oil price had risen in 1994, in 1995, with the exception of Daqing, Shengli, Liaohe, and Xinjiang, there were still several enterprises that made losses despite selling their crude oil at the grade II oil prices of 1,240 yuan per tonnes, much higher than the world oil price at that time. In 1999, more than ten enterprises incurred losses of approximately 6.5 billion yuan.

From the mid-1980s, China's enterprise reform stressed the autonomy of the individual production enterprise in conducting businesses including retaining profits and making investments. During the 1990s, facing the critical situation of a steep decline in profits, CNPC adopted the policy of transforming oil enterprises into 'legal person' entities responsible for their own profit and losses as well as for their growth. However, Daqing felt deeply let down by CNPC's policy of giving loss-making enterprises autonomy rather than supporting profitable enterprises to grow stronger. For example, loss-making enterprises could get subsidies for oil production from CNPC. Moreover, they were allowed to sell their oil at grade II prices or market prices and were granted autonomy in conducting businesses. For the profitable Daqing, CNPC required it to 'hand over' money above the agreed amount. In 1998, Daqing handed over more than 8.6 billion yuan to CNPC. In the first six months of 1999, Daqing handed over more than 5.0 billion yuan to CNPC. Daqing argued that this mechanism of 'controlling the strong and letting go the weak' was no different from the 'iron bowl' system under the command economy. Moreover, CNPC had no control on capital spending. Subordinate enterprises competed with each other for funds from CNPC's headquarters and spend them without any limit on the returns from the investments. According to Daqing, this mechanism encouraged spending money but not creating value through careful investment. Furthermore, as China became increasingly integrated into the world economy, competition from global oil companies was bound to intensify. Daqing was fully aware of the fact that the oil multinationals have far greater capabilities in technology, economies of scale, financial strength and branding, and possess greater all-round efficiency.

Daqing's struggle for autonomy and independence brought it into conflict with CNPC's headquarters. Daqing's journey to transform itself into a 'real firm' was fraught with difficulties. In the early 1980s, Daqing was the first large state-owned enterprise that undertook reforms in infrastructure construction, material supplies and project management, as well as in its financial and compensation system. It experimented with the two-party responsibility system (*jia yi fang ze ren zhi*) and with investment contracts. However, these reforms were strongly criticised by the Ministry of Petroleum Industry. Despite the objections from the top, Daqing managed to keep to this reform path. In 1988, Daqing proposed that they should be allowed to operate independently following international practices. It promised to maintain the production volume and the amount of profits handed over to the government. In addition, it was willing to hand over to the government an additional 15 billion yuan, equivalent to the amount of profits handed over by the whole Sinopec every year. Again, this proposal was turned down. In 1992, the Production Office of the State Council (the predecessor of the State Economic and Trade Commission) started to set up fifty-five experimental enterprise groups across the country with core enterprises to be listed on the domestic or international stock market. Daqing was placed at the top of the first batch proposed by the Production Office. But CNPC rejected the proposal to get Daqing listed. CNPC stressed the idea of retaining 'unity' (*zheng ti xing*) of the company. The argument was that CNPC had certain governmental administrative functions and should keep the onshore oil industry firmly under its uniform administration. In the following effort to get Daqing as a pilot enterprise to establish a modern enterprise system, it failed again. Instead, supported by CNPC, Dagang, was given the opportunity. It was not even mentioned in the second batch for setting up enterprise groups organised by the SETC in 1995.

Daqing perceived itself as having great political importance in China's industrial reform. As the largest enterprise in China with revenues of more than 50 billion, Daqing felt that its mission was to lead the reform of China's state-owned enterprises. The battle for independence reached its climax in 1996 when Daqing, led by Ding Guiming, explicitly expressed its wish to become an integrated multinational company and started its own internal restructuring programme. Daqing's ambition was a direct confrontation with the authority of CNPC headquarters. CNPC consistently stressed that, because oil is a special natural resource and is of strategic importance to the country, the oil industry must be under direct state control, of which CNPC is the representative.

Internal restructuring: 1996

RESTRUCTURING GOALS

In the mid-1990s, Daqing made explicit its goal to construct itself into a multinational oil company with integrated upstream and downstream businesses as well as businesses in trading and financial service. Daqing was deeply concerned about its own survival and development, and it strongly wished to expand into downstream businesses and into the domestic and international market. Otherwise, Daqing realised it would be 'defeated' sooner or later in competition. Therefore, Daqing needed to restructure itself and establish the business model of a large global oil company.

Daqing's restructuring goals had seven aspects.

- *Daqing's position* Daqing should be a firm instead of being just a production site. A production site will be inevitably abandoned when the oil reserves run out whereas a vertically integrated firm with other businesses related to the oil industry can sustain development. Daqing should be reorganised into Daqing Petroleum (Group) Company, a joint stock company with limited liabilities, with CNPC as its controlling shareholder:

  > We must achieve three goals of *wen chan* (stablise production), *fa zhan* (development), and *gai ge* (reform). *Wen chan* refers to maintaining annual production at 50 million tonnes; *fa zhan* refers to entering the world market and increasing revenue from 170 billion yuan to 350–500 billion; *gai ge* refers to integration of production and trading.
  >
  > (Ding Guiming, interview, December 1999)

- *Business structure* Daqing should transform its business structure with oil as its sole business stream into an integrated structure with both upstream and downstream businesses, and should develop businesses in trading and financial services. Daqing should make oil business the core for development both at home and abroad.

- *Management system* A 'parent and child company' (*muzi gongsi*) system should be established. Daqing Petroleum Corporation Ltd should be the parent company engaging in the core businesses of oil and gas and be responsible for capital management and investment activities. Under the parent company, four branch companies should conduct businesses in oil and gas exploration, oil and gas development, refining and petrochemical enterprises. Subsidiaries (child companies) are those specialised companies engaging in businesses closely related to the core businesses and those companies should provide services in new areas such as trading, financial services, engineering services and public services. To maximise financial returns, investment decisions, financial control, purchasing, sales and marketing should be centralised.

- *Market* Daqing believed that it should operate in the market economy, but did not believe that there should be competition within Daqing itself. Daqing believed that it should organise its production in response to market conditions, and should become a unified entity, mobilising all its resources to compete more effectively in the market.

- *Responsibility of the top management team* The top management team should be responsible for devising key policies for long-term development, and for formulating strategies and plans to ensure sustainable development.

- *Human resources* Human resources are vital for Daqing's development, and talents should be nurtured for the twenty-first century. In pursuit of this aim, Daqing should build a company culture as a cohesive force to unify the whole company.

THREE STAGES OF RESTRUCTURING

The first phase was from the second part of 1996 to the end of 1998. During this phase, Daqing PAB was to be reorganised into Daqing Petroleum Group. Branch companies were set up for developing core businesses in oil and gas exploration and development. The Petrochemical General Works was set up for refining and petrochemical businesses. Technical service company groups were organised to provide support for oil and gas exploration and production. The Material and Equipment Company and General Sales Company was established to centralise purchasing and sales. The Business Development General Company was set up to look after the diversified businesses. The second stage began in 1999. Daqing obtained support from CNPC to undertake ownership reforms. It was to be restructured into a company with limited liabilities. The third stage began in early 2000. Daqing Group Company was to be transformed into a joint stock company with limited liabilities. The company's ownership was to be diversified by means of alliances, mergers and acquisitions.

Up until July 1997, the restructuring process was progressing well. The twenty-three management departments in the headquarters of Daqing had been reduced to just ten. Ten specialised companies were set up. Supporting and service businesses and social functions had been separated from the core businesses of oil, gas and petrochemicals, and transferred to specialised companies. The reorganisation involved more than 1,500 units, 105,000 employees and assets worth 6 billion yuan.

Development strategies

Ding Guiming believed that an industrial entrepreneur should deeply understand the industry and management as well as being an investor with strategic vision. An industrial entrepreneur should have 'strategic insight, systematic thinking capability, engineering awareness, and practical experience to apply theory to technology and production'. An industrial entrepreneur should also have integrity of character. Ding Guiming established concrete plans for strengthening Daqing to prepare for further business expansion. Plans were devised to set up a company intranet, a science park in Daqing, and to obtain an ISO-9000 certificate for the company. Moreover, Daqing was to create a new corporate culture characterised by science and technology, but based on its traditional spirit. The main development strategies were as follows:

MARKET DEVELOPMENT PLAN

Daqing realised that the market for its crude oil and oil products was crucial for its growth. The domestic markets that Daqing targeted were the following:

- *Northeast China* Daqing planned to build a pipeline to transport refined oil products from Daqing, through Harbin, Shenyang, and Tianjin to Beijing. The refined products pipeline would help to market refined products in these areas and prepare Daqing for expanding into downstream businesses through mergers and acquisition. The logic was that compared with an oil pipeline, a refined oil product pipeline is more economical since the diameter of the latter is smaller. Moreover, refined oil product is more profitable than crude oil.
- *East China* This area covers Jiangsu, Zhejiang, Fujian, Shanghai and is economically the most developed area in China. Daqing had built oil tanks in Zapu Port to store crude oil from Dalian and Qinghuangdao ports. The oil tanks would serve as the base for marketing crude oil along the Grand Canal, covering the eastern part of China.
- *Changjiang River area* Daqing invested $6 million in the construction of a port in Chongqing.
- *Pearl River Area* This area includes Guangdong, Guangxi, and the southwest part of China. Daqing had built a refinery in Beihai, Guangxi to process crude oil from the Middle East.

HUMAN RESOURCES

Daqing realised the importance of the 'battle for talent'. It planned to recruit first-class personnel from prestigious universities such as Beijing and Tsinghua universities. Daqing's educational institutions were to be changed into training centres that could provide regular training programmes for the 280,000 employees.

MERGERS AND ACQUISITION

According to Ding Guiming, there are four prerequisites for successful mergers: sufficient capital, professional management practice, professional managers, and a market-oriented corporate culture. The top leadership of Daqing emphasised the growth that could be achieved by merging with or taking over other strong companies 'through the market' and 'following companies' wishes', in order to meet the business interests of the merging entities. Daqing planned to merge with other strong companies rather than with weak companies.

Daqing planned a series of large-scale mergers with other strong Chinese companies. It held talks with Shanghai Petrochemical Company (SPCC) in Jinshan, Shanghai. Around one-third of SPCC's crude oil was supplied by Daqing and Daqing's low sulphur oil was suitable for the refining facilities in Jinshan. For Daqing, Jinshan's location would have provided Daqing with a base in the coastal area with the highest income in the country, possessing a huge and highly dynamic market. Also the base in Shanghai would permit low transport costs to supply other highly developed parts of China. In addition, Daqing held talks with Yanshan Petrochemicals in Beijing to explore the possibility for a merger with the objective of developing downstream businesses. It even held talks with China's largest automobile companies, Yiqi and Erqi, with the objective of establishing joint ventures to co-operate in the development of high quality lubricants.

In retailing, Daqing planned to develop a network of service stations along highways in the coastal areas. It planned to take over developing high margin retail stores along with service stations through mergers and acquisitions. In transportation, Daqing planned to develop an oil tanker fleet of its own. It held talks with Dalian port, through which Daqing's oil is exported, with a view to merger. As we have noted, it invested in setting up a new port in Chongqing along the Changjiang River. In oil trading, Daqing even contemplated merging with Sinochem in order to provide Daqing with a direct link to international markets. Moreover, Daqing devised strategies for overseas exploration and development, and planned to develop its business globally.

R&D

Daqing has developed new technologies of 'third-time oil extraction' (*sanci caiyou*), which grew out of a long-term programme of scientific research. Daqing developed a distribution structure of oil-extracting machines, with 600 metres between rows and 500 hundred metres between each machine, aiming to sustain oil production at Daqing for another fifty years. In Daqing's initial development period, the projected total recoverable oil was 1 billion tonnes. By utilising the 'second-time oil extraction' (*erci caiyou*) technology of water injection, the recoverable oil in 1995 had reached two billion tonnes. However, by utilising the 'third-time oil extraction' technology of polymer injection, the recoverable oil in Daqing was projected to reach three billion tonnes. Daqing planned to further develop its technology in exploration and production to sustain its development.

SERVICE COMPANIES AND SOCIAL FUNCTIONS

Daqing planned to separate gradually the oil-field 'technical service' companies from the core businesses and establish a service contract relationship between the core businesses and the service companies. Daqing also planned to transfer its schools, hospitals and other social service activities to local government.

Defeat

Daqing's 1996 restructuring was resolutely rejected by CNPC. The headquarters gave a blunt message to Ding Guiming that he would be treated as a criminal if he led Daqing to independence. Only after fifteen months as the Director of

Daqing, Ding Guiming was moved to CNPC headquarters and beame the assistant to the President of CNPC. Shortly afterwards, Ding Guiming was appointed as one of the 'special inspectors' sent by the State Council to monitor large state-owned enterprises under the administration of the State Council. Ding Guiming left the oil industry together with his ambition to build up a internationally competitive Chinese oil company.

Following the abortion of Daqing's restructuring programme, CNPC announced its restructuring programme in 1999, which triggered massive resentment in Daqing. The argument now boiled down to two issues: Daqing's legal person status and who should be floated, Daqing or a new company created by grouping together the core businesses of the whole of CNPC.

LEGAL PERSON STATUS

In CNPC's restructuring programme, Daqing would be deprived of its legal person status, as would any other PAB under CNPC. Daqing found it unacceptable that it should lose its legal person status, which ought to have guaranteed its independent development by law. Without the legal person status, Daqing would become merely a regional branch company or a production unit with no possibilities for self-development. The strategy for sustainable development no longer made sense.

It seems at first sight that CNPC's restructuring programme was similar to Daqing's 1996/97 restructuring programme. However, in essence, they were completely different as the idea of which entity constitutes the firm had been totally changed. CNPC now became *the firm*. For Daqing, without their legal person status, their initiatives and ambitions were at stake.

Another concern was that the brand of 'Daqing' would became useless and meaningless without the legal person status. Daqing pointed out that the elimination of Daqing's brand name served no one's interests including that of CNPC. It was strongly argued that the decline and disappearance of Daqing would be a disaster for China's oil industry.

WHO WILL BE FLOATED?

Along with their fight to retain their legal person status, Daqing argued that the approach to creating a new company that grouped together the core businesses from each enterprise by administrative measures might be fatal. This was because the new company would not have a 'soul', and the challenge to integrating this company would be immense. In the meantime, Daqing proposed to set up Daqing Petroleum Corporation Ltd as a joint stock company with limited liabilities and get it floated. Daqing's core business assets would be more attractive to investors and Daqing could capitalise on its intangible assets. The floated Daqing could serve as the core for development and gain resources to merge or acquire other companies to further build up competitive strength. Daqing wished to see CNPC be transformed into a government supervising body rather than a firm.

The reality

CNPC responded to Daqing's argument by stressing that the oil business was of national strategic importance and its reorganisation must follow the state's command. It was pointed out that the restructuring programme had been decided by the state (*guojia*) and that CNPC had been chosen by the state to reorganise the oil industry. Moreover, CNPC argued that Daqing's assets were those of the state and its people, and that it must follow the command of the state in the disposition of those assets. Daqing's fight resulted in the following arrangement: the core businesses of Daqing formed Daqing Oilfield Corporation Ltd (Figure 7.1), and, as a special exception, was granted legal person status within the newly-created PetroChina (Chapter 6). However, Daqing's proposal to create and subsequently float Daqing Petroleum Corporation Ltd. was vetoed.

THE FLOATED DAQING: CORE BUSINESSES

By 1999, Daqing's proven crude oil reserves were 5983.3 million barrels, accounting for 55.6% of PetroChina's's total proven oil reserves. In the first nine months of 1999, Daqing produced 2.97 million barrels, accounting for 52.3% of PetroChina's output (PetroChina, 2000). In the 1999 internal reorganisation of CNPC, Daqing Oilfield Corporation was created by grouping together twenty-four enterprises separated from Daqing PAB and engaged in the core business activities of exploration and development, refining and marketing, chemicals, scientific research and design. With net fixed assets estimated at 56.8 billion yuan ($6.8 billion) and 106,000 employees, it is regarded as a 'child company' (*zi gong si*) with legal person status but wholly owned and controlled by PetroChina. A senior official in Daqing commented: 'The "legal person" is just of purely nominal significance. This is a political arrangement.' Legal person status does not guarantee freedom in conducting businesses. Daqing Oilfield Corporation is no different from a regional branch company under the tight control of PetroChina. PetroChina has achieved centralised power in financial management, capital expenditure and business planning.

THE RELATIONSHIP WITH PETROCHINA

- *Assets* As part of CNPC's 1999 restructuring, Daqing's assets were divided into two parts. The core assets of Daqing, which is now the Daqing Oilfield Corporation, were owned and controlled by PetroChina, whereas the non-core assets of Daqing remained in CNPC. In 1999, of a total workforce of 292,000 in Daqing, about one-third were employed by Daqing Oilfield Corporation Ltd and the rest of the workforce were with the non-core businesses in CNPC. Although Daqing Oilfield Corporation was granted a legal person status, PetroChina took full control of its assets. It turned out that Daqing Oilfield Corporation did not have the ownership of its own assets, which, according to China's Company Law, should be guaranteed by

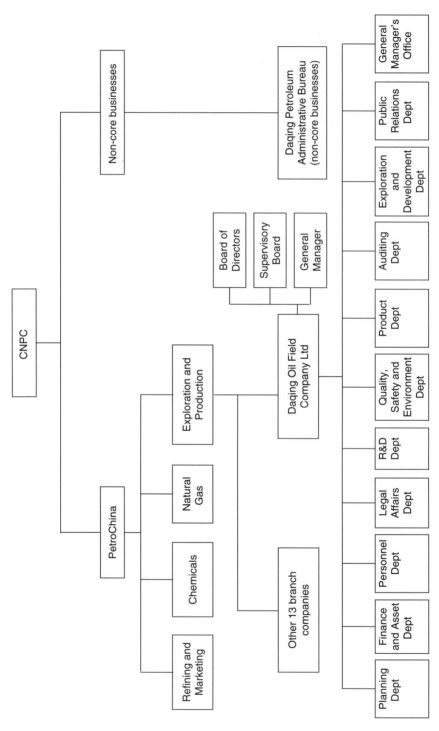

Figure 7.1 Daqing within PetroChina and CNPC, 2000.

legal person status. It was very difficult for people in Daqing to accept the fact that Daqing's core assets would become a 'mere production plant' within PetroChina with no autonomy in management and investment. One senior manager termed it 'quiet transfer of property rights' from Daqing to PetroChina. Another manager was concerned about the awkward position of Daqing Workers' Representative Congress who represented employees in the unified Daqing before CNPC's 1999 restructuring. He pointed out that the Workers' Representative Congress would no longer have the power to overturn any decisions from PetroChina that would not favour the workers' interests.

- *Planning* Production and profit targets are set by PetroChina. Daqing's primary task is to produce crude oil and gas. The refining and chemical businesses will be further consolidated within PetroChina and their future is uncertain. In 2000, Daqing was required to hand over 32.2 billion yuan (approximately $3.9 billion), more than half of the total profit target of PetroChina. The annual profit growth rate and rate of return on capital are set at 10% and 10.2% respectively.
- *Investment* PetroChina devises investment targets each year. In 2000, the total sum of investment was 50 billion yuan ($6 billion), of which 12 billion yuan ($1.6 billion) was invested in Daqing. Daqing was not allowed to exceed this total investment amount and every project invested in by Daqing needed to be reported to PetroChina. Investment in exploration and development that is more than 50 million yuan ($6 million) must be approved from PetroChina. Refining investment above 30 million yuan ($3.7 million) must be approved.
- *Finance* PetroChina has centralised power in finance. It has a single settlement account for all branch companies, which are required to follow the same rule. In 2000, the oil price for account settlement was set at $16.5 per barrel. Any profit that arose from prices rising above $16.5 per barrel had to be handed over to PetroChina. As a special consideration, Daqing has the right to set aside statutory surplus reserves (SSR) but not statutory public welfare funds (PWF), both of which are appropriated from a company's after-tax profit.

Non-core businesses

The remaining enterprises in Daqing include the non-core businesses (Figure 7.1) in the area of technical service, manufacturing supporting services, diversified businesses and social functions. There are approximately 186,000 employees remaining in Daqing's non-core businesses, many of whose companies are close to bankruptcy. CNPC is devising programmes to reorganise these non-core businesses but the pressing matter for Daqing now is how to give its people a job with a secure income to live on.

The separation of the oil and gas businesses from Daqing came as a blow to many people in the remaining businesses, most of which were plunged suddenly into a very difficult situation. There have already been companies failing to pay wages for half a year. People felt they now had lost the profitable oil businesses to back them up. The realisation that Daqing had been broken up proved very difficult for them to accept and the subject became highly emotional. CNPC provided a three-year phase-out period for these remaining enterprises, which meant these enterprises would be fully exposed to market competition after 2002. There would be no protection or subsidies in terms of related transactions within the same group. In Daqing in 2000, related transactions were still carried out under administrative orders. It was estimated that the ratio of work available to the capacity of the remaining businesses was 95 per cent in 2000; however, the ratio was projected to be 50 per cent for 2001. The construction group had businesses worth one to two billion yuan and just broke even. The power plant was operating at less than full capacity. The water plant still made a profit at a price of 3.5 yuan per tonnes, compared with the price of water supplied to households at 1.1 yuan per tonnes. There was tremendous pressure from the core businesses to decrease the water price. Moreover, the water consumption by the oil fields was declining drastically due to the decreasing activities in well drilling.

Most of the remaining enterprises are not psychologically prepared to face market competition and are not competent to compete in terms of technology, management, and the employees' mindset. The well drilling business in Daqing is the leading business among the remaining businesses. Before the separation, they were guaranteed business from Daqing's 2,400 wells every year. They faced serious problems after separation. In terms of costs, well drilling companies outside of CNPC are more competitive at 100 yuan per metre. In terms of technology and management, the drilling teams from Zhongyuan Oil Field are more competitive. The fear was that if the well drilling business lost out in the competition, the supporting businesses of water and electricity supply would also collapse as a result. CNPC was trying to devise plans to reorganise the well drilling teams within the group into a national well drilling company. The problem for Daqing was that what the workers in the well drilling business were going to do for a living before the reorganisation was completed. Moreover, if CNPC took away the drilling business, the businesses left with Daqing such as work-over would lose an 'anchor' for development.

Prospect

In 2000, the management team of Daqing PAB was devising plans to reorganise the remaining businesses into a holding company. The ownership structure of the subordinate companies would be diversified. The holding company would wholly own the core businesses. For businesses related to the core businesses, the holding company would either hold either a majority or minority equity shares. However, to decide what businesses had the potential to become core businesses was a big challenge. The businesses available were not competitive whereas new businesses such as information technology, e-commerce, bio-technology were remote concepts. Daqing did not have the human resources to develop these new businesses and it would be too risky for the management to invest in businesses they did not know. Moreover, moves to develop core businesses might clash with CNPC's reorganisation plans for the remaining businesses. The dilemma was that something needed to be done but in the meantime certain things might not be permitted. No one knew what was going to happen and the prevailing attitude was to 'wait and see'.

Summary

CNPC and Daqing have each struggled to become the 'firm' within China's oil industry. CNPC did not want to become a mere supervisory body just as Daqing did not want to be a mere production site. CNPC's restructuring for flotation in 1999 dashed Daqing's ambition to become an independent company. Daqing now is divided into two parts and may be divided into more parts in the near future. Daqing is powerful within PetroChina in terms of reserves and production volume. However, it is now a production region though it is likely that Daqing's oil will run out some day. In 1998, PetroChina scaled down the exploration and production activities in Daqing. Moreover, PetroChina will make a huge investment in developing natural gas in line with the government policy of developing clean primary energy. The reserves of natural gas are mainly located in western China.

For the remaining businesses in Daqing that used to rely and thrive on the oil businesses, things have already become difficult. It is very likely that CNPC is going to take the technical service businesses from Daqing. An area such as Daqing, developed from the oil businesses in a remote place but also close enough to Harbin, the capital city of Helongjiang Province, stands only a limited chance of becoming a large commercial centre in that region that can create abundant employment opportunities for its people. Some people have already left Daqing or are considering leaving. Will Daqing eventually become a deserted oil field? This is the situation that Daqing had been struggling to avoid.

Zhenhai Refining and Chemical Corporation

The predecessor of Zhenhai Refining and Chemical Company Ltd was established as Zhejiang Refinery Plant in 1974. Following the government's policy of 'industrial management' (*hangye guanli*), the Zhejiang Refinery Plant came under the direct supervision and control of Sinopec upon the establishment of the latter in 1983. The plant was renamed Sinopec Zhenhai General Petrochemical Works (ZGP). In 1994, ZGP was restructured into a joint stock company named Zhenhai Refining and Chemical Corporation (Zhenhai). In the same year, Zhenhai was listed on the Hong Kong Stock Exchange and raised HK$1.428 billion by issuing 600 million H shares. Sinopec, its parent company, controls 71.3 per cent of the issued shares. In 1996, Zhenhai issued $200 million of convertible bonds on the Hong Kong Stock Exchange and London Stock

Exchange. On 25 February 2000, Sinopec Group transferred the 71.3 per cent state-owned shares to China Petroleum and Chemical Corporation (Sinopec). In 2000, Zhenhai had around10,000 employees and total assets of 13.3 billion yuan and net assets of 4.4 billion yuan.

Ambition

Since it began production in 1977, Zhenhai strove to develop its scale and increase its efficiency. It strove for a sufficient crude oil supply and financial capital for development and built itself into a highly efficient and most competitive refinery within the Chinese refining industry. Moreover, it developed concrete corporate ambitions and a strong corporate identity. In the late 1990s, senior managers at Zhenhai emphasised that Zhenhai's ambition was to become a world-class company engaging in refining, marketing, transportation and chemical production.

Zhenhai's corporate culture was summarised as 'solidarity, seeking truth, pioneering, dedication'. Workers in Zhenhai take strong pride in being 'Zhenhai people' (*Zhenhai ren*). They have very strong sense of responsibility for the job they do and try their best to do it better. From managers to workers, a strong team spirit created powerful cohesion (*ningjuli*). Sun Weijun, the general manager of Zhenhai, commented in 1999:

> Every employee in Zhenhai realises they have a future with the Company and they want to do their job better. This is a kind of corporate spirit and cohesive strength. If a company has a bright prospect, its employees will be hopeful and confident. The more confidence they have in the company, the better they will do with their job. This is a virtuous circle.
>
> (quoted in *China Petroleum*, May 1999)

Struggle for autonomy

CRUDE OIL SUPPLY

At the time of its establishment in the 1970s, Zhenhai had an annual crude oil processing capacity of three million tonnes. Every year, Zhenhai was allocated 1 million tonnes of crude oil from the government at the price set by government, amounting to only one-third of its processing capacity. In 1983, the crude oil allocated to Zhenhai was reduced to 900,000 tonnes. In the same year, the Ministry of Petroleum Industry held a meeting in Zhenhai announcing that the government would adopt a dual pricing system for crude oil. Oil refineries would be allowed to buy crude oil produced by the oil fields in excess of the contracted volume at four times the government price. Refineries could sell the petroleum products at a higher price than that set by the government. Zhenhai's management team decided to buy 565,000 tonnes of crude oil at the high price. The logic was that an increase in processing volume could fully utilise the processing capacity, decrease energy consumption and reduce the unit processing cost. Thus it could improve the company's efficiency. In the meantime, the company could adjust and improve its product mix and look into opportunities for expanding into new businesses. Another contributing factor for the decision was that the market demand for petroleum products was increasing rapidly. However, in early 1983, the market mechanism in China was limited. Zhenhai was not sure that after buying high-priced crude oil for processing, it could sell the refined oil products at a higher price. Despite the doubts, the instinct to increase in scale, reduce costs and achieve growth encouraged Zhenhai's management take risks. The decision to purchasing high-priced oil proved to be successful. The profit and taxes created in 1983 were 150 million yuan, a 50 per cent increase from that of 1982.

In the late 1980s, the shortage of domestic crude oil supply became acute. The leadership at Zhenhai realised that the only way to guarantee sufficient crude oil for processing was to enter the international oil market. Zhenhai has its own dock for ocean shipping located in Ningbo, a coastal city open to the outside world. Zhenhai believed that these advantages should be fully utilised. The opportunity came in 1988 at a conference for exports sponsored by Sinopec in Shenzhen. Zhenhai learnt that an American company was looking for a refinery in China for co-operation. After negotiation, Zhenhai and American Union Oil International Supply and Trading Company signed a contract for processing 50,000 tonnes of crude oil supplied by American Union Oil. Zhenhai had made its first step into the international market. This contract is highly significant in the history of China's refining industry in that it is the first contract for a Chinese refinery processing crude oil supplied by a foreign company. The contract is now in the Museum of Chinese Revolutionary History in Beijing.

MARKETING

The huge profit from processing high-price crude oil attracted a sea of refineries to enter the business. But the channel to market high-price petroleum products was simply not in place. Local petroleum sales departments under the administration of the Ministry of Commerce did not allow its customers to buy refined petroleum products from refineries at a higher price. The penalty was to cut the supply of petroleum products at the low price set by the government.

Zhenhai had a high inventory of refined products and faced the challenge of how to market its products. A strategy was devised to develop a high-priced petroleum products market in the special economic zones that enjoyed special and flexible policies. Zhenhai sent out three sales teams to three areas: Hangjia (Hangzhou and Jiaxing) area, Fujian Province and Guangdong Province. Immediately, they found out that the market for petroleum products in Fujian had the greatest potential for development. In 1994, Zhenhai and Xiamen Oil Supply Station set up Xiamen Luyong Petroleum and Chemical Company Limited for trading petroleum products. A 30,000 cubic metres oil storage tank and a dock with a capacity of 5,000 tonnes were built up in Xiamen. The inventory of petroleum products was sold out shortly after the establishment of Luyong. The success greatly encouraged Zhenhai to further develop the market to sell high-priced refined products. Another eight associated companies were successively set up to market refined products in cities such as Zhuhai, Nantong, Xiaoshan, Shanghai, Wenzhou, Jinhua, and Ningbo. This gave Zhenhai good market access in the Jiangzhe region (Zhejiang and Jiangsu Province), Shanghai and Minyue region (Fujian and Guangdong). These coastal cities and regions have high incomes and growth rates. From 1984 to 1988, Zhenhai processed 4.5 million tonnes of high-priced crude oil, and generated 450 million yuan in profits and taxes.

Processing high-price crude oil was highly significant for Zhenhai. The strategy enabled Zhenhai to break through the old model of conducting businesses under the command economy and to participate actively in domestic market activities.

AUTONOMY IN IMPORT AND EXPORT OF CRUDE OIL

Zhenhai's ambition was more than being just a refinery processing crude oil from overseas customers. In early 1990s, Zhenhai planned to purchase crude oil itself from the international market for processing (*ziying jiagong*). However, there were two problems: shortage of foreign currency and no autonomy to conduct import and export business.

To get sufficient foreign currency to buy crude oil, Zhenhai applied to the Ningbo Foreign Currency Allocation Centre for a trading seat. But the amount of foreign currency Zhenhai could trade was strictly controlled by the centre. Zhenhai decided to go to other cities in China to buy foreign currency. Since Zhenhai had no rights to conduct import and export business, they needed to purchase crude oil from the international market through their agent Sinochem. Zhenhai could not directly monitor the constantly fluctuating international oil price and obtain the best buy for the company. Autonomy in conducting import and export businesses would enable Zhenhai to gain power to bargain for oil prices and the flexibility to purchase directly from the international market. It made great efforts in lobbying to obtain the right to conduct import and export businesses. Their effort paid off eventually, and in July 1992, MOFTEC granted Zhenhai this right. Zhenhai became one of the first companies in the oil and petrochemical industry that were granted autonomy to conduct import and export businesses.

In 1992, Zhenhai processed 500,000 tonnes crude oil purchased from the international market and made a profit of 55 million yuan. According to government regulation, 80 per cent of the petroleum products produced from processing imported crude oil had to be sold to overseas customers. Over the years, Zhenhai has developed stable customer accounts in the United States, United Kingdom, Japan, Singapore, Korea, and India. Among China's refineries, Zhenhai became the one that processed most crude oil from overseas. In 1999, 78 per cent of Zhenhai's total throughput consisted of imported crude oil (Zhenhai, 2000).

Zhenhai practised strict budgeting in infrastructure construction investment. In the course of the project to expand refining capacity to 8 million tonnes per year, they twice changed the programme and reduced the budget from the initial 10.9 billion yuan to 6.9 billion yuan. Careful and strict budgeting became a common practice, which was closely related to Zhenhai's pattern of growth. Over the years, Zhenhai relied on its own resources for development: 'We cannot bear any waste in our company. This good habit is handed down from generation to generation in Zhenhai' (Senior manager, interview in Zhenhai, July 2000).

MERGERS AND ACQUISITIONS

In addition to becoming a highly competitive refinery, Zhenhai intended to develop downstream chemical businesses and to set up a network of service stations. Plans were devised to merge with Shanghai Gaoqiao Petrochemical Company and Fujian Refinery, and to construct pipelines for shipping refined products up to Jiangxi Province. Zhenhai planned to co-operate with Zhejiang Petroleum Company to develop a network of service stations and control the market of petroleum products in Yunnan, Guizhou and Sichuan Provinces.

Restructuring for flotation: 1994

The shortage of financial capital necessary to increase scale and efficiency remained a persistent problem after its establishment in the 1970s. Before 1987, Zhenhai's growth was almost entirely funded by self-accumulation except for the funds of 700 million yuan allocated by the government. The second-phase of construction began in 1987. The government agreed to allocate the required funds of 1.1 billion yuan for the project. During the construction process, the funds from the government could not be realised due to the change in macroeconomic policy to control the scale of investment and to adjust the investment structure. In response to the setback, Zhenhai set out raise money. Investment funds were finally obtained through loans from the China Construction Bank, bonds issued through banks and Zhenhai's own resources. In 1990, Sinopec, Zhejiang Provincial government and Ningbo City agreed to build an ethylene cracker with an annual capacity of 600,000 tonnes per year in Zhenhai. If realised, this would greatly increase Zhenhai's capability in chemical production. The project was approved by the State Planning Commission in 1992 and had a construction budget of 6 billion yuan. However, the project was never realised due to shortage of funds.

In 1993, as recommended by Sinopec for overseas flotation, Zhenhai was restructured into a joint-stock company. Sinopec controlled 71.3 per cent of the total shares of Zhenhai and the rest of shares were to be traded on the stock market. In December 1994, Zhenhai was successfully listed on the Hong Kong Stock Exchange and raised HK$1.428 billion. Arco purchased 9.4 per cent of the shares issued. Zhenhai used the capital to upgrade its refining equipment and increase its refining capacity to 8 million tonnes per year, which ranked Zhenhai as the third largest refinery in China. From 1995, Zhenhai started to further expand its refining capacity and raised $200 million by issuing the same amount of convertible bonds in Hong Kong and London. In 1999, its comprehensive refining capacity reached 12 million tonnes per year and it became China's largest refinery. The successful flotation not only enabled Zhenhai to raise capital for further development but also helped Zhenhai establish the modern enterprise system.

From processing high-price crude oil to processing crude oil from overseas customers, from obtaining autonomy in importing crude oil to listing in the international capital markets, the leadership in Zhenhai was able to capture 'first mover' advantages and achieve growth in scale and improvements in efficiency.

Organisational structure

Zhenhai's Board of Directors is composed of seven Directors, eight outside Directors including four independent Directors and four Directors from different management departments within of Sinopec. The Supervisory Board has five members including one shareholder supervisor, two independent supervisors and two supervisors elected from Zhenhai's employees. The board has three Committees: Finance and Development Committee, Organisational Design and Reform Committee, and Audit Committee (Figure 7.2). The executive management team is composed of the company's general manager, five Deputy General Managers and one Chief Accountant. Zhenhai adopts the direct responsibility management model at three levels: the company headquarters, manufacturing plants and workshops. Plants and subsidiaries are set up according to product line and specialisation.

In 1994 and 1995, Zhenhai twice restructured its administrative departments, reducing the number of administrative departments from sixteen to nine and the number of department employees from 828 to 528 (Figure 7.2). The nine administrative departments at the company headquarters are as follows: General Manager's Office, Human Resource Department, General Management Department, Manufacturing Department, Economic and Trading Department, Finance Department, Safety and Environment Department, Security Department, and Audit Department. The General Management Department is an organisational innovation for SOEs at Zhenhai. It has a wide range of responsibilities from manufacturing planning to crude oil purchasing, from technological development to company management such as performance evaluation. It merged the functions of the usual planning department, company management department and science and technology department found in a typical Chinese SOE. This arrangement enabled the headquarters to devise overall plans and reduce the co-ordination disputes between departments. Zhenhai regards the General Management Department as the advice department in an army.

The Human Resource Department is responsible for HR development and training, employees' welfare, compensation and rewards, and so on. The

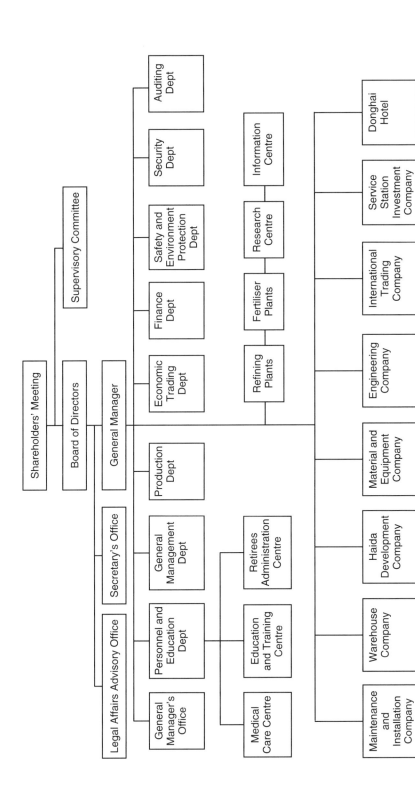

Figure 7.2 Organisational structure of Zhenhai, 2000.

functions of the Manufacturing Department are for scheduling operations, providing machinery power, resolving technical problems and checking product quality. The Economic and Trading Department supervises domestic and foreign trading, product transportation, and the management of petrol stations. Apart from the conventional financial management, the Finance Department has a Fixed Assets Section that centrally manages the Zhenhai's asset account. The Safety and Environment Department focusses on safety and environmental issues, and the Security Department is responsible for security matters and transportation within the company. This department also supervises the Community Committees of the residential area. The Audit Department undertakes internal audit, while also functioning as the office of the Supervisory Board.

Zhenhai has three centres for welfare functions for company employees all under the supervision of the Human Resources Department. These included the Medical Centre, the Education and Training Centre, and the Retired Employees Centre. The schools under the Education and Training Centre are expected to be gradually handed over to the local government. More than 1,600 retired employees and more than 1,000 so-called 'internal retired employees'[1] are under the management of Retired Employees Centre. The Research Centre and Information Centre are under the direct leadership of the General Manager.

The eight subsidiaries of Zhenhai each has legal person status and are supervised by the General Management Department. The Maintenance and Instillation Company has 1,500–1,600 employees engaging in general maintenance activities and the business of manufacturing pressure containers. The Warehousing Company has businesses in storing and transporting crude oil and company products. Its five berths have loading and unloading capabilities from 10,000 to 250,000 tonnes. The Haida Development Company looks after property management, kindergartens and canteens. In addition, it has the business of filling LNG canisters. The Materials and Equipment Company undertakes materials purchasing and transportation according to the purchasing plan from the General Management Department. The International Trading Company Ltd is located in the Ningbo bonded area and enjoys favourable policies in conducting foreign trade. The Gasoline Stations Investment Company originates from the Market Development Section of the company since state policy formulates that firms that engage in developing petrol stations must set up a company for this purpose. In addition, Zhenhai has nine associated companies in Shanghai, Zhuhai, Nantong, and Wenzhou for trading petroleum products.

In 2000, there were 10,000 employees in Zhenhai of whom 6,000 were in the parent company and 4,000 in the subsidiaries. More than half of the workforce were under the age of thirty-five. The management level consisted of 2,800 employees, about 49 per cent of whom were engineers, 27 per cent were in accounting, statistics, sales and supplies, 15 per cent were in education and health, and 9 per cent were in other occupations. Approximately 16 per cent of the company's employees were university graduates. Over 280 employees with postgraduate qualifications were working in the manufacturing shop floor.

Centralised management system

Management is highly centralised at the level of the company headquarters. The major manufacturing plants including the refinery plant and the fertiliser plant do not have legal person status. They are manufacturing units carrying out the monthly manufacturing plan set out by the company headquarters. They do not have any power to sell their products and they are not permitted to set up diversified businesses. The eight subsidiaries have second-tier legal person status but conduct their own businesses respectively under direct supervision from the company headquarters. The highly centralised management system was facilitated by the information technology system that the company invested in from the early 1990s.

In response to the volatile international oil market, Zhenhai set up a rapid reaction decision-making system for purchasing oil from the international market. The General Management Department is in charge of monitoring the daily oil price. The General Manager makes the final purchasing decision within a certain price range while the Chairman controls the overall price range for each period of time. If unexpected fluctuations take place, the three parties must get together whenever and wherever they are, and make a collective decision.

PRODUCTION MANAGEMENT

Zhenhai strives to improve its production system through technological upgrading and careful planning. In order to de-bottleneck production, Zhenhai invested in technological revamping of the existing production facilities. For example, instead of investing in new facilities, Zhenhai revamped a urea production facility of 520,000 tonnes per year capacity and increased the annual production volume up to 615,000 tonnes. Investment for the revamping project was less than 100 million yuan. Building up a new urea production facility with an annual capacity of 10,000 tonnes would have required 500 million yuan. With the technological progress in its production facilities, Zhenhai changed the traditional 'post operation system' into a modern 'systematic operation system'. The traditional system categorised posts for refining equipment in great detail and practised 'one post, one person'. Zhenhai divided the whole operating system into 'inside operation' and 'outside operation'. The former controlled and checked operating meters and the latter inspected the onsite equipment. The new operating system reduced the number of workers, maintained equipment in the best state of operation, and enhanced production efficiency. For example, the first workshop in Zhenhai's refining plant has 158 workers working on five production installations, compared with 300 workers under the traditional operation system.

In 1997, Zhenhai planned to downsize buying off about 1,200 workers. By 1999, 540 workers had been removed from existing production units and placed to work on new projects or projects for upgrading. From 1995 to 1999, Zhenhai's annual processing capacity increased from 8 million tonnes to 12 million tonnes, but the number of employees stayed constant. During the same period, the average profit and tax per employee reached 1 million yuan. In order to become a world-class enterprise, Zhenhai set up an internal auditing and performance monitoring system. After the flotation, Zhenhai's standard of business conduct and transparency won recognition from both the business world and the international capital market. In 1996, Zhenhai was designated one of 'China's best-run companies' by the Hong Kong press.

INFORMATION TECHNOLOGY SYSTEM

In the early 1990s, Zhenhai began to set up an information technology system to facilitate production and management. Over the years, Zhenhai established a computer network, including over twenty computer servers and more than 1,300 computers. Real time supervision became available to every management level through the network. The PI database system automatically collects, computes and manages data from more than 170 production facilities covering crude oil processing, refined oil product and feedstocks for chemical production. Octane gasoline can be supervised and blended on line. In addition, control is also implemented in the propylene-rectified facility and in some aromatic extraction units to further improve product quality and increase the level of propylene yield. The Planning Department also introduced the BP crude oil evaluation system. Laboratory Information Management System (LIMS) from United Kingdom facilitates data management, quality management, sample management and data sharing in the laboratory.

Zhenhai's management departments in finance, personnel, trade, production plan, material supply, safety and environmental protection and quality management have all been connected to the company's IT system. Information about oil products, processing and management are available from Zhenhai's intranet. Zhenhai can communicate with Sinopec through a satellite link and monitor the markets for oil, natural gas and refined products in New York, London and Singapore.

Relationship with Sinopec

As discussed in previous chapters, Sinopec negotiated and agreed with suppliers the terms of government-allocated crude oil on a group basis, which was then allocated among the subordinate companies, including Zhenhai. Major transactions between Zhenhai and Sinopec included reimbursement on crude oil purchased from Sinopec, surcharges on imported and offshore oil paid and payable to Sinopec, R&D fees paid to Sinopec, R&D funds received from Sinopec, insurance premiums, and subsidies received from Sinopec. From July 1998, a surcharge of 50 yuan per tonne was paid to Sinopec on imported and offshore oil processed by Zhenhai. If Zhenhai processed onshore oil supplied by companies outside Sinopec, a surcharge of 20 or 30 yuan per tonne based on different production area was paid to Sinopec. If Zhenhai processed onshore oil supplied by companies within Sinopec, a reimbursement of 40 yuan per tonne was made by Sinopec. Zhenhai paid Sinopec R&D fees, which amounted to 35 million yuan in 1999. In the same year, Zhenhai undertook certain R&D projects for Sinopec, from which Zhenhai received an amount of 6.45 million yuan from Sinopec. As required by Sinopec, Zhenhai arranged insurance coverage with a subsidiary of Sinopec, covering buildings, machinery, equipment and inventories. In 1999, Zhenhai received subsidies from Sinopec amounting to 7.01 million yuan for exclusive use to enhance Zhenhai's security and safety measures and to conduct specified research.

POST SINOPEC FLOTATION

Under the 2000 Sinopec restructuring programme, Zhenhai ceded to Sinopec headquarters its autonomy in the crude oil import and export businesses. Zhenhai's team in charge of monitoring and trading crude oil online were moved to the headquarters of Sinopec. The right to sell its products was taken from Zhenhai and returned to Sinopec. All the products produced by Zhenhai were now to be sold through Sinopec East China Sales Company. Zhenhai became simply a manufacturing plant within Sinopec. Capital investment exceeding 30 million yuan now needed to get approval from Sinopec headquarters. Zhenhai was chosen by Sinopec along with other three subsidiaries to participate in a pilot study to implement the integration of the Enterprise Resources Planning system.

It was suggested that Sinopec had plans to acquire the shares owned by other investors in Zhenhai and other three H-share companies, Shanghai Petrochemicals, Yizheng Chemical Fibres and Yanhua Petrochemicals and place the four companies under Sinopec's full control. In 2000, the combined assets of the four companies accounted for 18 per cent of Sinopec's total assets. There was also a suggestion that the four companies should merge.

Summary

Within the apparently large corporations of CNPC and Sinopec, there were many subordinate enterprises, as exemplified by Daqing and Zhenhai, which struggled fiercely for autonomy and independence. Daqing and Zhenhai each had its own history of development and its own traditions. Following the enterprise reform calling for autonomy in the mid-1980s, legal person status was granted to both the central corporations of CNPC and Sinopec as well as subordinate enterprises such as Daqing and Zhenhai. Each struggled forcefully to obtain business autonomy. Apart from the 'hand-over' of profits to the headquarters, each received limited performance monitoring from the headquarters. Led by their visionary leaders, each aspired to become a competitive world-class company. Each had a strong desire to expand into upstream and downstream businesses. Each devised plans for development through mergers and acquisitions. Their corporate ambitions were distinct from those of the central supervisory authorities. Daqing directly challenged the authority of CNPC headquarters to restructure and float the enterprise. Zhenhai, a much smaller scale enterprise than Daqing, was allowed to float on the Hong Kong Stock Exchange.

The industry restructuring in 1998 marked a hugely significant shift in the Chinese government's industrial policy. The government decided finally to choose CNPC and Sinopec as the firm instead of supporting strong and aspiring companies such as Daqing and Zhenhai. Key leaders in powerful subordinate companies such as Daqing and Zhenhai were replaced by CNPC and Sinopec's headquarters. The creation and flotation of PetroChina dashed Daqing's ambition for independent development. The creation and floatation of Sinopec upset Zhenhai's own plan to grow 'through the market'. Both PetroChina and Sinopec began to integrate their powerful subordinate companies through centralising production planning, capital investment, and marketing. PetroChina and Sinopec needed to establish a company structure and system to monitor and control from the headquarters while providing operational autonomy for the business branch companies. The task was formidable, considering the history of companies such as Daqing and Zhenhai. It required strong political will and subtle strategies. 'The process is analogous to the centralisation of power in the early modern state that broke down the decentralised power of feudal lords' (Nolan, 2001: 497). That process has only just begun.

8   Challenges for large Chinese firms

During the last decades of the twentieth century, in order to survive and prosper, the world's leading firms underwent a revolutionary transformation in organisational structure and business capabilities. During the same period, China's large enterprises undertook large-scale evolutionary change and encountered many internal difficulties. At the beginning of the twenty-first century, China joined the World Trade Organisation. As the country begins to closely integrate with the world economy and business system, China's ambition to build up large competitive firms appears to be as strong as ever. In addition to their internal difficulties, large Chinese corporations will encounter sharply increased competitive pressure on the 'global level playing field', which is now coming to China. The relationship between large Chinese corporations and large global firms has been immensely complicated, involving both competition and co-operation. In this process, China's large firms face great challenges.

The world oil and gas sector in the 1990s

During the 1990s, crude oil and natural gas remained central to the world's primary energy supplies. The contribution of oil to the world's primary energy consumption remained stable at around 40 per cent. The share of natural gas in world primary energy consumption rose from 20.3 per cent in 1990 to 24.7 per cent in 2000.

The distribution of world oil and gas reserves, production and consumption remains geographically uneven (Table 8.1). This simple fact is of great importance for the global political economy. The Middle East and the former Soviet Union (FSU) account for 69.7 per cent of the world total oil reserves and 72.8 per cent of the world's total natural gas reserves. The five countries of Saudi Arabia, Kuwait, Iran, Iraq and the United Arab Emirates between them account for over three-fifths of the world's total oil reserves. Russia alone accounts for more than one-third of the world's total gas reserves. The Middle East remains the world's most important oil supplier. Its oil production for 1990–2000 grew at an average annual rate of 3.1 per cent alongside a 1.3 per cent growth rate of the world average for the same period. By 2000, Middle Eastern oil production had reached 1112.4 million tonnes, accounting for 31 per cent of total world production, 75 per cent of which was exported. The FSU is the largest gas producer in the world, accounting for 28 per cent of total world production in 2000.

The United States remains the world's biggest oil and gas consumer (Table 8.1). Its share of world oil production declined from 13.2 per cent in 1990 to 9.8 per cent in 2000 while its share of world oil consumption rose from 24.9 per cent in 1990 to 25.6 per cent in 2000. In 2000, the United States imported 446 million tonnes of oil, accounting for over one quarter of total world oil imports and nearly half of the country's total consumption. Fifty-six per cent of the USA's oil imports are from the Middle East and South America, and the rest are from Canada, the North Sea, Mexico, and Africa. The United States accounts for 23 per cent of the world's gas production but its gas production still lags behind its gas consumption, which accounts for 27 per cent of the world total. In Europe, more than 60 per cent of the of 752.6 million tonnes of oil consumption is met by imports from the Middle East and Russia, and half of the 458.8 billion cubic metres of gas consumption is supplied by Russia through pipelines. Japan relies totally on imports to meet its consumption of oil and gas (Table 8.1). More than 95 per cent of Japan's oil imports are from the Middle East and around three-quarters of its gas imports are from the Middle East and Southeast Asia.

China is poorly endowed with oil and gas, with its share of the world oil and gas reserves standing only at 2.3 per cent and 0.9 per cent (Table 8.1). In contrast, China's coal reserves are the second largest in the world, next to those of the United States. China was the world's largest producer and consumer of coal during the 1990s. The percentage of coal consumption in its total primary energy consumption, however, decreased from 76.2 per cent in 1990 to 67.1 per cent in 1999. More importantly, China plans to raise the share of gas consumption in total primary energy consumption from the current three per cent to 7.9 per cent in 2010, which means a further reduction in the share of coal consumption. During the 1990s, oil and gas consumption increased by a compound annual growth rate of 5.5 per cent and 5.7 per cent respectively. In 2000, China was the world's third largest consumer of oil, after the United States and Japan. Since 1993, China has become a net importer of crude oil. Oil imports reached 71 million tonnes in 2000 (BP, 2001), equivalent to 31 per cent of its total oil consumption. Approximately 65 per cent of the imported oil is from the Middle East and South East Asia. China's industrial experts predict that by 2005, 40 per cent of China's demand for oil will be met by imports (*China Petroleum*, June, 1999). The issue of oil supply security has been a major concern among the country's policy makers. President Jiang Zemin spoke at the economic working meeting of the central government in 2000, 'We must closely watch the trend of international oil prices and their impact on the economic and social development of our country. We must take precautions and earnestly work out our strategies'.

National oil companies

By 1999, among the world's top twenty-five oil companies ranked by operating performance, fourteen were still fully state-owned 'national champions' and all of

Table 8.1 Geographical distribution of world oil and gas reserves, consumption and production, 2000.

Regions and countries	Proven reserves		Consumption		Production		Net imports [exports]	
	Oil (bt)	Gas (tcm)	Oil (mmt)	Gas (bcm)	Oil (mmt)	Gas (bcm)	Oil (mmt)	Gas§ (bcm)
World	142.1 (100%)	150.19 (100%)	3503.6 (100%)	2404.6 (100%)	3589.6 (100%)	2422.3 (100%)	–	–
United States	3.7 (2.8%)	4.74 (3.2%)	897.4 (25.6%)	654.4 (27.2%)	353.5 (9.8%)	555.6 (22.9%)	442.8	101.53
Europe	2.5 (1.9%)	5.22 (3.5%)	752.6 (21.4%)	458.8 (19.1%)	329 (9.2%)	287.9 (12%)	389.6	197.33
Mexico	4.0 (2.7%)	0.86 (0.6%)	84.3 (2.4%)	35.5 (1.5%)	172.1 (4.8%)	35.8 (1.5%)	[86.7]	0
S/C America* of which:	13.6 (9.0%)	6.93 (4.6%)	218.7 (6.2%)	92.6 (3.8%)	348.2 (9.7%)	96.4 (3.9%)	[59.7]	[3.51]
Venezuela	11.1 (7.3%)	4.16 (2.8%)	22.6 (0.6%)	27.2 (1.1%)	166.8 (4.6%)	27.2 (1.1%)	–	–
FSU** of which:	9.0 (6.4%)	56.7 (37.8%)	173.1 (5.0%)	548.3 (22.8%)	394.4 (11%)	674.2 (27.8%)	[142.6]	[132.98]
Russia	6.7 (4.6%)	48.14 (32.1%)	123.5 (3.5%)	377.2 (15.7%)	323.3 (9.0%)	545 (22.5%)	–	[130.33]
Middle East of which:	92.5 (65.3%)	52.52 (35%)	209.0 (5.9%)	189 (7.9%)	1112.4 (31%)	209.7 (8.7%)	[831.7]	[23.44]
Saudi Arabia	35.8 (25%)	23 (15.3%)	62.4 (1.8%)	47 (2.0%)	441.2 (12.3%)	47.0 (1.9%)	–	–
Iran	12.3 (8.6%)	6.05 (4%)	56.9 (1.6%)	62.9 (2.6%)	186.6 (5.2%)	60.2 (2.5%)	–	2.65
Iraq	15.1 (10.8%)	3.11 (2.1%)	–	–	128.1 (3.6%)	–	–	–
Asia Pacific of which:	6.0 (4.2%)	10.33 (6.8%)	968.9 (27.8%)	289.3 (12.1%)	380.5 (10.6%)	265.4 (11%)	557.9	22.41
China***	3.3 (2.3%)	1.37 (0.9%)	226.9 (6.5%)	24.8 (1.0%)	162.3 (4.5%)	27.7 (1.2%)	59.9	–
Japan	–	–	253.5 (7.2%)	76.2 (3.2%)	–	–	214.9	72.46
Africa of which:	10.0 (7.1%)	11.16 (7.4%)	116.7 (3.3%)	58.9 (2.4%)	373.2 (10.4%)	129.5 (5.3%)	[251.1]	[67.05]
Nigeria	3.1 (2.2%)	3.51 (2.3%)	–	–	103.9 (2.9%)	11.0 (0.5%)	–	[5.61]

Source: BP Statistical Review of World Energy 2001.

Notes:
Figures in parentheses ( ) are percentage share of world total, in brackets [ ] are net exports.
*South and Central America **Former Soviet Union, ***Data exclude Hong Kong, §Trade movement of gas transported by pipeline and LNG, excluding intra movement.

bt = billion tones, tcm = trillion cubic metres, mmt = million tones, bcm = billion cubic metres.

them were based in developing countries (Table 8.2). There have been no cross-border mergers among these companies. These fourteen national oil companies (NOCs) together with the partially privatised Brazilian national champion Petrobrás, own over one-half of the world's oil and gas reserves, and are the world's largest oil producers. In 1999, the combined oil and gas reserves of these oil companies accounted for 77.3 per cent and 48.8 per cent of the world total oil and gas reserves respectively. Their aggregate oil production was 48 per cent of total world oil production, compared with a 17.9 per cent share of the global oil majors (GOMs) based in the United States and Europe.[1] The NOCs' gas production was 448.9 billion cubic metres in 1999, accounting for 18.8 per cent of the world total, compared with 424.1 billion cubic metres produced by GOMs in the same year. However, the top fifteen NOCs are weak in downstream refining and marketing. Their total annual refinery capacity in 1999 was 942.6 million tonnes, compared with 1064.1 for the GOMs. The gap in oil product sales was even more stark. The refined product sales of the fifteen NOCs were 872.9mmt (millions of tonnes) in 1999, substantially less than the combined amount of 1062.8mmt of refined products sold by Exxon Mobil, Royal Dutch/Shell and BP Amoco/Arco in the same period.

Compared with the other NOCs, PetroChina and Sinopec Group's oil and gas reserves were at the bottom of the league (Table 8.2). Even their combined oil reserves were 2.33 billion tonnes, only 6.6 per cent of that of Saudi Aramco and far behind even the 3.89 billion tonnes of Pemex. Their combined gas reserves of 1004.7 billion cubic metres were the smallest among NOCs. Both PetroChina and Sinopec rely entirely on domestic reserves for production. In 1999, PetroChina was ranked the eighth largest oil producer in the world (*Petroleum Intelligence Weekly*, December 18, 2000). The combined oil production of PetroChina and Sinopec Group would place China the fifth largest producer in the world in the same year. In contrast, the combined gas production of PetroChina and Sinopec Group was tiny, only 18.4 per cent of that of Petronas. Downstream, the combined annual refinery capacity of PetroChina and Sinopec Group was above 100mmt/y (millions of tonnes per year), but their combined oil product sales were only 117.1mmt, at the level of Chevron alone (and far below that of the combined Chevron Texaco). As we have seen, in 2000, the core businesses of Sinopec Group and CNPC were partially privatised.

Consolidation of the western oil majors

In sharp contrast to the NOCs, in the late 1990s, a wave of cross-border consolidation swept through the global oil majors based in western countries. In a short period of just two years from 1998 to 2000, the number of giant western oil companies was reduced from eleven to six (Figure 8.1). This fundamentally changed the competitive landscape among the global oil majors, and the nature of the competition facing oil companies from developing countries, such as CNPC and Sinopec.

Table 8.2 Top fifteen national oil companies, 1999.

Company	Reserves		Production		Refinery capacity (mmt/y)	Oil product sales (mmt)	Country
	Oil (bt)	Gas (bcm)	Oil (mmt)	Gas (bcm)			
Saudi Aramco	35.5	6040.7	402.2	31.4	99.6	132.5	Saudi Arabia
PDVSA	10.5	4155.1	147.5	41.3	154.8	125.0	Venezuela
National Iranian Oil Company	12.1	23134.1	181.0	53.3	76.7	67.1	Iran
Pemex	3.89	849.7	167.2	49.5	76.4	82.5	Mexico
Indonesia National Oil Company	1.08	3361.6	48.7	65.1	52.5	59.5	Indonesia
Kuwait Petroleum Corporation	13.2	1492.5	101.3	9.7	53.75	58.25	Kuwait
Algeria National Oil Company	1.21	3860.1	74.0	78.4	24.25	37.5	Algeria
PetroChina	1.51	696.8	106.2	7.0	103.3	48.3	China
Petrobrás*	11.1	302.0	59.6	12.8	97.65	90.9	Brazil
Abu Dhabi National Oil Company	6.95	5553.8	62.0	32.9	11.7	22.75	United Arab Emirates
Iraq National Oil Company	15.4	3109.5	126.4	3.3	17.4	26.0	Iraq
Libya National Oil Company	3.23	1309.6	60.6	6.2	19.0	20.0	Libya
Petronas	0.40	1825.8	31.8	52.7	14.5	21.25	Malaysia
Sinopec Group	0.82	307.9	31.5	2.2	118.65	68.8	China
Nigeria National Oil Company	1.85	2105.3	60.8	3.1	22.25	12.55	Nigeria
Total	118.8	58104.5	1660.9	448.9	942.6	872.9	

Sources: *Petroleum Intelligence Weekly*, 18 December 2000, and author's own research.

Notes:

*In 1999, 49 per cent of Petrobrás was state-owned.

bt = billion tonnes, bcm = billion cubic metres, mmt = million tonnes, mmt/y = million tonnes per year.

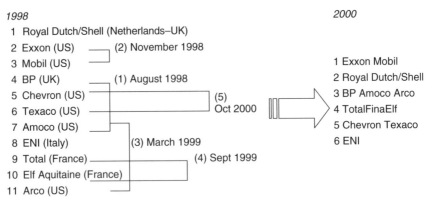

Figure 8.1 Five major mergers among eleven western oil companies during 1998–2000.

BP/Amoco: August 1998

The consolidation process in the oil and petrochemical industry was initiated by BP's trans-Atlantic merger with Amoco in a $55 billion stock and debt transaction in August 1998. With oil and gas production of 3.1 million barrels of oil equivalent per day (BP, 1998: 68), the combined group placed itself close behind the world leader Royal Dutch/Shell and Exxon in terms of market capitalisation, oil and gas reserves and production. The deal greatly strengthened BP's position in downstream marketing in the Mid-West and Eastern United States as well as in the petrochemicals production. The merger is highly significant in that it was one of a series of massive trans-Atlantic mergers and acquisitions, such as Daimler/Chrysler Deutsche Bank/Bankers Trust, Vodafine/ Voicestream, Ford/Volvo Autos, GM/Saab Autos, Glaxo/Smith Kline Beecham, and WalMart/Asda (also see Chapter 3).

Exxon Mobil: November 1998

Just three months after the BP/Amoco merger, Exxon, the then second largest western oil company, announced its intention to merge with Mobil, the third largest, in an $86.4 billion transaction. The merged company took over from Royal Dutch/Shell as the number one among the western oil companies in terms of revenue, profit, combined oil and gas reserves, oil and gas production, refining capacity. The new company Exxon Mobil had a much wider global spread of assets. With over 19 billion barrels of oil and oil equivalent of gas, the new company has a significant share in some of the world's most important emerging oil areas, including offshore in West Africa and in the Caspian Sea. It owns 60 per cent of the proven gas reserves in Europe and is actively exploring and developing gas fields in the Asia Pacific Area. The merger also filled the gap in Exxon's asset portfolio in liquefied Natural Gas (LNG), where Mobil owns the profitable Arun LNG business in Indonesia. With 14 billion cubic feet per day, Exxon Mobil is well positioned in the gas market for power generation, domestic use and even in advanced fuel cells installed in pollution-free automobiles (*Financial Times*, 30 November 1998; 2 December 1998). Downstream, Exxon and Mobil had 33,000 service stations world-wide, one quarter of which are in the United States. Both Exxon and Mobil have global brand recognition. In the fast-growing and profitable lubricants market, Exxon is the world's top producer of lubricant base stocks. Mobil is the market leader of lubricant, accounting for 12 per cent of the US market and 18 per cent of the European market at the time of merger. Exxon and Mobil also had complementary assets in major petrochemicals such as polyethylene and paraxylene (*Financial Times*, 30 November 1998; 2 December 1998). The Exxon Mobil merger fundamentally changed the long-standing competitive rivalry between Exxon and Royal Dutch/Shell. It enabled Exxon, which gradually lagged behind Royal Dutch/Shell in the last twenty years, significantly to overtake Royal Dutch/Shell in financial performance and in almost every aspect of operating strength.

BP Amoco/Arco: March 1999

Following hard on the heels of completing the BP/Amoco merger, in March 1999, BP Amoco agreed on a $26.8 billion all-stock take-over with the Atlantic Richfield Company (Arco). The acquisition of Arco significantly increased BP Amoco's oil and gas reserves from 12.9 billion to 17.5 billion barrels of oil and oil equivalent. More importantly, through Arco, the new company gained a much wider global reach with oil fields in Algeria, Venezuela, the Caspian Region and Russia as well as gas fields in the Gulf of Mexico, the North Sea, the South China Sea, Malaysia, Thailand and Qatar. Moreover, the new company has full operational control of the Prudhoe Bay oil and gas field in Alaska with 4.5 billion barrels of oil equivalent oil and gas reserves, equivalent to the total proved reserves of the entire United Kingdom. Through Arco, the new company owns 40 per cent of the Tangguh natural gas site in Indonesia, which has proven gas reserves of over 2.5 billion barrels of oil equivalent. The acquisition of Arco also enabled the new company to access Arco's large chain of service stations on the West Coast of the United States, thus effectively establishing a coast-to-coast network across the country. After the acquisition, BP's revenue, oil and gas reserves and production rivalled those of Shell. It became the world's third largest producer after Shell and BASF (*Financial Times*, 12 August, 1998), with leading technology and market shares in acetic acid, polypropylene and PTA. The deal of BP Amoco/Arco secured BP's position among the top 'big three' of western oil companies (see also Chapter 3).

TotalFina/Elf: September 1999

In late 1998, France's second biggest oil group, Total, acquired the Belgian PetroFina in a $7 billion stock swap and renamed the new company 'TotalFina'.

The take-over deal enabled Total to strengthen its downstream businesses in Europe and enhance its international exploration effort, especially in the North Sea. The principle significance of this deal was not its value, but the fact that it demonstrated the fading of national sensitivities associated with the former state-owned oil companies in Europe (*Financial Times*, 1 December 1998). Closely following behind the Total/PetroFina deal, TotalFina launched a $43 billion hostile bid for Elf Aquitaine, France's biggest oil group. The take-over was vigorously resisted by Elf Aquitaine but was supported by the French government who owned a 'golden share' in Elf Aquitaine. After months of protracted negotiation, TotalFina and Elf Aquitaine finally agreed to a friendly merger in September 1999. The oil and gas reserves of TotalFinaElf is over 9 billion barrels of oil equivalent, widely distributed across the world, with 28 per cent in Africa, 27 per cent in Europe, 25 per cent in the Middle East and 20 per cent across the rest of the world. Oil production of TotalFinaElf is close to that of BP Amoco/Arco. The new company also has powerful downstream capability in integrating its petrochemicals with its refining activities around six main hubs. Total/Fina/Elf greatly strengthened its position as the fourth largest global oil company.

Chevron/Texaco: October 2000

Despite extensive discussion, the merger of Chevron and Texaco was initially abandoned in 1999. Merger discussions were re-opened in early 2000 and in October, the two companies agreed to a $42 billion debt and stock merger. With reserves equivalent to 11.2 billion barrels of oil and production equivalent of 2.7 million barrels of oil a day, the new company became the world's fourth largest producer behind Exxon Mobil, Royal Dutch/Shell and BP. The combined company has a better position in most of the world's major and emerging exploration and producing areas, including North America, the North Sea, West Africa, the Caspian Region, Latin America and the Asia Pacific Region. Chevron has low-cost international oil projects offshore in Angola and Kazakstan, and is a 50:50 equity partner with Petrobrás in the Campos and Cumuruxatiba areas of Brazil. Texaco has made deep-water discoveries offshore in Nigeria, and is actively exploring and developing in the US Gulf of Mexico, Kazakhstan, deep-water Brazil, Venezuela and the Philippines. The new company became the third largest producer in the Gulf of Mexico next to BP and Exxon Mobil. Caltex, the refining joint venture between Chevron and Texaco established in 1936, was integrated into the new company. This greatly strengthened the new company's downstream businesses in Asia, Africa and the Middle East. Caltex has a refining capacity of 860,000 barrels per day and operates 8,000 service stations. In the profitable lubricants business, the new company accounts for 20–30 per cent of the lubricants additive market and 5–10 per cent of finished lubricants sales in Europe (*Financial Times*, 1 March 2001).

The recent round of mergers in the world's oil and petrochemical industry has created a group of new super-giants that stand in a position of greatly enhanced competitive advantage compared to firms in this sector from developing countries. These new giants greatly increased their size. They are constructing a portfolio of high quality oil and gas reserves widely distributed around the world. They are more able to invest large amounts in R&D to sustain and extend their technical lead over other companies, and to invest in large-scale information technology systems that enable them to integrate better their respective value chains. They are more able to develop integrated global marketing and purchasing capabilities and to develop their global brand. MSDW estimates that the super-majors, namely Exxon Mobil, Shell and BP, have a capability to sustain their competitive edge in the industry for at least fifteen years (MSDW, 1998).

Repsol/YPF

During the period of large-scale mergers among the western major oil companies, Spain's Repsol launched a hostile, $13 billion all-cash bid for Argentina's YPF in 1999. The deal is highly significant in that involved a large privatised western oil company taking over a major, formerly state-owned oil company from a developing country.

Before it was privatised by the government in 1991, YPF had had exclusive rights to exploration and production in Argentina. Demand for Argentina's domestic oil supply had been deficient, and domestic and international private companies had long participated in Argentina's oil businesses. YPF's oil production accounted for around one-half of domestic production. Following its privatisation, YPF was restructured for international flotation. Separated from the non-core businesses, the core businesses from upstream exploration and development to downstream refining, marketing, and petrochemicals, as well as electric power were grouped together and formed a joint stock company, the new YPF. In 1993, the new YPF was listed on the stock exchanges in Buenos Aires and New York. It was the largest publicly-traded oil company in Latin America.

By 1998, YPF owned proven reserves of 3.2 billion barrels of oil equivalent and produced 158 million barrels of oil, accounting for 51 per cent of Argentina's total production. Its three refineries, with an overall annual capacity of 122 million barrels, accounted for 51 per cent of Argentina's refining capacity. Its 2,500 service stations across Argentina held a 37 per cent market share. Under the strong leadership of its CEO, Roberto Monti, YPF had the ambition to build itself from a strong regional player, mainly based within Argentina, into a powerful international company. YPF pursued a series of international projects. In 1995, it purchased the US independent exploration and production company, Maxus Energy. It worked together with Petrobrás for a number of exploration blocks in Brazil and to develop its gas business in southern Brazil. It also had a joint venture with Petrobrás to develop a chain of service stations in Brazil. In addition, YPF had exploration interests in Bolivia, Ecuador and Venezuela. Through its affiliated companies, YPF also held stake in upstream operations in Russia and in downstream activities in Chile and Peru.

After its privatisation in the late 1990s, the Spanish oil company Repsol followed the strategy of international expansion, mainly in Latin America. It pursued growth in exploration and development, giving priority to natural gas reserves for the Spanish market. With 64 per cent of its assets in exploration and development, YPF was a strong upstream player and became an ideal target for Repsol's international expansion strategy. In January 1999, Repsol spent $2.011 billion for a 14.99 per cent stake in YPF under a purchase and sales contract from the Argentinian government, which then owned 20 per cent of YPF. In April 1999, Repsol launched a $13 billion all-cash bid for all of YPF's shares that it did not own. Repsol's hostile bid was opposed by the board of YPF. However, the deal was supported by the Argentinian government, which had 5.3 per cent of the shares in the company, three other provincial governments with smaller stakes and other private investors. Within just one week, the board of YPF conceded defeat. Chairman Roberto Monti commented, 'We have always maintained a business philosophy based on value creation, and it is the board's view, which I back, that Repsol's bid offers the best alternative for our shareholders in current market conditions' (quoted in the *Financial Times*, 12 May 1999, emphasis added).

The new company Repsol YPF combined YPF's powerful upstream businesses with Repsol's strong downstream capabilities. It became the world's eighth largest publicly traded oil companies in terms of oil and gas reserves. Repsol/YPF had reserves equivalent to 4.23 billion barrels of oil, and production equivalent to 1 million barrels per day, very close to that of ENI. Its assets were spread across the world in Europe, North Africa, Latin America and United States. It accounted for 59 per cent of the refining capacity and 47 per cent of the retail market in Spain, and 56 per cent of the refining capacity and 48.6 per cent of the retail market in Argentina.

Restructuring the Chinese oil industry

In the same period that the large-scale merger wave swept through the global major oil companies, and greatly influenced by this dramatic process, China's oil and petrochemical industry underwent a massive restructuring. After an intense debate on how to reform the oil and petrochemical industry, the Chinese government supported the creation of two large integrated oil companies through administrative measures.

The 1998 reorganisation of the Chinese oil industry

In 1998, the State Council comprehensively restructured China's oil and gas industry with the goal of creating internationally competitive large oil companies (Chapter 5). Three objectives were achieved in this asset reorganisation. First, through the massive assets swap, the new CNPC and Sinopec became two vertically integrated oil and petrochemical companies with assets across the whole value chain from upstream to downstream. The new CNPC accounted for

66 per cent of China's oil output, 66 per cent of its gas output, and 42 per cent of its refining capacity. Its assets were located in twelve provinces and regions in northern and western China. The new Sinopec accounted for 23 per cent of China's oil output, 11 per cent of its gas output and 54 per cent of its refining capacity. Its assets were located in nineteen provinces and regions in eastern and southern China. With sales revenue of $25–30 billion each, both of the two groups would have been listed in the world's top 500 companies by revenue. Second, the administrative functions of CNPC and Sinopec were separated from their business management functions. As part of the major government restructuring programme in the same year, the State Petroleum and Chemical Industry Bureau under the State Economic and Trade Commission was formed to take over the administration functions from CNPC and Sinopec. Third, starting from June 1998, China's crude oil price was pegged to the Singapore FOB prices, which was a significant step to integrate China's oil industry with that of the world. Before that, the crude oil price in China was set by the government, which resulted in constant disputes between CNPC and Sinopec with each lobbying intensely for prices favourable to their respective businesses. In line with the restructuring, the State Development and Planning Commission now publishes monthly a benchmark crude oil price based on the average Singapore FOB prices. CNPC and Sinopec each negotiate a premium relative to the benchmark price.

The 2000 flotation of PetroChina and Sinopec

Closely following the 1998 asset reorganisation, CNPC and Sinopec each restructured the respective company in preparation for international flotation. The businesses and structure of the two companies were changed fundamentally. In each of the companies, core businesses covering oil and gas exploration and development, storage and transportation, refining and marketing, petrochemicals were separated from non-core businesses, including enterprises that provide engineering, technical and infrastructure services to core businesses as well as social functions such as schools and hospitals. On 5 November 1999, CNPC grouped together its core businesses and created PetroChina as a joint stock company with limited liability. On 25 February 2000, China Petroleum and Chemical Corporation, known as Sinopec, was established on the basis of the core businesses from the old Sinopec, now known as Sinopec Group (Chapter 6).

In April 2000, PetroChina was listed on the New York and Hong Kong Stock exchanges. The IPO raised $2.89 billion. Among the shares issued, 32.1 per cent were bought by strategic and corporate investors including BP Amoco, Hong Kong Cheung Kong Enterprise, Sing Hung Kai, and Hutchison Whampoa. After this global listing, CNPC controlled a 90 per cent interest in PetroChina. Six months later, in October 2000, Sinopec was listed on the stock exchanges in New York, Hong Kong and London. The IPO raised $3.73 billion. After the global flotation, 56.06 per cent of the interests of Sinopec were controlled by its parent company Sinopec Group, 22.73 per cent by the State Development Bank and three asset management companies, Cinda, Orient and Huarong, 21.21 per cent by overseas investors including the three largest global oil companies Exxon Mobil, Shell and BP. The share purchase by the global giants was crucial for the success of the two companies' flotation.

Global leading firms and Chinese large companies

Business capabilities

RESERVES AND OUTPUT

China's total oil reserves were estimated at around 24 billion barrels by 2000 (Table 8.1), of which PetroChina owned 11.03 billion barrels, equivalent to that of Exxon Mobil and exceeding those of Shell and BP (Table 8.3). PetroChina's natural gas reserves were 58 per cent of those of Exxon Mobil and around 10,000 billion cubic feet more than that owned by TotalFinaElf and Chevron Texaco, respectively (Table 8.3). In terms of output, PetroChina is already close to the level of the world's leading companies, with an oil output of around 2.1 million barrels per day, compared with 1.93 million at BP, 2.27 million at Shell and 2.55 million at Exxon Mobil. Sinopec is similar to Repsol YPF in terms of oil reserves and oil production, but is a much smaller scale in natural gas reserves and production. However, even the combined production volume of both PetroChina and Sinopec lags considerably behind the global giants in terms of natural gas production (Table 8.3).

There are, however, crucial differences between the reserves and output of the two leading Chinese oil companies and those of the global giants. First, the global distribution is strikingly different. PetroChina and Sinopec produce entirely within China. CNPC has international operations in Canada, Venezuela, Kazakhstan, Sudan, Thailand, Indonesia and Malaysia. In 2000, approximately 5.5 million tonnes of oil were obtained from overseas operations, equivalent to 7.8 per cent of China's total crude oil imports in the same year. But CNPC retained ownership of these international projects and PetroChina did not have any foreign operations. Sinopec had virtually no overseas reserves or production. By contrast, BP has production and exploration activities in twenty-seven countries and Exxon has them in thirty countries. Second, the quality of the portfolio of oil and gas assets is very different. China's main onshore oil reserves are declining seriously.

Fifty per cent of PetroChina's 11 billion barrels of crude oil reserves are from the Daqing oil field alone, China's largest producing region, and one-third of the natural gas reserves are in the Tarim Basin. However, 89 per cent of PetroChina's proven crude oil reserves have already been developed. Daqing is in the secondary recovery stage and polymer flooding has been applied to about 14 per cent of its production. Tarim is in the remote western part of the country and the reserves are geographically extremely complex, requiring advanced technology to extract and involve high costs to transport the gas to the main consuming

Table 8.3 Operating data compared: global majors vs PetroChina and Sinopec, 2000.

Company	Reserves		Production			Refinery throughput (mmb/d)	Oil product sales (mmt/y)	Chemical production (mmt)	Number of service stations
	Oil (bb)	Gas (bcf)	Oil (mmboe/d)	Gas (bcf/d)					
Exxon Mobil	11.56	55,866	2.55	10.34		5.64	400	25.6	45,000
Royal Dutch Shell	8.67	50,842	2.27	8.22		2.92	278.5	20.29	46,000
BP	6.51	41,100	1.93	7.61		2.92	188	22.07	27,545
TotalFinaElf	6.96	20,705	1.43	3.76		2.41	185	15.4†	17,700
Chevron Texaco*	6.83	19,176	2.30	3.70		2.26	233.5	–	39,000‡
ENI	3.42	14,762	0.80	2.50		0.86	53.5	8.5	12,085
Repsol YPF	2.38	14,394	0.64	2.22		1.21	51.4	2.8	7,200
PetroChina	11.0	32,532	2.10	1.38		1.50	56.4	6.7	11,350
Sinopec Corporation	2.95	999	0.68	0.22		2.12	67.0	20.03	20,259

Sources: Compiled from company reports.

Notes:
* Figures are combined estimates after announced merger in October 2000.
† Capacity.
‡ Numbers include 8,000 service stations of Caltex.
bb = billion barrels, bcf = billion cubic metres, mmboe/d = million barrels of oil equivalent per day, bcf/d = billion cubic feet per day, mmb/d = million barrels per day, mmt/y = million barrels per year, mmt = million tonnes.

areas in the eastern part of the country. Through their financial and technical resources, the global giants have attempted to construct a portfolio that can make a profit at as low as $10 per barrel of oil. In 2000, Exxon Mobile's finding costs reached as low as $0.67 per oil equivalent barrel. In contrast, less than five of PetroChina's oil fields could make a profit with an oil price of $10–15 per barrel, which Shell sets as the benchmark for profitable operations.

REFINING

PetroChina and Sinopec between them have a total of forty-nine refineries, among which twenty-one have annual refining capacities greater than 5 million tonnes. None of PetroChina's refineries and only four of Sinopec's refineries have capacities greater than 10 million tonnes. In 2000, the refinery throughput of PetroChina's refineries was 75 million tonnes and those of Sinopec averaged 105.5 million tonnes, only around one-third of the average for the global giants (Table 8.3). Moreover, the average cost of processing one tonne of crude oil for Sinopec's refineries was 200 yuan, compared with 167 yuan for some foreign refineries (Chen, 2001). The utilisation rate of refineries owned by PetroChina and Sinopec rose from 61 per cent in 1998, the lowest in the 1990s, to 80 per cent in 2000. This is due to the increasing amount of crude oil available for the two companies' refineries and, to some extent, to the government's campaign to close down small refineries with an annual capacity of less than 1 million tonnes and refineries outside the state crude oil allocation plan. Since 1999, the SETC has ordered the closure of 111 refineries across the country (SETC, 1999, 2000). The small refineries usually have support from the local government for tax revenue and employment and closure has proved a complex task. Despite the government's campaign, an investigation by SETC showed that small refineries in Sha'anxi, Shangdong and Henan that should have been closed down were still active in production and marketing (Zhang, 2001).

At the end of 2000, China's total refining capacity was 279.5 million tonnes, exceeding the country's total oil consumption by 53 million tonnes in that year. However, the refining sector needs revamping, upgrading and expanding. First, most of China's refining facilities are equipped to process low-sulphur oil and are unable to process high-sulphur crude oil from the Middle East except for a few refineries on the east coast such as Maoming and Zhenhai. With more than half of the oil imports from the Middle East, refineries need to add capabilities to use sour crude oil. The effort of PetroChina and Sinopec to increase their capabilities to process sour crude oil requires technological and financial capabilities. Second, more stringent environmental regulations on refined products calls for high-conversion refineries. Third, China's accession to the WTO is reducing the tariffs on refined products from 6–12 per cent to a uniform rate of 6 per cent. Few of PetroChina's refineries can survive the competition from imported refined products. Sinopec estimated that the reduction in tariff for oil products and chemical products would reduce its sales revenue by 3 billion yuan a year.

Since 1999, both PetroChina and Sinopec have been aggressively expanding their network of service stations all over China. By 2000, PetroChina reported to have 11,350 service stations, compared with 20,259 for Sinopec. Each almost doubled the number of service stations in 1999–2000. This was strongly supported by the government, which granted the two companies exclusive licences to operate new service stations in China. However, the two companies engaged in a 'blind competitive clash' in the race to acquire service stations, which led to 'less than stringent evaluations and inflated prices for the service stations targeted for acquisition' (Zhang Zhigang, Vice Minister of SETC). Around one quarter of each of the two companies' service stations are franchised retail outlets bearing the companies' brands, 'PetroChina' and 'Sinopec' respectively. These 8,000 'franchised' service stations, accounting for 30 per cent of the total number of service stations outside the two companies, still run as separate entities. Refined product supplies and prices of selling refined products and accounting are not uniformly controlled or consolidated. A centralised supply of refined products on a regional basis has not been realised even to the network of service stations owned and operated by the two companies themselves. Moreover, the annual average transaction volume per petrol station of Sinopec is less than 1,500 tonnes, compared with the average international level of 5,000 tonnes. Between them, PetroChina and Sinopec have around 2,100 wholesale entities that have no effective co-ordination over supply, price and customers. Many of the storage facilities are obsolete. PetroChina and Sinopec still have a long way to go before they develop the logistics expertise of the global giants or are able to develop a comparable brand name.

PETROCHEMICALS

- *Ethylene crackers* By the end of 2000, China had a total ethylene capacity of 4.3 million tonnes, ranking the eighth largest in the world and the third in Asia after Japan and Korea (*Oil and Gas Journal*, 23 April 2001). Of the total of eighteen ethylene crackers in China, only seven had an annual capacity above 400,000 tonnes (four owned by Sinopec and one by PetroChina) and the other eleven had less than 200,000 tonnes. The annual capacity of the largest cracker is 480,000 tonnes, compared to the world's largest at 2.8 million tonnes. Compared with the integrated large sites of the global majors, the average capacity of each petrochemical complex is extremely small (Table 8.5). Instead of being large integrated sites situated in a few concentrated areas, these eighteen ethylene crackers are located in sixteen production plants in fifteen cities.
- *Product mix* A high proportion of China's petrochemical and refined products are low value-added products. In the year 2000, high-value added petrochemical production accounted for only 30 per cent of the value of the total petrochemical production. Only 73 per cent of the diesel produced can

Table 8.4 Top ten ethylene producers* vs PetroChina and Sinopec Corporation.**

Ranking	Company	No. of sites	Capacity (million tonnes per year)		Company interest (per cent)
			Entire complexes	Company interests	
1	Dow Chemical Co.	16	12.467	10.076	0.8
2	Exxon Mobil Chemical Co.	14	10.609	7.071	66.7
3	Equistar Chemicals	7	5.265	5.265	100
4	Shell Chemicals Ltd	6	6.188	4.539	73.4
5	Chevron Phillips Chemical Co.	3	3.674	3.674	100
6	Saudi Basic Industries Corporation	4	5.65	3.95	69.9
7	BP	5	4.151	3.036	73.1
8	Nova Chemicals Corporation	2	3.54	2.968	83.8
9	Atofina	7	3.725	2.378	63.8
10	Enichem SPA	7	3.005	2.196	73.1
–	Sinopec Corporation	5	1.99	1.99	100
–	PetroChina	2‡	0.8	0.8	62†

Sources: *Oil and Gas Journal*, 23 April 2001, and author's own research.

Notes:
* As of 1 April 2001.
** End of 2000.
† Percentage of total capacity of company.
‡ Sites of annual capacity over 350,000 tonnes.

be classified as 'first class' and just 70 per cent of lubricants are of middle or high premium. By 1997, China could only produce 128 differential synthetic resins, compared with over 10,000 produced by Japan (Chen, 2001). The total petrochemical output and low-value added products cannot keep up with the rapid growth of China's economy, which leads to surging petrochemical imports. By 2000, imports of refined products and major petrochemicals accounted for one half of the Chinese market (Table 8.6). With further reductions in import tariffs after China's accession to WTO, even these low-value added petrochemical products face enormous competition not only from global majors but also from low-cost producers in the Middle East and the South East Asia.

RENEWABLE ENERGY

Both BP and Shell have renewable energy in their business portfolios. There has been extensive co-operation and partnership in fuel cell technology between the global energy companies including BP, Shell and Exxon Mobil, the world's leading automobile manufacturers such as Ford, DaimlerChrysler, GM, Toyota, Nissan, Honda, Hyundai, and Volkswagen, as well as specialised technology companies International Fuel Cells and Ballard Power Systems.

Table 8.5 Market share of imported oil products and petrochemicals in China, 2000.

Imported product	Market share
Refined products	20%
Lubricants	25%
LPG	50%
Synthetic resins	48%
Synthetic fibres	30%
Synthetic rubbers	44%

Source: Sinopec.

In the solar energy business, consolidation has been underway in recent years, with BP and Shell at the forefront of this process. Shell intends to invest $500 million to $1 billion on developing new energy businesses between 2001 and 2005. Shell recognises that 'solar photovoltaics, which offer abundant direct and widely distributed energy' and 'hydrogen fuel cells, which offer high performance and clean final energy from a variety of fuels' are the two 'potentially disruptive energy technologies' (Shell, 2001: 22). In September 2000, Shell agreed to form an equal joint venture with United Technologies of the United States to develop, manufacture and sell fuel cell processors. The two companies will target applications of fuel cell processors in road transport, power generation and retail outlets such as filling stations that can convert petrol into hydrogen on-site. In early 2001, Shell Solar went into partnership with the solar business of Siemens and Eon of Germany and set up a joint venture that was intended to capture 15 per cent of the world market, compared with 20 per cent for BP. In October 2001, Shell signed a joint venture agreement with Akzo Nobel to develop low cost solar cell technology. The joint venture was to test an automated production line to apply a thin 'solar cell coating' virtually continuously to rolls of flexible foil. The mass production process is expected to bring the cost of flexible solar cells at only a fraction of that of the traditional silicon and glass cells (*Financial Times*, 16 October 2001). In 2000, BP's solar business generated revenue of $200 million and BP aims to achieve $1 billion revenue from its solar business in 2007. In July 2001, BP agreed to acquire Agere System's semiconductor plant in Madrid as a base for a five-fold expansion of its solar photovoltaic cell manufacturing in Spain. The new plant, in which BP was to invest over $100 million, will produce 60 megawatts a year of high-efficiency crystalline silicon solar cells.

In sharp contrast, neither PetroChina nor Sinopec has businesses in renewable energy. The Chinese market for renewable energy such as solar, wind power, bio-mass and terrestrial heat is developing but very fragmented and technologically backward. By the end of 2000, over 1,000 enterprises engaged in the research, production, sales and installation of solar water heaters (*taiyangneng reshuiqi*), generating a total revenue of 6 billion yuan. Over

40 manufacturing and sales enterprises produced solar cells with total capacity of 5 megawatts, compared with BP's single plant in Spain with 60 megawatts capacity. The technology for solar cells is equivalent to the international level of the 1980s. There were twenty-six wind farms generating 340,000 kilowatts of electricity. The annual methane production capacity was 600 million cubic metres. The electricity generation capacity through terrestrial heat reached 30 megawatts by the end of 2000 (SETC, 2001). Neither CNPC, Sinopec nor CNOOC is engaged in the development of renewable energy. Whereas BP, Shell and Exxon Mobil are actively participating in the research and application of fuel cells together with the world's leading automobile manufacturers and specialised technology companies, neither CNPC, Sinopec nor CNOOC has activities in fuel cell technology. CNPC (PetroChina), Sinopec, and CNOOC lag behind the global giants in renewable energy.

More significantly, the global giants have moved into China's renewable energy market. For example, Shell has recognised that China is a major potential market for solar energy with its vast rural population. Shell has participated in a solar photovoltaic project in Xinjiang sponsored by the Dutch Government under the China Brightness programme, organised by the State Development and Planning Commission of the Chinese government. The $25 million Chinese–Dutch project will use Shell's photovoltaic panels to generate electricity for around 78,000 homes in rural areas of Xinjiang.

TECHNOLOGY

Both PetroChina and Sinopec have made many important technical advances. However, both companies are still far behind the global giants in their development of world-leading technologies. Compared with an average of more than 1,000 patents produced annually by each of the global petrochemical companies, Sinopec produces only around 300. In 2000, PetroChina and Sinopec reported to have spent $212 million and $200 million respectively on research and development, about one-fifth to two-fifths of that spent by the 'big three' (Table 8.4). The R&D spending/revenue ratio of PetroChina and Sinopec (0.07 per cent) is no less than that of Shell and higher than Exxon Mobil and BP (0.04 per cent). However, the global majors are able to spend more on research and technological development in absolute terms due to their sheer size in sales revenue.

The technological capabilities of both upstream and downstream are backward. This is reflected, for exploration and production, in the fact that oil field development equipment is equivalent to world level in the late 1980s and exploration equipment is equivalent to world level in the early 1990s. Oil extracting machinery and oil and gas treatment equipment are either imported complete or assembled in China. Key electronic instruments and software for exploration and production are imported. China's industrial experts pointed out that China's capability for technological innovation in upstream oil and gas industry is still at the level of a 'third world' country, which is a great constraint on the industry's competitiveness and efficiency (*China Petroleum*, January 1999). The backwardness in technology is also reflected, for petrochemical production, in the high energy consumption level. In ethylene production, PetroChina consumed an average of 872 kilograms of standard oil per tonne in 2000 while the world average level is 500–690 kilograms of standard oil per ton. In addition, the rate of ethylene loss is high. The average rate of ethylene loss in PetroChina was 1.3 per cent in comparison with the world average of one per cent in 2000. The high energy consumption level and high ethylene percentage loss contribute to the high cost of ethylene production. Energy consumption accounted for 76 per cent of the total cost of production compared with the world average of 63 per cent. Moreover, only 55 per cent of the chemicals from the cracking process in China are further processed and utilised (Chen *et al.*, 1998: 29).

FINANCIAL PERFORMANCE

- *Revenue* The sales value places Petrochina and Sinopec alongside the leading second tier of global oil and petrochemical companies, such as ENI and Repsol YPF. However, the sales of PetroChina and Sinopec still fall considerably short of those of the industry leaders, Exxon Mobil, Shell and BP (Table 8.4).
- *Profit* Net profits at PetroChina and Sinopec dramatically improved in 2000 at $6.67 billion and $2.30 billion compared with $0.33 billion and $0.56 billion in 1999. The gap of net profits with the global leading giants has been narrowed considerably from only a small fraction in 1999 to almost one-third and half that of the 'big three'. However, if one looks at the profits per worker at PetroChina and Sinopec, they are minuscule compared with those at the world's leading companies in the sector. Each of PetroChina and Sinopec has a workforce 4–5 times as big as the top three global oil and petrochemicals giants (Table 8.4).
- *Market capitalisation* The market capitalisation of PetroChina and Sinopec is only a small fraction of that of the leading global companies. Even if one assumed that 100 per cent of the company had been floated, the market capitalisation of PetroChina and Sinopec would be $35 billion and $14 billion respectively, compared with $286.4 billion for Exxon Mobil, $206.3 billion for Royal Dutch/Shell and $178 billion for BP (Table 8.4). Analysts estimate PetroChina's average annual growth rate in the next five years at 4.9 per cent, 50 per cent of that of Exxon Mobil and only 33.3 per cent of that for the whole global oil industry. This is due to the serious doubts about PetroChina's operational efficiency and high uncertainty about its performance after China's accession to WTO. PetroChina's P/E/G (price/equity/growth rate) ratio is predicted to be less than 1.0, compared to 1.7 for Exxon Mobil due to the 'institutional risk' involved in China (*Caijing*, April 2001).

Table 8.6 Financial indicators compared: global majors vs PetroChina and Sinopec, 2000.

Company	Revenue ($billion)	Net profit ($billion)	R&D spending ($million)	Market Cap** ($billion)	Employee numbers	Profit/revenue (per cent)	Profit/Employee ($)
Exxon Mobil	210.4	17.7	936.0	286.4	99,600	8.4	177,711
Royal Dutch Shell	149.2	12.7	1144.0	206.3	90,000	8.5	141,111
BP	148.1	11.9	599.0	178.0	107,200	8.0	111,007
TotalFinaElf	105.9	6.4	631.0	102.9	123,303	6.0	51,905
Chevron Texaco*	99.2	7.6	922.0	84.5	53,621	7.7	141,736
ENI	45.1	5.3	315.3	48.8	69,969	11.8	75,748
Repsol YPF	42.3	2.2	61.6 (1999)	20.6	37,194	5.2	59,149
PetroChina	29.2	6.7	212.0	3.5†	441,000	22.9	15,193
Sinopec	39.7	2.3	200.0	1.4‡	508,000	5.8	4,528

Sources: *Fortune Global 500,* 2001, *FT500,* 2001, company annual reports.

Notes:

* Figures are combined estimates after announced merger in October 2000.

** Market capitalisation on 4 January, 2001.

† Flotation of 10 per cent of company value.

‡ Flotation of 20 per cent of company value.

Organisational capabilities

STRUCTURE

The organisational structure of PetroChina and Sinopec are not very much different from that of an international integrated oil company with the establishment of a board of directors, senior management team and core businesses segments from upstream to downstream. However, two structural issues stand out: the integration of powerful subordinate companies and their relationship with their parent companies.

The internal organisational structure of PetroChina and Sinopec has major differences from that of the global giants. The latter have a strong 'one company' corporate identity and culture. Under both PetroChina and Sinopec, there exist powerful entities that over the years developed strong corporate identities and ambitions. They struggled for autonomy in business management and aspired to become independent competitive companies. With a history of over forty years, Daqing, China's largest oil field now under PetroChina, had developed a strong corporate identity and its employees took great pride in being 'Daqing people' (*Daqing ren*). Daqing had the corporate ambition to build itself into a leading oil company able to compete globally. It strongly believed that it should be *the firm* to be floated. Under Sinopec four companies including Zhenhai, Shanghai Petrochemicals Corporation, Yizheng and Yanhua were listed on the stock exchanges in Hong Kong and New York. Zhenhai and Shanghai Petrochemical Corporation each with a history of more than thirty years had developed strong corporate identities. Each devised plans and strategies for development through mergers and acquisitions. Both PetroChina and Sinopec took measures to integrate these powerful subordinate companies by centralising planning, investment and finance. Nevertheless, the challenge to establish a unified corporate identity and culture still remains formidable.

The relationship between the two listed companies and their parent companies remains ambiguous. As discussed above, CNPC controls 90 per cent of PetroChina and Sinopec Group controls 56 per cent of Sinopec. A principal part of the annual income of CNPC and Sinopec Group is from the dividend payment made by each of the two listed companies. In 2000, CNPC received approximately $3.1 billion in dividend payments from PetroChina,[2] accounting for 53 per cent of its net profits. CNPC retained the non-core businesses as well as social functions employing more than 800,000 people, most of whom incurred huge losses. The non-core businesses of Sinopec Group employs more than 600,000 people but none of the businesses made a profit in 1999. To what extent PetroChina and Sinopec have the decision-making autonomy in business strategy, dividend payment and appointment of senior management, remains unclear. Moreover, of the thirteen directors on the board of PetroChina (including three independent non-executive directors), five concurrently hold top positions with CNPC. Of the ten directors on the board of Sinopec (including three independent non-executive directors and one employee representative director), two also have top positions with Sinopec Group. Ma Fucai, Chairman of PetroChina, and Li Yizhong, Chairman of Sinopec, are concurrently the President of the two respective parent companies. Issues of corporate governance in creating shareholder value and protecting the rights of minority shareholders are a serious concern among investors.[3]

PERFORMANCE MONITORING

Despite the differences in their governance structure, both BP and Royal Dutch/ Shell adopted the 'business units' model from the mid-1990s (Chapter 3). The business units have operational autonomy in conducting their businesses but are subject to the strategic direction set for the whole company and to rigorous monitoring from the headquarters. In the case of BP, the performance contract serves as the 'vehicle' linking the business units together to ensure BP delivers its performance. In Shell, the annual assurance letter set the standards and performance targets for business activities.

During and after its flotation, PetroChina attempted to adopt performance contracts and hired McKinsey to work out a system of key performance indicators (KPIs). However, it proved impossible to implement the performance contract within the company. Senior officials of PetroChina seriously questioned the feasibility of the performance contract. Over-staffing was a serious difficulty in setting up metrics with which to evaluate performance: 'The work in my Department can be done by five people but now I have ten. That will definitely affect my performance (as the head of the Department) following the "scientific" measurement system. But I don't have the right to and I can't just ask five of them to go' (senior official, interview, June 2000). In addition, PetroChina lacked a uniform and scientific management accounting system, which made it impossible to collect and validate data on the KPIs set out in the performance contract. In early 2002, it was decided that the performance contract could not be implemented in PetroChina. For a publicly-traded company on the international market, this was a serious issue, which damaged investors' confidence in the company's ability to implement international management practices.

REWARD POLICY

The reward policy for executives of both BP and Shell is to set compensation at a competitive level for the industry in order to attract and retain high quality personnel. For PetroChina and Sinopec, the issue of the reward policy is highly sensitive, affecting the 'stability and psychological balance' within the company.

The difficulties arise on three fronts. First, until today, executives with CNPC and Sinopec Group are ranked as bureaucrats. For example, both Ma Fucai and Li Yizhong have the rank equivalent to vice-minister. They have the basic salary for bureaucrats, which is less than $500 per month; meanwhile, they have certain privileges for bureaucrats such as those relating to housing and car provision. We have seen that some executives with PetroChina and Sinopec have a dual position with their respective parent companies. PetroChina and Sinopec reported that the remuneration for their executives consisted of basic salary, bonus and stock appreciation rights. Another issue is that of how to reconcile the fact that the remuneration for senior managers within PetroChina is higher than it is for those who are with CNPC. CNPC has tried to increase the income of its senior managers, but their income still lags behind that of PetroChina's senior managers.

Second, we have seen both PetroChina and Sinopec have a huge workforce to downsize and their parent companies have tens of thousands of employees in the non-core business sectors. The major approach to shedding workers is to pay an employee a lump sum on the basis of the number of years they have served. This is a costly and complex process. In 2000, CNPC paid 16 billion yuan to 10,000 employees who were made redundant. It was reported in 2001, that Yanshan Petrochemical Corporation under Sinopec paid a total amount of 2 billion yuan to 16,000 redundant workers, of which some 70 per cent was from Sinopec Group and the remaining 30 per cent was raised by Yanshan itself. The amount that it has agreed to pay per year of service differs among enterprises under Sinopec: 4,300 yuan for Yanshan, 4,350 yuan for Shanghai Petrochemical, 4,550 yuan for Yangzi Petrochemical, 3,900 yuan for Qilu Petrochemicals, 3,750 yuan for Tianjin Petrochemicals, and 4,100 yuan for Shengli Oilfield. In addition to the huge cost involved for the Sinopec Group and the individual enterprises, the process had a tremendous psychological impact on the employees. Most of the employees, and in many cases their entire families, had worked in the industry for decades. They were proud of being 'oil people' (*shiyouren*), regarded as the vanguard of China's industry. It has been a painful 'transitional process' for them to accept the fact that they are no longer the 'master' (*zhuren*) of their company and that they are not 'needed' any more. In Yanshan, a significant proportion of employees said they were actually not willing to be paid to cease the labour contract with the company. Instead, they were, to some extent, 'forced' into accepting the settlement. They were told that it was a good opportunity to take the money now when the company could afford it. They were warned of the intense competition for jobs with the company and their own relative strengths and weaknesses in that competition.

Third, with China's accession to the WTO, global giant corporations such as BP, Shell, Exxon Mobil now have more freedom to expand their businesses in China. They are better placed in competition with the Chinese companies to attract high-quality local personnel with superior pay offers and better training provision. 'Brain drain' has become a serious concern for the Chinese companies.

LEADERSHIP

- *Lord Browne of BP* Lord Browne aged fifty-five in 2003; he graduated with a first-class degree in physics from the University of Cambridge and joined

BP in 1966. He started his job with BP as a trainee in petroleum engineering for eighteen months in Alaska, followed by postings to New York, San Francisco and Canada. In the early 1980s, he was in charge of turning around the Forties oil field in Aberdeen. He 'exploited a tax loophole and sold off pieces of oil field to smaller companies', which made profits of £200 million for BP (*Financial Times*, 21 March 2000). Shortly afterwards, Lord Browne was promoted to the position of Group Treasurer in 1984, at the age of thirty-six. In 1989, he became the Director of BP Exploration. During his tenure at BP Exploration, Lord Browne implemented a massive cost-cutting programme and adopted the performance contract system. He sold off non-core businesses worth $1.3 billion and cut 10 per cent of the workforce. In 1995, Lord Browne became the Group Chief Executive Officer of BP and he has committed himself to staying in office until he is sixty.

Lord Browne was dubbed as 'BP's daring deal-maker' (*Financial Times*, 21 March 2000). Since he became the GCEO in 1995, he has transformed BP from a 'two-pipeline company'[4] into a company of global reach in assets, and from a significantly under-performing company into a global energy group with a market capitalisation of $178 billion in 2000. This was achieved through a series of large-scale mergers and acquisitions in the industry. He initiated the consolidation process in the oil and petrochemical industry through BP's transatlantic merger with Amoco in 1998. The merger made BP the world's third largest oil company after Exxon Mobile and Royal Dutch/Shell. Subsequently, Lord Browne announced the take-over of Arco in March 2000 and the acquisition of Burmah Castrol in 2001. 'John is several steps ahead of most people, not just one step' (Daniel Yergin, quoted in *Fortune*, 5 July 1999). Moreover, he rapidly disposed of the 'bones' that came along with the 'meat' in the acquisition process. Lord Browne aims to sell about 3–5 per cent of BP's capital base each year (*Financial Times*, 20 January 2002).

After these large-scale mergers, Lord Browne has not stopped global expansion. First, BP has entered German petro retailing by acquiring Eon's Aral chain of service stations, which gives BP a leading market share ahead of Shell. Second, BP is sharply stepping up its activities in Russia. BP is considering increasing its equity share in Russian Sidanco,[5] in which BP now has 10 per cent equity share and management control. BP is also looking into opportunities beyond its interests in Sidanco and the Kovykta gas field in East Siberia. Lord Browne sees Russia as 'a place where we could deepen our interest' and 'our philosophy is to work through a Russian company' (quoted in *Financial Times*, 20 January 2002). Third, Lord Browne is interested in expanding into Iran, which is now under US sanctions. BP has 40 per cent of its assets in the United States and it is the biggest gas producer in the United States. In early 2001, Lord Browne was very cautious about the possibility for BP to enter Iran, following Royal Dutch/Shell and TotalFinaElf. He stressed the need to take US foreign policy considerations into account in areas such as the Middle East. It would be 'inappropriate' to ignore the US sanctions on Iran, even though BP is a UK-registered company (quoted in *Financial Times*, 17/18 February 2001). In January 2002, Lord Browne was more assertive with the issue of Iran: 'We are very struck by the precedent set by TotalFinaElf and Shell [which have gone into Iran] that we believe we should be able to follow. In spite of being a very big American company, we are British-based' (quoted in *Financial Times*, 20 January 2002). Lord Browne frankly pointed out that BP would like to go back to Iran, where BP was born as the Anglo-Iranian Oil Company in 1909, through negotiating the right deal.

When announcing BP's take-over of Amoco, the then Sir John Browne said BP/Amoco would not settle for the third place among the big three. The new group would compete with Shell and Exxon for the most attractive projects in the industry but would also want to set the pace of competition (*Financial Times*, 13 August 1998). Lord Browne's ambition paid off through the series of mergers and acquisitions, which have given BP 'the physical scale to present itself to governments as fully capable of taking on bigger projects – and a bigger share of those projects' (quoted in *Financial Times*, 20 January 2002). Scale helped BP beat its rivals in the international bidding process and was chosen by China to build the country's first LNG terminal. It was also advantageous to BP to be chosen by Saudi Arabia to build gas projects in the country for the first time after the 1970s nationalisation of oil and gas assets.

Lord Browne is keen on creating a learning organisation and delivering performance in BP. He adopted the business units structure and performance contract system in the whole company after he became the GCEO. The simple rule of the game, according to Lord Browne, is to know all the people around you. You must feel it is 'my success' if 'my department' achieves success (*China Petroleum*, September 2000). He believes that ultimately the role of top management in the learning organisation is to make decisions on the organisational architecture and the way forward. The most senior managers

> set policies, standards, and target, and create processes to ensure that people achieve or adhere to them ... What determines whether it does is the questions leaders ask and the way they approach what is going on. Leadership is all about catalyzing learning as well as better performance.
>
> (quoted in Prokesch, 1997: 168)

At the beginning of 2002, Lord Browne's ambition remained as strong as ever: 'I would like to be able to overtake our competitors in profitability and size' (quoted in *Financial Times*, 20 January 2002). He believes that what distinguishes a company in the oil industry whose products, oil and gas, change less than in most other sectors is how to invest for the future, how to divest, how to acquire as well as how to make cost savings. The essence is to remain big and nimble.

- *Sir Mark Moody-Stuart of Shell* Sir Mark was awarded a PhD by the University of Cambridge. He joined Shell in 1966, working as a geologist. Following his posts in exploration in Spain, Oman, Australia, and Brunei, Sir Mark served as the leader of Shell's exploration teams in the North Sea. He then moved on to more general management positions, working in Africa, Asia, and Europe. When he worked as a senior manager in Turkey and Malaysia, Sir Mark played an instrumental role in working with national governments to launch a number of major projects. In 1990, Sir Mark took over duties as the Co-ordinator of Exploration and Production in The Hague. He was appointed Group Managing Director in 1991 and became Chairman of the Committee of Managing Directors of the Royal Dutch/ Shell Group in 1998. Sir Mark retired in June 2001 and succeeded by Phil Watts.

   While consolidation was sweeping through giant corporations in the oil industry, Sir Mark concentrated on his 'internal merger' (*The Independent*, 12 April 2000). Not ruling out the possibilities of an external merger 'if the right opportunity arises', Sir Mark believed that his company had 'a great deal of work to do in (its) own shop' and was 'large enough to be the leading company on our own without any merger' (quoted in *NPN*, February 1999). During his tenure as Chairman of Royal Dutch/Shell, Sir Mark accelerated change within the company through stringent control over capital investment, reducing cost, and setting financial targets: 'When you clearly burn your boats it acts as a powerful weapon internally' (quoted in *Financial Times*, 2 November 2000). Moreover, he changed Shell's business structure from business committees into CEOs and executive committees running each of the company's business streams with the objective of speeding up business decisions. This was a move away from collective decision-making to a system emphasising greater personal responsibility among executives. He closed previously powerful national head offices in the United Kingdom, the Netherlands, Germany and France and stripped Shell Oil in the United States of its autonomy over capital expenditure. Under his leadership, Royal Dutch/Shell significantly reduced costs and increased profitability. Costs had been cut by $4 billion from 1998 to 2001, beating the projected target. The company's average return on capital employed reached 19.5 per cent in 2000, well above the projected 15 per cent by 2001. Instead of pursuing mega-merger strategies as other oil majors did, Shell expanded globally through smaller acquisitions and other investments. Shell acquired Fletcher Challenge Energy, the largest oil and gas company in New Zealand. It was also awarded a leading position in two of the three natural gas projects in Saudi Arabia. With projects in Oman and Nigeria, Shell increased its LNG business by 40 per cent.

   Unlike Lord Browne who enjoys an open-ended tenure, Sir Mark was obliged by internal company rules to retire after a four-year term of office with Royal Dutch/Shell. In running such far-flung and complicated company as Royal Dutch/Shell, Sir Mark admitted that four-year is too short a time. 'In principle, six or seven years might be better' (quoted in *Financial Times*, 2 November 2000).

- *Ma Fucai of CNPC and PetroChina* Ma Fucai, aged fifty-seven in 2003, is the Chairman of the Board of Directors of PetroChina and the President of CNPC. He graduated from Beijing Petroleum Institute and is a senior engineer. From February 1990 to December 1996, Mr Ma worked in Shengli Petroleum Administration Bureau as the Deputy Director, Standing Deputy Director and eventually Director. He was an Assistant President of CNPC for a brief period of two months from November 1996 to December 1996 and then became the Vice President of CNPC in December 1996. In June 1997, Mr Ma succeeded Ding Guiming and became the Director of Daqing Petroleum Administration Bureau (Chapter 7). Ma Fucai has been the President of CNPC since April 1998 and became the Chairman of PetroChina when the company was created in 1999.

  Under Ma Fucai's leadership, CNPC defeated Daqing's attempt to gain independence, completed the huge task of separating the core from the non-core businesses, and created and listed PetroChina in the international market. Along with the parallel transformation of Sinpec under Li Yizhong (see below), these were colossal events in CNPC's history and of great significance in China's transition from a planned economy. The whole process was completed within one year and each step was fraught with difficulties. Mr Ma pushed through the restructuring while managing to hold the company together. Mr Ma keeps a low profile and is seldom to be seen at high-level conferences, forums, or seminars. He is economical with his words with the press both at home and abroad. His company believes in 'action' instead of 'words'. Despite great difficulties with the company, Chairman Ma Fucai is confident that PetroChina can be constructed into a first-class global oil company. Speaking as President of CNPC at the CNPC annual meeting[6] at the end of 2000, Mr Ma stressed CNPC's strategy of 'overall development'. He said that 'overall development' was the objective of restructuring and flotation.

  > We will construct PetroChina into a 'lean' company with high efficiency, standardised operation, and international competitiveness. For the other enterprises within CNPC, we will build up a group of competitive regional service companies and specialised technology companies that are able to operate independently and are responsible for their own profit and loss. We must sustain the increase in domestic oil and gas production; meanwhile, we must accelerate overseas oil development'
  >
  > (*China Petroleum*, January 2001).

- *Li Yizhong of Sinopec Group and Sinopec* Li Yizhong, fifty-nine in 2003, he is Chairman of the Board of Directors of Sinopec as well as the President of Sinopec Group. Mr Li graduated from Beijing Petroleum Institute in 1966 specialising in refining engineering. From January 1985 to October 1987,

Mr Li was President of Qilu Petrochemical Company under the old Sinopec. From October 1987 to August 1997, he was the Vice President and then Managing Vice President of the old Sinopec. From August 1997 to April 1998, Mr Li was the Chairman and President of China East United Petrochemical Group Ltd. (*Dong Lian*), responsible for the experiment which demonstrated that 'merging companies under the administration of different government ministries can work'. Li Yizhong has been the President of Sinopec Group since April 1998 and became the Chairman of Sinopec when the company was created in 2000.

Within just one year, Mr Li led Sinopec Group through the separation of core businesses from the non-core businesses and listing Sinopec on the international market. He implemented a series of measures to centralise control over capital investment and financial operations. He is highly enthusiastic about information technology. He decided to invest 994 million yuan to develop the ERP (Enterprise Resource Planning) system, which he hopes will make the financial data, procurement, production, and marketing activities transparent and cost-effective. His ambition is to build Sinopec into 'a world-class integrated energy company with strong core businesses, high-grade assets, technological innovation, scientific management, stringent financial control, and international competitiveness' (Li Yizhong, speech at the International Forum on China and the World in the 21st Century, Beijing, 12 September 2001). However, Li Yizhong is under no illusion about the scale of the challenges posed by direct competition from global giants such as BP, Shell and Exxon Mobil after China's entry into the WTO.

'What I am most concerned about is Sinopec's competitiveness and capabilities to control its domestic market share. In the world market, the supply of oil products and chemical products exceeds demand. China is the only market that keeps stable growth. Foreign large companies will definitely try to capture our most valuable market, relying on their strong capabilities, products of better quality, lower cost, and more effective competitive measures. Therefore, whether we can maintain and expand our market share and enhance our control over the market after WTO is my biggest worry' (http://www.oilnews.com.cn, 3 December 2001, translated by the author).

Competitive landscape

Domestic players

The competitive landscape among the three major Chinese oil companies is changing rapidly, with each speedily expanding their business across the value chain. In 2001, Sinopec bought Sinopec National Star[7] from its parent, Sinopec Group. Sinopec National Star has total proven oil and gas reserves of about 622 million barrels of oil equivalent, mainly in the western regions of China such as Tarim. The acquisition of Sinopec National Star has significantly increased Sinopec's oil and gas reserves and production. In August 2001, Sinopec announced that the company was studying the feasibility of acquiring part of the equity of PetroChina's West to East natural gas transmission project. PetroChina has made a significant move by expanding businesses into the marketing of refined products in Jiangxi Province, a key province under Sinopec, and acquiring and building service stations along the main roads connecting major cities of Nancang, Jiujiang and Ganzhou in the province. Having already accounted for 14 per cent of China's oil and gas production in 1999, CNOOC[8] is emerging as the third integrated oil company in the country. After twelve years' negotiation, in 2001, CNOOC and Shell agreed to jointly establish a petrochemical complex in Huizhou, Guangdong Province. With a total investment of $4.5 billion, the petrochemical complex will have an annual ethylene capacity of 800,000 tonnes, ranking it the second largest ethylene producer in China (Table 8.7). Currently, CNOOC is rapidly moving into imported LNG (Liquefied Natural Gas) supply and sales to the Pearl River Delta as well as imported natural gas and LNG supply and sales to the coastal provinces. The latter is perceived to be a potential rival to PetroChina's West to East natural gas project.

Global leading firms

The global giants are deeply interested in developing their business in China from upstream to downstream. In upstream exploration and development, by 1999, a total of 167 onshore blocks had been opened to foreign companies for exploration and development. Total foreign investment reached $1.1 billion in onshore upstream and $6.45 billion in offshore upstream (SETC, 2001). There are altogether seventy oil companies from eighteen countries that have participated in upstream activities (SETC, 2001), including the global giants Exxon, Shell, BP and other major players such as Chevron Texaco, and Conoco Phillips. In petrochemicals, five global majors will each set up a major joint venture petrochemical complex by 2005 (Table 8.7). These projects involve investment from $2.5 billion to $4.5 billion and are mostly located in the coastal regions, which have China's highest incomes and output growth rates.

BP'S BUSINESSES IN CHINA

- *Upstream* BP began its upstream exploration and production in China in 1979. Today, BP has three main upstream assets in China: the Yacheng 13–1 gas field, the Liuhua 11–1 oil field, and the North China unit which consists of a coal bed methane appraisal project and a non-operated interest in a Bohai Bay oil development called QHD. First, the Yacheng gas field has estimated reserves of 3 trillion cubic feet. It is located in the South China Sea, approximately 100 kilometres south of Hainan Island. BP is the operator of Yacheng and owns 34.5 per cent of the gas field, together with CNOOC, which owns 51 per cent and the Kuwaiti Kufpec, which owns 14.5 per cent. Since 1995, 85 per cent of the gas from Yacheng supplies the

Table 8.7 Five major proposed Sino-foreign petrochemical joint ventures by January, 2000.

Major partners	Ethylene capacity (thousand tonnes per year)	Investment ($billion)	Location	Date of completion
Sinopec SPCC/BP*	900	2.7	Shanghai	2005
Sinopec Yangzi/BASF*	650	2.7	Nanjing	2005
Sinopec Fujian/Exxon Mobil/ Saudi Aramco	600	2.5	Fujian	2005
Sinopec Tianjin/Dow Chemical	600	–	Tianjin	
PetroChina Lanzhou/Phillips	600	–	Lanzhou	–
CNOOC/Royal Dutch/Shell*	800	4.5	Guangdong	2005

Sources: *Chemical Week*, 13 October 1999, *Oil and Gas Journal*, 23 April 2001, author's own research.

Note: *In construction.

Black Point Power Station to the northeast of the New Territories in Hong Kong through an underwater pipeline and the rest of the gas is transported by pipeline to Hainan Island for power generation and fertiliser production at Fudao Chemical Plant. Production of Yacheng in 2001 was approximately 350 million cubic feet per day of natural gas and 15 barrels of oil per day. Second, Liuhua oil field has estimated reserves of 1.2 billion barrels and is located 200 kilometres south-east of Hong Kong in the South China Sea. CNOOC owns 51 per cent of the oil field, BP, 24.5 per cent, and Kerr McGee of the United States, 24.5 per cent. Liuhua is operated by a joint operating group consisting of the main owners, primarily BP and CNOOC. The field has passed its peak of production and is slowly declining with production at approximately 22,000 barrels of oil per day in 2001. Third, QHD oil field is operated by CNOOC. Reserves are estimated at approximately 200 million barrels and maximum field production is expected to be at 80,500 barrels of oil per day. Fifty-one per cent of the project is owned by CNOOC, 24.5 per cent by BP and 24.5 per cent by Texaco. Texaco provides primary technical assistance to CNOOC. Finally, the coal bed methane project is in Hebei Province, 51 per cent of which is owned by China United Coal Bed Methane, 24.5 per cent by BP and 24.5 per cent by Texaco. The project was under appraisal and evaluation in 2001.

- *Chemicals* BP has been selling chemical technology licences in China since 1973. Up to the year 2000, twenty-two chemical licence agreements had been signed between BP and Chinese chemical producers. BP's polyethylene (PE) production process, called Innovene, has been sold to twenty-three licensees in sixteen countries for plants with a combined production capacity of above 4.5 million tonnes per year. In China, BP has sold three licences for producing PE using Innovene technology at Panjin in Liaoning Province, Lanzhou in Gansu Province, and Dushanzi in Xinjiang Autonomous Region. China is the world largest importer of PE and BP has been a major supplier of PE to China. For acetic acid, BP supplies 25 per cent of total world demand through its production capacities in Europe, America and Asia. In 1998, Yangtze River Acetic Company Ltd. (YARACO), a joint venture between BP and Sinopec's Sichuan Vinylon Plant, completed construction. BP owns 51 per cent of the joint venture. YARACO has a total investment of $200 million and an annual production capacity of 150,000 tonnes of acetic acid, supplying the markets in southern, southwest, central and northwest China. BP is now upgrading the production capacity at YARACO to 200,000 tonnes per year, the highest production capacity for acetic acid in China. For acrylonitrile, BP is the proprietor of the world's leading acrylonitrile production technology, accounting for more than 90 per cent of global production capacity. This technology has been licensed ten times in China for nine plants with a total capacity of 400,000 tonnes per year including Daqing, Jinlin, Fushun, Zibo, Lanzhou, Jinling, Jingmen, Anqing, and Jinshan. BP also sells acrylonitrile directly into China. BP is the world's largest producer of purified terephthalic acid (PTA), with a total production capacity over 7 million tonnes, accounting for one-third of the world's capacity. BP's PTA technology has been licensed to Yanshan, Luoyang, Yangzi, Yizheng. In 1997, BP went into partnership with Fu Hua Group Holding Company and China National Chemical Fibre Company to build a world-scale PTA production plant in Zhuhai, in which BP owns an 80 per cent of the equity share. The plant places BP in a leading position in the fibre, film and textile market in China, all of which are growing at high speed.

- *Marketing* BP's marketing activities in China cover oil products retail, LPG, lubricants, aviation and marine fuels. In 1995, BP began to set up a retail network in Guangdong Province and by the beginning of 2001, BP had had forty-three retail outlets in the province. A retail training centre provides training programmes to staff across China on health and safety standards, customer services, and marketing skills. Since the 1980s, BP lubricants have been distributed and sold in the Chinese market through a sales network covering all major cities across China including Beijing, Tianjin, Shanghai, Guangzhou, Shenzhen, and Xiamen. Lubricants sales reach 60,000 tonnes per year. In addition, BP has blending plants producing more than 500 types of lubricants and greases supplying the industrial, marine and automotive sectors. From 1997, BP began its LPG business in China and now has three joint ventures, importing LPG. The BP Fujian Ltd LPG Terminal, in which BP has 67 per cent equity share, began operating in 1997 with a total investment of $20 million. The annual throughput is 300,000 tonnes. Huaneng Amoco Clean Energy Company, in which BP, through its merger with Amoco, owns 46.4 per cent share is located in Taicang. The total investment for the project was $32 million. The BP Ningbo Huadong LPG

Company plans to invest $96.5 million in building a terminal with throughput expected to be over one million tonnes. In 1991, BP set up the joint venture Shenzhen Chengyuan Aviation Oil Company Ltd in partnership with China Aviation Oil Supply Company (CAOSC) and Shenzhen Airport. Since then BP has been the only foreign oil company operating aviation fuel supplies in China. In 1997, BP went into partnership with CAOSC and Fortune Oil, and set up the South China Bluesky Aviation Oil Company. Bluesky has become the sole supplier of aviation fuel at sixteen airports throughout Guangdong, Guangxi, Hunan and Hubei. The two joint ventures account for 25 per cent of the total Chinese jet fuel market. BP Marine was the first foreign company in China to stock duty free lubricants through the China Marine Bunker Supply Company, BP Marine lubricants are stocked as consignment stock in the ports of Dalian, Shanghai, Huangpu, Qingdao, Tianjin, Shekou, Zhanjiang, Nantong, Ningbo and Xiamen.

In March 2001, BP was selected to take a stake in the first LNG terminal in Shenzhen in Guangdong Province. The terminal has a total investment of $600 million. BP has a 30 per cent equity share in the joint venture, CNOOC 33 per cent, each of the Hong Kong Electric and Light Company and the Hong Kong Gas Corporation each 3 per cent, and the remaining 31 per cent is held by a consortium of companies of Guangdong consisting of Shenzhen Investment Holding Corporation, Guangdong Electric Power Holding Company, Guangzhou Gas Company, Dongguan Fuel Industrial General Company and Foshan Municipal Gas General Company. The joint venture will import 3 million tonnes a year on a twenty year contract, worth around $10 billion in total. By winning the bid for the Shenzhen LNG terminal, BP was better placed in the growing Chinese LNG market than Shell, which, ironically, had been 'instrumental in persuading Chinese authorities in the early 1990s of the benefits of importing LNG' (*Financial Times*, 20 March 2001).

SHELL'S BUSINESSES IN CHINA

- *Upstream* Shell started exploration activities in China in the early 1980s, when the country first opened its offshore areas for foreign participation. Since then, Shell companies have invested around $800 million in exploration and production activities in China. The focus of upstream activity in China now is moving away from risk exploration into gas development and production. Shell Exploration (China) Ltd represents Shell's upstream businesses in China. In addition to staff working in China, a technical team based in the Exploration and Production Research and Technical Service Centre in Rijswijk, the Netherlands, undertakes project evaluation studies for Shell's China projects.

  Shell's exploration and production activities in China include the following projects. First, the Xijiang fields in the South China Sea, 120 kilometres south of Hong Kong, were discovered between 1985 and 1986 by a Phillips/Pecten[9] partnership. The development of the two fields, Xijiang 30–2 and 24–3, is a joint venture between CNOOC, Pecten and Phillips. Average daily production from the two fields is 85,000 barrels of oil per day. Since 1994, the Xijiang crude oil began to supply Chinese refineries. Second, the West Xijiang Block 15/23 was awarded as a production sharing contract (PSC) at the beginning of 1997. The first well, XJ 28-2-1, was drilled in December 1997 using the Japanese semi-submersible drilling rig Hakuryu III to a depth of 3,050 metres in the western part of the block. Third, in September 1998, Shell entered into a Geophysical Survey Contract (GSA) with CNOOC for the 15/12 block in the South China Sea, which is adjacent to the Xijiang production blocks, to study the potential reserves. Fourth, in September 1999, Shell and CNPC signed a contract to jointly develop the Changbei natural gas field in Shaanxi Province and Inner Mongolia Autonomous Region. The contract sets out the framework for an integrated project that includes gas production, building new pipelines, and developing gas markets in Beijing, Hebei, Shandong and Tianjin. Total investment is estimated at $3 billion, of which Shell will invest $500 million.

- *Gas and power* Through its 68 per cent share in InterGen, Shell owns 30.5 per cent of Fujian Pacific Electric Co, a coal-fired power plant jointly owned by InterGen (45 per cent), the Lippo Group (25 per cent), El Paso Energy (24.8 per cent) and the Asian Development Bank (5.2 per cent). The joint venture has a total investment of $700 million and began operation in February 2001 with a generation capacity of 700 megawatts.

  In February 2002, it was reported that PetroChina had reached an agreement with a consortium led by Royal Dutch/Shell to participate in the massive West to East Gas Transmission Project. The consortium includes Shell International Gas Ltd, Russia's Gazprom and Stroytransgaz, and Hong Kong and China Gas Company. The agreement also includes joint exploration and development of gas fields under a PSC, a co-operative joint venture and a unified sales company for natural gas. The total cost of the project is estimated to be 150 billion yuan, approximately $18 billion. Shell estimate the cost of upstream development to be 26 billion yuan, building the pipeline to be 46.3 billion yuan, and separate development of gas markets in East China between 70 to 80 billion yuan.

- *Chemicals* The first Shell chemicals joint venture in China was a $10-million chemicals storage and transport terminal in Tianjin. Shell's second chemicals joint venture was with Jinling Petrochemicals Corporation to increase the capacity of Jinling's expandable polystyrene plant in Nanjing from 10,000 to over 30,000 tonnes a year. Shell has a 60 per cent share of the total investment of around $30 million. In 1998, Montell, a wholly-owned Shell subsidiary, signed an agreement with Sinopec Maoming Petrochemical Company to evaluate the feasibility of establishing a joint venture to produce polypropylene for sale in China, using Montell technology.

  The Nanhai project is currently Shell's largest joint venture project in China. It involves the construction of a $4.5-billion petrochemical complex near Huizhou in Guangdong Province and is expected to begin operation in 2005. The project became the largest petrochemical Sino-foreign joint venture in China. In October 2000, after sixteen years of negotiation, the Nanhai joint venture contracts were signed by the partners including Shell Nanhai BV (50 per cent), CNOOC (40 per cent), Guangdong Investment and Development Company (5 per cent), and China Merchants Holdings Company Limited (5 per cent). The plants and facilities to be constructed include a petrochemical complex with an ethylene cracker of 800,000 tonnes per annum (tpa) capacity; a 560,000 tpa styrene monomer and 250,000 tpa propylene oxide plant; a 320,000 tpa monoethylene glycol plant; a 240,000 tpa polypropylene plant; a linear low density polyethylene/high density polyethylene plant of 300,000 tpa; and a low density polyethylene plant of 150,000 tpa. A refinery is planned to be built with a capacity of 8 million tpa. The refinery would be able to process both heavy Chinese crude oils and light Middle Eastern crude oil.

- *Marketing* Shell's marketing activities in China cover oil trading, retail, lubricants, and bitumen. Shell is one of the largest international traders of crude oil with China, supplying crude oil from Oman, Brunei, West Africa and the North Sea. Shell also sells the Chinese market a full range of oil products including gasoline, naphtha, kerosene, and fuel oil, sourcing from Shell's Singapore refinery as well as Shell's refineries in the Arabian Gulf, Northwest Europe and the United States. In retail, Shell opened its first service station in 1996 in Guangdong and by the end of 2000, Shell had had forty service stations in Guangdong, Tianjin, Beijing, Nanjing and Wuhan. Shell opened three lubricants plants in 1997: the wholly-owned blending plant in Tianjin producing 35,000 tonnes per year, the joint venture lubricants plant in Zhejiang Province producing 40,000 tonnes per year, and a joint venture plant in Zhuhai. In addition, Shell has established a lubricants distribution network with over 400 outlets in over 250 cities across China. Shell accounts for 10 per cent of the global market for bitumen. In China, Shell has bitumen manufacturing plants in Zhapu, Zhejiang and Tianjin. Since 1997, Shell has sold into China over one million tonnes of bitumen used in highway projects such as Beijing–Tianjin, Jinan–Qingdao, and Shanghai–Nanjing highways, the Zhuhai Formula One race track, Beijing's Changan Avenue, as well as in other industrial sectors. For aviation fuels, Shell does not have operations in China but has formed a strategic alliance with Sinopec to develop its aviation business within China.

THE GLOBAL GIANTS AS STRATEGIC INVESTORS

The latest development of foreign investment in China's oil industry is that the global majors have become strategic investors in PetroChina and Sinopec. Before its international listing, Sinopec signed an agreement with each of its strategic investors to develop businesses both upstream and downstream in China. In the upstream sector, Royal Dutch/Shell will go into partnership with Sinopec to develop natural gas resources in the Ordos Basin and Tarim oil and gas region, both key areas for the supply of gas to the West to East Gas Transmission project. In the Ordos Basin, the joint study by Shell and Sinopec covers the Tabamiao exploration block and the Daniudi development blocks, about 500 kilometres north of Xi'an. In the Tarim Basin, the joint study is on two exploration blocks and one development block in the Shaya Uplift area. If the joint studies in Ordos and Tarim are both successful, Shell will enter into PSC with Sinopec for exploration and development. In addition, Shell and Sinopec agreed to jointly explore gas reserves in the Xihu Trough. Meanwhile, Shell and CNOOC, through their strategic alliance concluded in 2000, agreed to co-operate in the Xihu Trough, where CNOOC has development rights. Shell and CNOOC also agreed to explore jointly and develop a number of oil and gas fields in the Bohai Bay. The reserves in these fields are estimated at 1 trillion cubic feet of gas and 600 to 700 million barrels of oil. It was suggested that a joint marketing venture should be set up to supply 0.4-0.8 cubic metres of gas per year from these fields to customers in Shandong Province.

In refining and marketing, Exxon Mobil will establish a joint venture with Sinopec for retail marketing in Guangdong Province and 500 service stations will be set up within three years. Exxon Mobil will study the feasibility of doubling the current refining capacity of 150 thousand barrels per day at the Guangzhou Petrochemicals Company. Royal Dutch/Shell has established a joint venture with Sinopec for retailing marketing in 500 service stations in Jiangsu Province. BP has established a joint venture with Sinopec to acquire, renovate or build 500 service stations in Zhejiang Province. These service stations will have the logos of both BP and Sinopec and will sell petrol supplied by Sinopec and other refined products supplied by both companies. For the three global giant companies, 'this is but the beginning of their attempts to capture a share of [what will become] the world's largest retail market' (*Petroleum Economist*, October 2000).

In petrochemicals, Exxon Mobil will build a joint venture petrochemical complex in Fujian Province with an annual ethylene production capacity of 600 thousand tonnes. Shell and Sinopec will invest $150 million in building a 50:50 joint venture at Dong Ting fertiliser plant in Hunan Province, using Shell's technology for coal gasification. This technology will also be introduced into Sinopec's fertiliser plants in Hubei and Anhui provinces. BP will establish a world-class PTA production facility with Sinopec. BP's PTA technology holds 37 per cent global market share (BP, 1998). ABB will co-operate with Sinopec to develop new technology in ethylene production. ABB and Sinopec have jointly developed an ethylene cracker to increase China's ethylene production capacity. ABB is the major supplier of the technology used in ethylene production in China.

In April 2001, PetroChina established a retail marketing joint venture with its strategic investor, BP, in Guangdong Province, with PetroChina holding a 51 per cent equity share and BP the remaining ones. The joint venture will consolidate the 366 service stations owned by PetroChina and the 43 service stations owned by BP in Guangdong. A further 100 service stations were acquired in 2001. PetroChina's current storage system in Guangdong will be renovated to guarantee supplies to these service stations. Similar projects with BP have been carried out in Fujian and Zhejiang as well. Despite disputes over project capacity, PetroChina is still in negotiation with Chevron Phillips Chemical Company to build a petrochemical complex in Lanzhou with annual ethylene capacity of at least 600,000 tonnes.

Conclusion

The reform of China's large state-owned enterprises in the 'pillar industries' (*zhizhu chanye*) evolved from the former government ministries such as oil and petrochemicals, the creation and international listing of PetroChina and Sinopec was a serious attempt to create modern industrial enterprises to compete internationally. The whole process of restructuring and flotation was achieved through administrative measures within just one year. Alongside China's struggle, the global giant oil and petrochemical corporations underwent large-scale and high-speed consolidation. They rapidly acquired assets with high returns and sought to capture those global markets with the greatest value or strategic importance. They radically changed their business structure into the 'business unit' model, characterised by a federation of autonomous business units operating within the boundary of principles and broad strategies set by the headquarters, and subject to close monitoring of their performance by the headquarters.

In relation to oil and gas reserves, PetroChina and Sinopec are at a disadvantage compared with the national oil companies. In terms of technology and financial strength, they are at a disadvantage compared with the global majors. They still face the tough task of establishing a cohesive corporate culture necessary to integrate their powerful subordinate companies and maintain a unified company. Across the value chain, PetroChina and Sinopec have been actively forming 'strategic alliances' and establishing joint ventures with global oil and petrochemical companies. How stable will these partnerships be, especially after China's accession to the WTO? Will PetroChina and Sinopec emerge as *the firm* to compete globally? For the two companies, it is a battle on all fronts. Is it conceivable that at some point the majority of state-owned companies, CNPC, Sinopec and CNOOC, could merge to become a global 'super giant'?

At a meeting convened by the State Planning Commission at the end of September 2001, (Xinhuanet, 2001), China's industrial experts emphasised that the accelerating trend of globalisation and consolidation means that China's petrochemical industry 'faces critical challenges from many aspects' after China's entry to the WTO. Their verdict on the state of the industry was blunt:

> The overall technological level of the petrochemical industry of our country lags behind the advanced countries about 10–15 years and has a fairly large gap compared with the world's advanced level. The energy and material

consumption level of the majority of the refineries and ethylene crackers is higher than the average level in Asia. The capabilities of technological innovation are weak. Patented self-developed technologies are few. Development and introduction of high and new technologies and products is weak. Engineering capabilities are weak and lacking in potential for further development.

PetroChina and Sinopec have both been successfully restructured and floated on international markets. However, everyone within the Chinese industry is fully aware of the deep challenges posed by globalisation and China's deepening integration with the global economy and business system. The future institutional structure of PetroChina and Sinopec is far from certain. It remains an open question whether PetroChina and Sinopec will succeed where YPF failed. Moreover, the institutional experiment in China's oil and petrochemical sector is being closely watched by all concerned to understand the future course of China's industrial strategy regarding large firms and their relationship with the global giants.

9 Conclusion

By the late 1990s, there was a high degree of firm-level concentration on a global scale in industries covering aerospace and defence, pharmaceuticals, automobiles, power equipment, mining, pulp and paper, brewing, banking, insurance, advertising and the mass media (Nolan *et al.*, 2002). The headquarters is at the centre of the business system of the leading global firms. In the same period, the Chinese government initiated the strategy of 'restructuring and flotation' to reform the large state-owned enterprises in oil and petrochemicals, telecommunications, and financial services. Evolved from government ministries, these large corporations are regarded as China's 'pillar industries' in both economic and strategic terms. Following PetroChina, Sinopec, CNOOC, China Unicom, and Chalco were each listed successfully on the international stock exchanges in New York, Hong Kong and London. The reform has now progressed into the financial service sector. The Bank of China was listed in Hong Kong in 2002. It became the first of the 'big four'[1] state-owned banks floated on the international market. However, large Chinese corporations face deep challenges in their organisational restructuring and building up their competitive capabilities.

The function of corporate headquarters

Leadership and control

During the epoch of the global business revolution, successful giant global corporations have fundamentally transformed their business structure. The 150 business units of BP are organised into four business streams from upstream exploration and production to downstream refining and marketing, gas and power, as well as chemicals. They are led by the BCEO and the Exco of each business stream, who are in turn monitored by the GCEO and the board of directors. The headquarters consists of the board of directors including the GCEO and the executive management team. In addition, the headquarters is supported by executives in functional areas such as finance and human resources. The headquarters formulates business policies including ethical conduct; employment practices; relationships; health, safety and environmental performance; control and finance. The business policies provide boundaries within which business units must conduct their activities. The headquarters set up internal control process that hold managers at various levels from line managers, functional heads, and regional presidents to business executives and GCEO accountable for conforming with the business policies in the domain under their responsibilities. The performance contract system monitors the performance of employees at various levels and in various functions. Meanwhile, the headquarters sets reward policies for executives and employees through bench-marking with peers in the same industry in order to make sure that the company can attract high-calibre personnel.

The structure of Royal Dutch/Shell is complex due to the historical alliance of Royal Dutch Petroleum in the Netherlands and the Shell Transporting and Trading Company in the United Kingdom on a 60:40 equity share basis. The two Group Holding Companies under the parent companies are Shell Petroleum NV based in the Netherlands and the Shell Petroleum Company Ltd based in the United Kingdom. The parent companies appoint the directors in the GHC. Under the two GHC, operating companies in more than 135 countries, many of which are stand-alone business units, are organised into five business streams – exploration and production, gas and power, oil products, chemicals and other businesses including renewable energies, customer and financial services. The business headquarters is the Committee of the Managing Directors consisting of managing directors from both GHCs. The headquarters determines Shell's business policies comprising Shell General Business Principles, Health Safety and Environment Commitment and Policy, and Risk and Internal Control Policy. All Shell businesses, including joint ventures, are subject to these policies and principles. The headquarters exercises internal control through devising group and business policies and standards, and by establishing the governing relationship across the different layers of management. The implementation of group policies and standards in Shell's businesses is monitored through the annual assurance letter process at various levels of management. Reward policies for executives and employees are set through bench-marking with peers in the same industry.

In the 1990s, the headquarters of global leading firms stripped away the autonomy that used to be enjoyed by their powerful subsidiaries, the 'feudal baronies', and centralised control from capital investment to performance evaluation: 'For the lack of any real integrating mechanism at the top of a feudal system implied by this type of polity posed a permanent threat to its stability and survival' (Anderson, 1975: 151). The business unit structure adopted by the giant global firms delegates operating autonomy to the business units or operating companies that spread all over the world. It emphasises the learning and sharing of knowledge between the business units, facilitated by advances in information technology. However, the business units must operate within the boundaries of principles and standards formulated by the headquarters. They must follow the strategic directions set by the headquarters and employ the resources determined by the headquarters. Moreover, the performance of the business units is under remorseless scrutiny from the headquarters. They must deliver their performance targets, or otherwise, they will be sold as under-performing assets. In sum, the headquarters' function in monitoring and controlling the business units was greatly enhanced during the 1990s. The complexity involved in the monitoring process was greatly facilitated and rendered easier and more transparent by the implementation of information technology systems.

Planning and co-ordination

With BP, the headquarters is the 'brain' which determines strategic moves such as mergers and acquisitions, provides strategic directions for business development, and creates asset portfolios with high returns across the globe. Moreover, facilitated by investment in information technology, the headquarters is able to centralise capital investment and financial reporting, as well as integrating the procurement process through e-businesses. The headquarters integrates the brands within the company under one global brand 'bp' and renovates the brand image and the value it carries. The headquarters, through the performance contract, monitors the performance of the subordinate business units and ensures the delivery of shareholder value. With Shell, the headquarters sets the strategic direction of the businesses and manages the Shell brand world-wide. The headquarters centralises control over the rights to make capital investments, which used to be in the hands of the powerful regional companies. The headquarters invests in R&D centres across the advanced countries to provide leading technologies for Shell's businesses.

Since the mid-1990s, the global oil industry has witnessed high-speed and large-scale concentration among the major western oil companies. They restructured their business portfolio across the value chain through keeping their businesses with a leading global position, selling off those businesses that were in a weaker position and with low growth prospects, while moving swiftly into new markets that were closed during the Cold War. They are able to obtain the most promising high-quality oil and gas reserves across the world. They are able to enhance the global influence of their powerful brands, facilitated by expanding their businesses into economies that liberalised their economies after the Cold War. They are able to strengthen their favourable position with stock markets and banks through their positive long-term prospects, which enables them to raise capital more economically. They are able to make vast investments in R&D and produce cutting-edge technologies, thus maintaining their leading position in technologies through developing patents. Through large investments in information technology, they have been able to set up IT-based business and management systems, enabling them to cut costs and share knowledge instantaneously across the whole company.

Corporate headquarters within large Chinese companies

Over the course of five decades, the Chinese oil industry underwent three major stages for development. In the early years after 1949, China's oil industry was developed in the fashion of a military-style 'massive campaign'. The objective was to develop oil production as fast as possible to support the national economic growth. Under the leadership of the State Council, the Ministry of Petroleum Industry was the administrative headquarters of China's oil industry. It made strategic decisions concerning the location of exploration and development. It planned the campaign, organising human and material resources nation-wide to support the campaign. It undertook and co-ordinated the production, transportation and marketing of oil and oil products based on the overall national plan formulated by the State Planning Commission. It negotiated for investment funds from the government, and allocated them to its subordinate petroleum administrative bureaux all over the country. The various PAB were production units responsible for carrying out the production and investment plan.

China began to liberalise its post-Mao economy in the late 1970s. During the 1980s, China's oil industry experienced significant institutional change. In 1983, China Petrochemical Corporation (Sinopec) was created by merging the assets from the refining and petrochemical section of the MPI, as well as some of the chemical and synthetic fibre manufacturing enterprises under the Ministry of Chemical Industry and the Ministry of Textile Industry. In 1988, the MPI was transformed into the China National Petroleum Corporation (CNPC). In this period, the headquarters of CNPC and Sinopec had both government and business functions. Created as state-owned companies, CNPC and Sinopec still carried government administrative responsibilities for the industry, such as formulating technological standards and devising environmental regulations. The critical function of organising production was controlled by the government. The headquarters of the two companies were expected to carry out the government's plans related to resource allocation and production. They co-ordinated amongst themselves the implementation of the plans. CNPC and Sinopec were entrusted by the State Council with managing the state's assets and were made responsible for generating revenue to hand over to the government treasury. They had no rights over product pricing, marketing or capital investment above 500 million yuan (CNPC) and 200 million yuan (Sinopec). These business decision-making rights were tightly controlled by the central government. In this sense, CNPC and Sinopec were 'administrative entities' rather than 'economic entities'.

China's enterprise reform strongly emphasised the expansion of enterprise autonomy at the level of the production unit. CNPC and Sinopec's subordinate enterprises were able to retain a greatly increased share of profits. They gained the autonomy to make investments in both core and diversified businesses. They were able to finance their expansion through bank loans and bonds, and were responsible for debt repayment. They were listed on domestic and international capital markets, which reduced the ownership rights of CNPC and Sinopec over listed companies. They negotiated and set up joint ventures with multinational companies. In both CNPC and Sinopec, strong subordinate enterprises initiated mergers and acquisitions in order to increase their domestic market share of particular products. CNPC and Sinopec's headquarters' control over finance, performance monitoring, procurement, and R&D was weak. This put CNPC and

Sinopec into an awkward situation. In their execution of government functions, the headquarters of CNPC and Sinopec were simply an extension of government administration. In exercising business functions, the headquarters of CNPC and Sinopec lacked the right to decide product pricing, capital investment above a certain amount, and product marketing. They did not possess effective control over their subordinate enterprises even in the most important question of finance and performance monitoring. They exercised their control over subordinate enterprises mainly through the appointment of senior managers in subordinate enterprises. The growing autonomy at enterprise level created tension between the headquarters and the subordinate enterprises. Powerful enterprises under CNPC and Sinopec, such as Daqing and Zhenhai, aspired to grow independently through expanding their business across the value chain both upstream and downstream, and through mergers and acquisitions. The question 'Where is the headquarters?' arises.

The reorganisation of China's oil and petrochemical industry in 1998 marked the immensely significant second stage in the development for China's oil industry. It indicated that the headquarters of CNPC and Sinopec had won the struggle to become 'the headquarters' leading the industry's development. Instead of allowing powerful constituent enterprises to become the 'core' of emerging large indigenous oil companies, the Chinese government supported CNPC and Sinopec in their ambition to become integrated oil and petrochemical companies. The subsequent restructuring for flotation in 1999 involved massive assets reorganisation. The productive core assets were separated from the non-core assets including service providers and social functions. CNPC and Sinopec Group each created a 'child company' – PetroChina and Sinopec – that amalgamated the core businesses of each company. The 'one-tier' legal person system established within the two child companies dashed the subordinate enterprises' aspirations for independence.

The international flotation of PetroChina and Sinopec in 2000 was a critical milestone in the development of China's oil industry. It indicates China's large oil companies had moved away from the institutional structure characteristic of the command economy. This third development stage began as China joined the WTO. PetroChina and Sinopec each have obtained from the government rights over product pricing, production, and investment in core businesses. They are centralising their control over their branch companies in capital investment, finance and marketing. They are investing integrated information technology systems within the company to facilitate centralisation. They have begun to monitor the performance of managers through performance contracts. The task of centralisation is formidable, considering the enormous autonomy the subordinate enterprises came to enjoy in the 1990s.

However, the question of 'Where is the headquarters?' still remains. PetroChina and Sinopec are independent legal persons able to conduct business autonomously but the degree of their independence remains unclear. The non-core businesses as well as social services retained by both CNPC and Sinopec Group employ 800,000 and 600,000 people respectively and produce huge losses.

Each year, both CNPC and Sinopec Group have to commit huge funds to finance the downsizing of their workforces. PetroChina and Sinopec both have to struggle to obtain more resources to finance their expansion. As listed companies, they are under pressure to create shareholder value. However, there are conflicts of interest and development strategy between CNPC and PetroChina. In sum, it is still uncertain where, ultimately, the headquarters will be located.

Policy implications

IMPLICATIONS FOR LARGE CHINESE COMPANIES

A study of the functions of headquarters with global leading firms has deep implications for large Chinese companies that aspire to become competitive 'world-class' firms. We have seen that during the 1990s, the global leading firms greatly strengthened their headquarters' functions in planning and co-ordinating business activities on a global scale, in setting strategic directions for the whole company, and in establishing mechanisms to govern and monitor their business units. Meanwhile, we have seen that CNPC and Sinopec Group created PetroChina and Sinopec, respectively, that were both listed on the international market. PetroChina and Sinopec subsequently made great efforts to rationalise their businesses and strengthen the headquarters' functions in integrating and controlling the subordinate enterprises.

However, the Chinese oil majors face serious challenges in respect of their business and organisational capabilities. Compared with the national oil companies, PetroChina and Sinopec are at disadvantage in terms of the quantity of oil and gas reserves. Compared with the global majors, they are at a disadvantage in terms of global distribution and quality of reserves, and in terms of technology and financial strength. The headquarters' function in monitoring and control is still at a very early stage. There remains a deep internal battle to establish a cohesive corporate culture to integrate powerful subordinate companies and construct a truly unified company.

We have seen that across the value chain, PetroChina and Sinopec have been actively forming 'strategic alliances' and establishing joint ventures with global oil and petrochemical companies. How stable will these partnerships be, especially after China's entry to WTO? Even if they were stable, this would only mean that the best assets of PetroChina and Sinopec had 'joined' the global business system of the world's leading firms. Many of their best assets have been 'integrated' into the business portfolio of the global firms. Where then, is the headquarters? Is it in Beijing or in London? This question is crucial for the prospect of development for China's large companies.

IMPLICATIONS FOR THE CHINESE GOVERNMENT

As the reform progressed in the late 1990s, the Chinese government tried explicitly to establish a group of globally competitive large firms in telecommunications and financial services. China Mobile, China Unicom and the Bank of China, with their massive international flotations, were at the forefront of this process. On the eve of China's entry to the WTO, the country's commitment to building globally competitive large firms remained undiminished:

> The state will encourage big state-owned businesses to become interna-
> tionally competitive corporations by listing on domestic and overseas stock
> markets, increasing research and development expenditure, and acquiring
> other businesses. The country will develop thirty to fifty large state-owned
> enterprises in the next five years through public offerings, mergers and
> acquisitions, restructuring and co-operation.
>   (Bai Rongchun, Director General, Industrial Planning Department,
>   State Economic and Trade Commission, July 2001)

As China begins closely integrating into the world economy, large Chinese firms face deep challenges. Given the government's undiminished commitment to construct globally competitive large firms, it is of vital importance to understand the deep challenges that large Chinese corporations are facing, even in the oil sector that has achieved apparent success. It is important to appreciate fully that China has already become the competitive battlefield among the global leading firms from almost every sector with each capturing an increasing share of the Chinese market. It is also important to recognise that the 'global level playing field' is not 'level' for large Chinese companies. It requires deep thoughts and a subtle strategy to determine the best way for China's large companies to join the global value chain. The Chinese government faces serious challenges in system reform related to the restructuring of the country's large companies in the 'strategic' sectors such as oil, aerospace, telecommunications, and financial services.

IMPLICATIONS FOR GLOBAL GIANT CORPORATIONS

Each of the global leading oil companies has major investment commitments in China and has formed various partnerships with the Chinese majors. The global leading firms must recognise that the transformation of the business capabilities and organisational structure of the Chinese majors is not easy to predict. In operating or forming joint ventures or strategic alliances with large Chinese firms, the global giant corporations need to understand the question: 'Where is the headquarters?'

It is necessary for them to keep in mind the fact that large Chinese companies operate in a different political-economic environment from theirs. China's political leaders have to consider the huge difficulties that stem from the existence of around one billion poor people within their boundaries, and the complexities involved in the reform of China's political system. Locking China into the world economic system by agreeing to accept the rules of the WTO does not guarantee a politically stable and economically rational environment for investment. China still has a long way to go in its 'transition' from the planned economy. The final destination of this 'transition' is still under intense debate among Chinese policy makers. If China's large firms were to experience widespread defeat, especially in key 'strategic industries', in the battle on the global level playing field of the WTO, that would raise deep issues not only for the Chinese government, but also for international relations, and, ultimately, for the large firms headquartered in the high-income countries.

Epilogue

In November 2002, China held the Sixteenth Congress of the Chinese Communist Party. This historic congress announced a new Central Committee and elected a new Party General Secretary, Hu Jintao. In March 2003, the tenth National People's Congress convened in Beijing. The Congress elected a new government led by Chairman Hu Jintao and Premier Wen Jiabao. On 10 March, the congress approved a government reform programme. Only five years after the comprehensive government reform in 1998, the State Council undertook another major restructuring. The State Economic and Trade Commission (SETC), the Ministry of Foreign Trade and Economic Co-operation (MOFTEC), and the State Council Office of Economic System Reform were abolished. The State Development and Planning Commission (SDPC) was renamed the State Development and Reform Commission (SDRC). The SDRC took over the State Council Office of Economic System Reform. It also took over from the SETC functions of sectoral planning, industrial policy, economic co-ordination, investment administration for technological upgrading, macro-supervision of enterprises with diversified ownership, promoting the development of small and medium-sized enterprises, as well as the planning functions of importing and exporting key industrial products and raw materials. The Ministry of Commerce was established on the basis of the MOFTEC, integrating the planning function of importing and exporting agricultural products from SDPC and functions from the SETC covering domestic trade administration, foreign economic co-ordination, and implementing the plan of importing and exporting key industrial products and raw materials.

Two new commissions were established to supervise the state-owned assets and regulate the financial sector: the State-owned Assets Supervision and Administration Commission (SASAC) and the China Banking Regulatory Commission (CBRC). The SASAC and CBRC were set up on the basis of the respective Central Work Commission of Large State-owned Enterprises and the Central Financial Work Commission. The SASAC currently has 196 large SOEs under its direct supervision, including CNPC, Sinopec, CNOOC and China National Chemicals Import and Export Corporation (Sinochem). The SASAC is headed by Li Rongrong, former Minister of the SETC. Li Yizhong, former Party Secretary and Managing Director of Sinopec Group, was appointed SASAC's

Party Secretary and Vice-Minister. SASAC is expected to integrate the administrative functions in personnel, assets and overall management from the former Central Work Commission of Large State-owned Enterprises, the CCP Organisation Department, the Ministry of Finance and the SETC. This is highly significant for the reform of large state-owned enterprises.

For the energy sector, the new government decided to set up an Energy Bureau under the SDRC, merging the energy sections in the former SDPC and SETC.[1] The Vice-Minister of SDRC Zhang Guobao is expected to be the Director of the Energy Bureau. The Energy Bureau regulates industries including oil, coal and power and is responsible for China's energy policy. The pressing tasks include establishing strategic petroleum reserves, co-ordinating between CNPC, Sinopec and CNOOC in their overseas expansion, and formulating mid- and long-term energy policy.

China stepped up its acquisition of overseas oil and gas assets in the late 1990s.[2] CNPC was the sole entity to invest in overseas oil and gas assets before 2002, when Sinopec and CNOOC started their overseas expansion. Currently, CNPC has major investments in Sudan and Kazakhstan and a presence in Syria, Venezuela, Peru, Canada, Myanmar, Thailand and Indonesia. In 2002, CNPC obtained 10.2 million tonnes of oil from its overseas assets. Sinopec has assets in Algeria, Yemen and Indonesia. CNOOC acquired assets in Australia and Indonesia. It is notable that Sinochem, approved by the State Council in 2001, joined the three Chinese oil majors for overseas acquisition. In March 2002, Sinochem Oil Exploration and Development Corporation was established. Its chief geologist is from CNPC. In February 2003, Sinochem acquired the Atlantis project from the Norwegian oil-filed service company PGS. Sinochem aims to become 'a vertically-integrated state-owned oil company' (Wang, 2003). More significantly, oil companies across the Taiwan Straits began to work together for oil exploration and development. At the beginning of 2003, China and Taiwan agreed to a proposal by the Chinese Petroleum Corporation, Taiwan's state-owned oil company and CNOOC to prospect jointly in the Tainan Basin in the Taiwan Straits. The two companies plan to form a joint management committee, comprising four officials from each, to devise a plan for oil field development.

However, the major Chinese oil overseas investments have had serious setbacks. At the end of 2002, CNPC bid for the Russian government's 74 per cent holding in Slavneft, the eighth largest oil company in Russia. However, just two days before the bidding date, the Russian Duma passed a resolution, forbidding any entity controlled by foreign governments to bid for Slavneft. CNPC withdrew from the bidding process. In early 2003, the proposed oil pipeline from Angarsk in eastern Siberia to Daqing was held up due to a rival proposal supported by Japan to construct the oil pipeline to the Russian port of Nakhodka on the Sea of Japan. In May 2003, CNOOC and Sinopec's purchase of an 8.3 per cent stake from BG in the North Caspian Sea oil and gas project in Kazakhstan was blocked by the other partners Shell, Exxon Mobil, TotalFinaElf, Conoco Philips and ENI, exercising their pre-emption rights. The project was considered 'the largest oil field discovered in the last half century'. Commentators regarded the pre-emption as '[flying] in the face of the traditional practice among Western businesses to court Chinese interests at all costs' (*South China Morning Post*, 3 June 2003). CNOOC thinks the deal was 'a business decision' and will not 'affect any future co-operation [between CNOOC and the global majors]' (*South China Morning Post*, 30 May 2003).

In March 2003, the Saddam Hussein regime was overthrown and the world embarked on a post-Iraq war era. Before the War, global majors called for a 'level playing field' for all oil companies in the post-Saddam Iraq. The Russian, Italian, French and Chinese oil companies have made deals with Saddam Hussein's government, amounting to $38 billion.[3] In the same month, the Resources and Energy Research Council under Japan's Ministry of Economy, Trade and Industry proposed three subsidiaries under Japan National Oil – Japan Oil Development, Inpex and Sakhalin Oil and Gas Development – merged to match 'second-tier western oil majors or national flag companies' in terms of oil reserves (*South China Morning Post*, 19 March 2003). Japan Oil Development owns 12 per cent of five oil fields off the coast of Abu Dhabi, supplying 200,000 barrels of crude oil daily to Japan. Inpex has extensive oil field developments in Indonesia and Sakhalin Oil Development has operations on the Russian island. In Russia, BP combined its Sidanco holdings with Tyumen Oil (TNK) for $6.75 billion, creating Russia's third largest oil and gas company, together with Alfa Group and Access-Renova (AAR). Only two months later, in April 2003, Russia's largest oil producer, the Yukos Oil Company, took over Sibneft, the fifth Russian oil company for $13 billion. The new company YukosSibneft became the world's fifth largest publicly traded oil company in terms of production. At 2.4 million barrels of oil a day, the new company ranks behind Exxon Mobil, Royal Dutch/Shell, BP and Chevron Texaco.

Despite their overseas investments, the Chinese oil majors are emphatically China-oriented. They are in the process of reforming their internal business structure. In November 2002, CNOOC (Group) floated its oil field services unit, China Oilfield Services Ltd (COSL). CNOOC also intends to float its petrochemical businesses in 2004. The core of the floated company will be the Nanhai project, a joint venture of CNOOC and Shell. In 2002, CNPC has set up BGP, a geophysical services company and China Petroleum logging, a well logging and drilling services operation. These oil exploration services units are expected to merge and float in 2003 (*South China Morning Post*, 10 December 2002). In the meantime, CNPC, Sinopec, and CNOOC still face the huge task of downsizing.

Despite the deep internal and external challenges for its large firms in the global business revolution, China's ambition to construct globally competitive large firms remains strong. The consistent goal was to 'nurture 30–50 globally competitive large enterprises and enterprise groups' (Li Rongrong, SASAC Press Conference, 22 May 2003). To achieve global competitiveness, China's aspiring large corporations still have a long way to go. Their institutional structure remains fluid. Their interaction with the large global firms remains highly complex. The future is dynamic.

Notes

1 Introduction

1 For an overview of restructuring SOEs for international listing from the international bankers' point of view, see (Walter and Howie, 2001: 117–25).
2 Also there are only a few in-depth studies of large companies in the newly industrialised countries such as Japan and South Korea (Amsden, 1989; Bartlett and Ghoshal, 2000; Cusumano, 1985; Janelli, 1993).

2 The function of corporate headquarters

1 Entrepreneurial decisions and actions refer to those that affect the allocation or reallocation of resources – funds, equipment or personnel – for the enterprise as a whole (Chandler, 1962: 11).
2 Operating decisions and actions refer to those that are carried out by using the resources already allocated.
3 Information is asymmetrically distributed between buyer and seller and can be equalised only at great cost. It is costly to apprise an arbiter of the true information condition should a dispute arise between opportunistic parties who have identical knowledge of the underlying circumstances (Williamson, 1975: 31–7).
4 The other two factors are the enterprises' existing capabilities and their success in developing capabilities to complement the existing ones.
5 For an excellent review and analysis of post-Fordism, see Ruigrok and Van Tulder, 1995: Chapter 2.
6 This refers to business organisations in Hong Kong, Taiwan and the overseas Chinese community in Southeast Asia.
7 This refers to the state-owned enterprises in mainland China.

3 Corporate structure and headquarters' function

1 Currently all BCEOs are male.
2 The discussion in this section is based on BP Business Policies, June 2000.
3 For the creation of the Royal Dutch/Shell Group of companies, see Yergin (1991).
4 Costs or surpluses are passed back to the companies that use them.

4 Government centralisation and corporatisation

1 Industrial added value = total industrial output − intermediate input (direct material input, production cost, management cost, sales cost, and financial cost) + income tax.

5 Restructuring for vertical integration and flotation

1 Chongqing, Liaoning, Jilin, Helongjiang, Shaanxi, Inner Mongolia, Gansu, Qinghai, Ningxia Hui, Sichuan, Xingjiang Uygur, Tibet.
2 Beijing, Shanghai, Tianjin, Jiangsu, Shangdong, Zhejiang, Fujian, Hebei, Henan, Shanxi, Hunan, Hubei, Anhui, Jiangxi, Guangdong, Guangxi Zhuang, Hainan, Guizhou, Yunnan.
3 They are China Oil & Gas Exploration and Development Company and China (Hong Kong) Petroleum Company.

6 Corporate structure and headquarters' function

1 The three asset management companies Cinda, Huarong and Orient were set up to take over the bad debts or loans from China Construction Bank, Bank of China and China Industrial and Commercial Bank, respectively.
2 Reserve replacement refers to the amount of oil and gas produced at the end of a year being replaced by new findings in oil and gas reserves in that year. Expressed in percentage terms, it is an indication of future production increase.
3 Including 3,600 service stations owned by CNPC but exclusively supplied by PetroChina.
4 Based on PetroChina's dividend payment of $0.02 per share and the weighted average number of 171,630 million shares issued and outstanding in 2000.

7 From production unit to autonomous enterprise and back to production unit

1 Employees who have retired before the legal age of retirement (60 for men and 55 for women). These retired employees will usually reach the legal age of retirement within five years.

8 Challenges for large Chinese firms

1 They are Exxon Mobil, Royal Dutch/Shell, BP Amoco/Arco, TotalFinaElf, Chevron, Texaco, Eni, Repsol YPF, and Conoco.
2 Based on PetroChina's dividend payment of $0.02 per share and the weighted average number of 171,630 million shares issued and outstanding in 2000.
3 The issues of creating shareholder value and protecting minority shareholders are discussed in *China Petroleum*, April 2000, pp. 18–29 and an article 'Oil industry: choices after flotation' in *Caijing*, November 2000. The article comments: 'For the listed state-owned companies, this kind of structure involves risks that cannot be anticipated. It will affect the profits of a company and distort the behaviour of a company, which in fact jeopardises the interest of shareholders. As a common problem, it will eventually damage the credibility of the Chinese concept shares (*zhongguo gainian gu*)'.
4 Referring to BP's heavy reliance on the Forties oilfield in the North Sea and Prudhoe Bay fields in Alaska.
5 BP bought 10 per cent of Sidanco for $484 million in 1997. However, Tyumen Oil, BP's fellow shareholder and owns 85 per cent of Sidanco, used bankruptcy proceedings to remove the Chernogorneft oil field and other key assets from Sidanco. BP eventually reached an agreement in 2001 with Tyumen Oil that the removed assets should be returned to Sidanco and gave BP the right of operating control over the company.
6 The annual meeting is usually held at the end of a calendar year and attended by senior and middle managers. The meeting reviews performance in the previous year, sets performance target for the coming year and announces strategy for future development.

7 Sinopec National Star was the former China National Star Petroleum Corporation (CNSPC) (Chapter 5). In March 2000, CNSPC was merged into the Sinopec Group.
8 CNOOC was listed on the Hong Kong Stock Exchange and New York Stock Exchange in February 2001. CNOOC is regarded as an efficient and well-organised oil company with extensive experience in co-operating with foreign oil companies.
9 Pectan is a US-based Shell company.

9 Conclusion

1 They are the Industrial and Commercial Bank of China (ICBC), Bank of China (BOC), Construction Bank of China (CBC), and Agricultural Bank of China (ABC).

Epilogue

1 The eight industrial 'state bureaux' under the administration of the SETC (Chapter 5), including the State Bureau of Petroleum and Chemical Industry and the State Bureau of Coal Industry, were abolished in February 2001.
2 For China's investment in overseas oil and gas resources in the 1990s, see Andrews-Speed, 2002: 33–6.
3 *Financial Times* accessed at ft.com, 25 February 2003.

Bibliography

Amsden, Alice, H. (1989) *Asia's Next Giant*, New York: Oxford University Press.

Anderson, Perry (1975) *Passages from Antiquity to Feudalism*, London: NLB.

Andrews-Speed, Philip, Xuanli Liao and Roland Dannreuther (2002) *The Strategic Implications of China's Energy Needs*, Adelphi Paper 346, the International Institute for Strategic Studies.

Aoki, Masahiko (1988) *Information, Incentives, and Bargaining in the Japanese Economy*, Cambridge: Cambridge University Press.

Bahrami, H. (1992) 'The emerging flexible organisation – perspectives from Silicon Valley', *California Management Review* 34, 4, 33–52.

Barnard, Chester (1938) *The Functions of the Executive*, Cambridge, MA: Harvard University Press.

Barney, Jay B. and William G. Ouchi (eds) (1986) *Organizational Economics*, London: Jossey-Bass Publishers.

Bartlett, Christopher A. (1986) 'Building and managing the transnational: the new organizational challenge', in Michael E. Porter (ed.) *Competition in Global Industries*, Boston: Harvard Business School Press.

Bartlett, C. and S. Ghoshal (2000), *Transnational Management* (3rd edition), Boston: McGraw-Hill.

Best, Michael (1990) *The New Competition: Institutions of Industrial Restructuring*, Cambridge: Polity Press.

BP (2001) *BP Annual Report 2000*, BP.

—— (2002) *BP Statistical Review of World Energy 2002*, BP.

BP/Amoco (1999a) Booklet for presentation to the financial community, London and New York, 15/16 July 1999.

—— (1999b) *Annual Report and Accounts 1998*.

—— (2000a) Presentation to the financial community, London and New York, July 2000.

—— (2000b) *BP Amoco Statistical Review of World Energy, 2000*, BP Amoco.

—— (2000c) *BP Amoco Annual Plan*, 1999, BP Amoco.

Brodie, Patrick (1990) *Crescent over Cathay: ICI and China*, 1898–1956, Oxford: Oxford University Press.

Brooke, Michael Z. (1984) *Centralization and Autonomy*, London: Holt, Rinehart and Winston.

Brown, David and Robin Porter (1996) *Management Issues in China: Volume I, Domestic Enterprise*, London: Routledge.

Byrd, W. A. (1992) *Chinese Industrial Firms under Reform*, New York: Oxford University Press.

Campbell, N. (1989), *A Strategic Guide to Equity Joint Ventures in China*, Oxford: Pergamon Press.

Cassis, Youssef (1997) *Big Business: the European Experience in the Twentieth Century*, Oxford: Oxford University Press.

Castells, Manuel (1996) *The Rise of the Network Society*, Oxford: Blackwell Publishers.

Chandler, Alfred D. Jr (1962) *Strategy and Structure: Chapters in the History of the American Industrial Enterprise*, Cambridge, MA: The MIT Press.

—— (1977) *The Visible Hand: The Managerial Revolution in American Business*, Cambridge, MA: Harvard University Press.

—— (1990a) *Scale and Scope: The Dynamics of Industrial Capitalism*, Cambridge, MA: Harvard University Press.

—— (1990b) 'The functions of the HQ unit in the multibusiness firm', in Richard P. Rumelt, Dan E. Schendel and David J. Teece (eds) *Fundamental Issues in Strategy: A Research Agenda*, Boston, MA: Harvard Business School Press, pp. 323–60.

—— (ed.) (1997) *Big Business and the Wealth of Nations*, Cambridge: Cambridge University Press.

Chen, Derong (1995) *Chinese Firms between Hierarchy and Market: The Contract Management Responsibility System in China*, London: St Martin's Press.

Chen, Huai *et al.* (1998) *Assets Restructuring of the Chinese Oil and Petrochemical industry (zhongguo shiyou yu huagong chanye de zichan chongzu)*, Beijing: Economic Science Press.

Chen, Min (1996) *Asian Management Systems*, London: International Thomson Business Press.

Chen, Yongkai (2001) 'Opportunities and challenges before Sinopec', http://www.worldoilweb.com.

Child, John (1984) *Organization: A Guide to Problems and Practices*, London: Harper & Row.

—— (1994) *Management in China during the Age of Reform*, Cambridge: Cambridge University Press.

Child, John and Sally Heavens (1999) 'Managing corporate networks from America to China', in Malcolm Warner (ed.) *China's Managerial Revolution*, London: Frank Cass.

Child, John and Yuan Lu (1996) *Management Issues in China: Volume II, International Enterprises*, London: Routledge.

China National Petroleum and Gas Corporation (CNPC) (1998), *China Petroleum Industry Yearbook (zhongguo shiyou gongye nianjian)*, Beijing: Petroleum Industry Press (*shi you gongye chubanshe*).

China Petrochemical Corporation (Sinopec Group) (1997), *China Petrochemical Corporation Yearbook (zhongguo shiyou huagong jituan gongsi nianjian)*, Beijing: China Petrochemical Publishing House (*zhongguo shiyou huagong chubanshe*).

—— (1999) *Annual Report 1998*.

Choung, E. and D. Terreson (1998), *China's Emerging Energy Landscape: A Bird's Eye View*, Hong Kong: MSDW.

Cluna Petroleum and Chemical Corporation (Sinopec Corporation (2001)) *Annual Report 2000*, BP.

Cusumano, M. A. (1985), *The Japanese Automobile Industry: Technology and Management at Nissan and Toyota*, Cambridge, MA: Harvard University Press.

Ding, D. Z., L. Ge and M. Warner (2002) 'Beyond the state sector: a study of HRM in Southern China', University of Cambridge: Research Papers in Management Studies, WP 21/2002.

Ding Guiming and Wang Yuxin (1999) *The Critical Situation of Oil Enterprises and the Orientation of Reform and Adjustment* (*shiyou qiye mian lin de yanjun xingshi ji gaige tiaozheng fangxiang*), Beijing: Petroleum Industry Press.

Dosi, Giovanni, Christopher Freeman, Richard Nelson, Gerald Silverberg and Luc Soete (eds) (1988) *Technical Change and Economic Theory*, London: Pinter.

Drucker, Peter (1946) *The Concept of the Corporation*, reissued 1964, New York: The New American Library.

Ferlie, Ewan and Andrew Pettigrew (1996) 'The nature and transformation of corporate headquarters: a review of recent literature and a research agenda', *Journal of Management Studies* 33, 4, 495–523.

Forrester, P. and R. Porter (1999) 'The politics of management in people's China: from CMRS to modern enterprise and beyond' in M. Warner (ed.) *China's Managerial Revolution*, London: Frank Cass.

Galbraith, J. V. (1972) *The New Industrial State* (2nd edn) London: Andre Deutsch.

Ghoshal, S and C. Bartlett (1990), 'The multinational corporation as an inter-organizational network', *Academy of Management Review* 15, 4, 603–25.

Goold, Michael (1991) 'Strategic control in decentralized firms', *Sloan Management Review* 69, Winter, 69–80.

Goold, Michael and Andrew Campbell (1989) *Strategies and Styles: The Role of the Centre in Managing Diversified Corporations*, Oxford: Basil Blackwell.

Goold, Michael, Andrew Campbell and Marcus Alexander (1994) *Corporate-Level Strategy*, New York: John Wiley & Sons.

Gulati, Ranjay, Nitin Nohria and Akbar Zaheer (2000) 'Strategic networks', *Strategic Management Journal* 21: pp. 203–15.

Hagstrom, Peter and Gunner Hedlund (1998) 'A three-dimensional model of changing internal structure in the firm', in Alfred D. Chandler, Jr., Peter Hagstrom and Orjan Solvell (eds) *The Dynamic Firm*, Oxford: Oxford University Press, pp. 166–191.

Hassard, J. J. Sheehan and J. Morris (1999) 'Enterprise reform in post-Deng China', *International Studies of Management and Organization* 29, 3, pp. 54–83.

Hay, D., D. Morris, G. Liu, and S. Yao (1994) *Economic Reform and State-owned Enterprises in China*, Oxford: Clarendon Press.

He, Jia (1999) 'Back to the basics: what is oil?', *China Petroleum*, January, 52–4.

Hendry, Chris (1990) 'The corporate management of human resources under conditions of decentralization', *British Journal of Management* 1, 91–103.

Hill, Stephen, Roderick Martin and Martin Harris (2000) 'Decentralization, integration and the post-bureaucratic organization: the case of R&D', *Journal of Management Studies* 37, 4, 563–85.

Hong, Ng Sek and Malcolm Warner (1998) *China's Trade Unions and Management*, Basingstoke: Macmillan.

Hungenberg, Harald (1993) 'How to ensure that headquarters add value', *Long Range Planning* 26, 6, 62–73.

Hymer, Stephen (1975) 'The multinational corporation and the law of uneven development', in Hugo Radice (ed.) *International Firms and Modern Imperialism*, London: Penguin Books.

Jackson, S. (1992) *Chinese Enterprise Management: Reforms in Economic Perspective*, Berlin: Walter de Gruyter.

Janelli, Roger L. (1993) *Making Capitalism: The Social and Cultural Construction of a South Korean Conglomerate*, Stanford, CA: Stanford University Press.

Jefferson, G. and I. Singh (1999) *Enterprise Reform in China*, New York: Oxford University Press.

Kang, T. W. (1989) *Is Korea the Next Japan?*, New York: The Free Press.

Kanter, Rosabeth Moss (1989) *When Giants Learn to Dance*, New York: Simon and Schuster.

Katz, Jorge (ed.) (1987) *Technology Generation in Latin American Manufacturing Industry*, London: Macmillan.

Kay, John (1993) *Foundations of Corporate Success*, Oxford: Oxford University Press.

Kono, Toyohiro (1984) *Strategy and Structure of Japanese Enterprises*, London: Macmillan.

—— (1999) 'A strong head office makes a strong company', *Long Range Planning* 32, 2, 225–36.

Laaksonen, O. (1988) *Management in China: During and After Mao*, Berlin: Walter de Gruyter.

Lazonick, William (1991) *Business Organization and the Myth of the Market Economy*, Cambridge: Cambridge University Press.

Lazonick, William, Ronald Dore and Henk W. de Jong (1997) *The Corporate Triangle: The Structure and Performance of Corporate Systems in a Global Economy*, Oxford: Blackwell Publishers.

Liu Changming, Zhou Dengli, Li Baiqi and Zhang Dianyou (1998) *Strategic Conception of China's Petroleum Market* (*zhongguo shiyou shichang de zhanlue gouxiang*), Beijing: Economic Science Press.

Lo, D. (1997) *Market and Institutional Regulation in Chinese Industrialization, 1978–94*, London: Macmillan.

Lu, Yuan and John Child (1996) 'Decentralization of decision-making in China's state enterprise', in David Brown and Robin Porter (eds) *Management Issues in China: Volume I*, London: Routledge.

March, James G. and Herbert A. Simon (1959) *Organizations*, Graduate School of Industrial Administration, Carnegie Institute of Technology.

Marris, Robin (1967) *The Economic Theory of 'Managerial' Capitalism*, London: Macmillan.

Morgan Stanley Dean Witter (MSDW) *The Competitive Edge*, 16 July 1998, New York: MSDW.

Naughton, B. (1995) *Growing Out of the Plan: Chinese Economic Reform, 1978–1993*, Cambridge: Cambridge University Press.

Nolan, Peter (1995) *China's Rise, Russia's Fall: Politics, Economics and Planning in the Transition from Stalinism*, London: Macmillan.

—— (1998) *Indigenous Large Firms in China's Economic Reform: The Case of Shougang Steel and Iron Corporation*, London: Contemporary China Institute.

—— (1999) *Coca-Cola and the Global Business Revolution: A Study with Special Reference to the EU*, Cambridge: Judge Institute of Management.

—— (2001) *China and the Global Business Revolution*, Basingstoke: Palgrave.

Nolan, Peter and Wang Xiaoqiang (1999) 'Beyond privatization: institutional innovation and growth in China's large state-owned enterprises', *World Development* 27, 1, 169–200.

Nolan, Peter and Jin Zhang (2002) 'The challenge of globalization for large Chinese firms', *World Development* 30, 12, 2089–107.

Nolan Peter, Dylan Sutherland and Jin Zhang (2002) 'The challenge of global business revolution', *Contributions to Political Economy* 21, pp. 91–110.

Ouchi, William G. (1984) *The M-form Society: How American Teamwork Can Recapture the Competitive Edge*, Reading, MA: Addison-Wesley.

Penrose, Edith T. (1995) *The Theory of the Growth of the Firm* (2nd edn), Oxford: Basil Blackwell.

PetroChina (2000) Prospectus for Global Offering.

—— (2001) PetroChina Annual Report 2000.

Porter, Michael (1990) *The Competitive Advantage of Nations*, London: Macmillan.

Powell, W. W. (1990) 'Neither market nor hierarchy – network forms of organization', in G. Thompson, J. Frances, R. Levacic and J. Mitchell (eds) *Markets, Hierarchies and Networks*, London: Sage.

Prahalad, C. K. and Yves L. Doz (1981) 'Strategic control – the dilemma in headquarters-subsidiary relationship', in Lars Otterbeck (ed.) *The Management of Headquarters–Subsidiary Relationships in Multinational Corporations*, England: Gower, pp. 187–203.

Prokesch, Steven E. 'Unleashing the power of learning', *Harvard Business Review*, September-October 1997.

Redding, S. G. (1993) *The Spirit of Chinese Capitalism*, Berlin: Walter de Gruyter.

Royal Dutch/Shell (2001a) *Group Governance Guide*, Shell International Limited.

—— (2001b) *Annual Report on Form-20F 2000*.

—— (2001c) *Annual Reports 2000*.

Rubenstein, Albert H. (1989) *Managing Technology in the Decentralized Firm*, New York: John Wiley & Sons.

Ruigrok, Winfried and Rob Van Tulder (1995) *The Logic of International Restructuring*, London: Routledge.

Rumelt, Richard, P., Dan E. Schendel and David J. Teece (eds) (1990) *Fundamental Issues in Strategy: A Research Agenda*, Boston, MA: Harvard Business School Press.

Sabel, C. (1991) 'Moebius-strip organizations and open labour markets: some consequences of the reintegration of conception and execution in a volatile economy', in P. Bourdieu, and J. Coleman (eds), *Social Theory for a Changing Society*, Boulder, CO: Westview Press, 23–54.

Sachs, J. and Wing Thye Woo (1994) 'Structural factors in the economic reforms of China, Eastern Europe, and the former Soviet Union, *Economic Policy* 18, 31–9.

Shanghai Petrochemical Corporation (SPCC), *Annual Report 1998*.

Shell (2001) *Energy Needs, Choices and Possibilities: Scenarios to 2050*, Shell International Ltd.

Shell Transport and Trading Company (Shell), Annual Report 1999.

Sloan, A. P. (1965) *My Years with General Motors*, London: Sidgwick and Jackson.

State Economic and Trade Commission (SETC) (1999) 'Notification on distributing the list of the first batch of small refineries that should be closed down', oil and petrochemical section, No. 584, 1999.

—— (1999) 'Notification on distributing the list of the second batch of small refineries that should be closed down', oil and petrochemical section No. 234, 2000.

—— (2001) 'The tenth five-year plan: oil industry', http://www.setc.gov.cn.

State Statistical Bureau (SSB), *Chinese Large and Medium-sized Enterprises Yearbook*, (*zhongguo daxing qiye nianjian*) (ZDQN) (various years), Beijing: China Statistical Publishing House (*zhongguo tongji chubanshe*).

—— *China Statistical Yearbook 1997* (*zhongguo tongji nianjian*) (ZTN), Beijing: China Statistical Publishing House (*zhongguo tongji chubanshe*).

Steers, Richard M., Y. K. Shin and G. R. Ungson (1991) *The Chaebol: Korea's New Industrial Might*, London: Harper Collins.

Steinfeld, Edward (1998) *Forging Reform in China: the Fate of China's State-Owned Enterprises*, Cambridge: Cambridge University Press.

Stopford, John M. and Susan Strange (1991) *Rival States, Rival Firms*, Cambridge: Cambridge University Press.

Strange, Susan (1994), *States and Markets* (2nd edn), London: Pinter Publishers.

Thorelli, H. B. (1990), 'Networks – between markets and hierarchies', in D. Ford (ed.) *Understanding Business Markets*, London: Academic Press.

Tyson, Laura d'Andrea (1992) *Who's Bashing Whom? Trade Conflict in High-technology Industries*, Washington, DC: Institute of International Economics.

Volberda, Henk W. (1998) *Building the Flexible Firm*, Oxford: Oxford University Press.

Walter, Carl E. and Howie, Fraser J. T. (2001), *'To Get Rich is Glorious!': China's Stock Market in the '80s and '90s*, Basingstoke: Palgrave.

Wang Yichao, 'Sinochem' self-salvation', *Caijing*, 5 June 2003.

Warner, Malcolm (1995) *The Management of Human Resources in Chinese Industry*, London: Macmillan.

Whitley, Richard (1994) *Business Systems in East Asia: Firms, Markets and Societies*, London: Sage Publications.

—— (2000) *Divergent Capitalism: the Social Structuring and Change of Business Systems*, Oxford: Oxford University Press.

Williamson, Oliver E. (1975) *Markets and Hierarchies: Analysis and Antitrust Implications*, New York: The Free Press.

—— (1985) *The Economic Institutions of Capitalism*, New York: The Free Press.

—— (1986) *Economic Organization*, London: Wheatsheaf Books.

—— (1990) 'Strategizing, economizing, and economic organisation', in Richard P. Rumelt, Dan E. Schendel and David J. Teece (eds) *Fundamental Issues in Strategy: A Research Agenda*, Boston, MA: Harvard Business School Press, pp. 361–401.

Xinhuanet, 'Our national petrochemical industry faces a severe situation', 27 September 2001, http://www.xinhuanet.com

Yan Xuchao (ed.) (1998) *Major Restructuring of China's Petroleum Industry* (*zhongguo shiyou da congzu*), Beijing: Petroleum Industry Press.

Yergin, Daniel (1991) *The Prize*, London: Simon & Schuster.

Zhang, Zhigang (2001) 'Proceed to regulating the market of refined products', http://www.setc.gov.cn.

Zhenhai Refining & Chemical Corporation (Zhenhai) (2000), Annual Report 1999.

Index